東南亞史研究6

島夷志略中英文對照本

Dao-yi Chi-lue (Chinese v. English Version)
(Concise Record on the Island Barbarians)

作者：（元）汪大淵

Author: (Yuan) Wang Da-yuan

校註及中譯英者：陳鴻瑜

Annotation and Chinese-English Translator:
Chen Hurng Yu

（附白話文翻譯）

(with vernacular translation)

蘭臺出版社

譯者序

Translator's Preface

島夷志略一書應是中國人遊歷海外撰寫的第一本遊記，對遍佈東南亞、南亞、地中海南岸和東非等 99 個國家和城市做了簡略的介紹。其因是汪大淵個人的親身經歷，故更是珍貴。

The book *Dao-yi Chi-lue* should be the first travel diary written by the Chinese who traveled overseas. It briefly introduced 99 countries and cities in Southeast Asia, South Asia, the southern coast of the Mediterranean Sea, and East Africa. Because it is Wang Da-yuan's personal experience, it is even more precious.

汪大淵是江西南昌人，南昌不靠海，也不是鄉人大量外移南海諸國的僑鄉，不知何種因緣際會，讓汪大淵出洋兩次，投身大海，尋訪各國？無論汪大淵以何種身份出洋遊歷，並將遊歷所見筆記下來，傳諸後世，讓後世得窺第十四世紀時這些國家和城市的樣貌，都是值得讚揚。

Wang Da-yuan is a native of Nanchang, Jiangxi. Nanchang is not close to the sea, nor a hometown of overseas Chinese where many villagers immigrated to the South China Sea countries. I don't know what kind of karma made Wang Da-yuan go abroad twice, devote himself to the sea, and seek to visit many vital port-city? No matter in what capacity Wang Da-yuan traveled abroad, he wrote down what he saw. He passed it on to future generations, so those future generations could have a glimpse of what these countries and cities looked like in the 14th century, which is worthy of praise.

譯者在 2018 年參加一次研討會，評論一篇菲律賓學者的文章，她引用島夷志略中有關三島的內容，見其英文譯文與原文意思有出入，故極思將該書譯成英文，俾讓外國人得瞭解該書的內容。

The translator participated in a seminar in 2018 and commented on an article by a Filipino scholar. She quoted the content about the three islands in *Dao-yi Chi-lue*. Seeing that the English translation was different from the original, at that time I hope to translate the book into English, So that foreigners can understand the content of the book.

當本書完成英文翻譯時，內人說，你翻譯古文為英文，是方便了英文讀者閱讀，但有許多中文年輕一代讀者，對古文言文不甚瞭解，你應該將之譯成白話文。所以筆者又花了些時間將文言文譯成白話文。

When the English translation of this book was completed, my wife said that you translated ancient Chinese into English, which is convenient for English readers, but there are many young Chinese readers who do not know much about ancient classical Chinese, so you should translate it into the vernacular. Therefore, I spent some time translating classical Chinese into vernacular.

于今終於譯成，願與讀者諸君分享之。

I have finally translated it today, and I would like to share it with readers.

陳鴻瑜謹誌
Chen Hurng Yu

2023 年 5 月 4 日
May 4, 2023

張序

Chang's Preface

九州環大瀛海，而中國曰赤縣神州。其外為州者復九，有裨海環之。人民禽獸，莫能相通。如一區中者乃為一州，此騶氏之言也。人多言其荒唐誕誇，況當時外徼未通於中國，將何以徵驗其言哉！漢唐而後，於諸島夷力所可到，利所可到，班班史傳，固有其名矣。然考於見聞，多襲舊書，未有身遊目識，而能詳其實者，猶未盡之徵也。

白話文**(Vernacular)**：

九州四周環繞大海，稱中國為赤縣神州。它的外圍還有九州，有小海環繞。人民和禽獸之間，無法相溝通。如一區為一州，這是騶氏所說的。大家多說他的說法荒唐誇張，當時外國未通中國，何能驗證他的說法可靠呢！自漢唐以來，可到達各個島夷，也能獲得利益，歷史都有記載，每個人都知道。然而研究見聞，多數是抄襲舊書，未有親身遊歷親眼看到，而能確實記下來的，還未盡可靠。

Jiǔzhōu (nine continentals) is surrounded by the great sea, while China is called Chixian Shenzhou(Red County and God Continental). Outside it has another nine continentals, which are also surrounded by a small sea. People and animals can't communicate with each other. If a district is continental, this is what Zou's saying. Many people say that it is absurd and exaggerated, and since the foreigners were not communicating with China then, how could he test his words? After the Han and Tang Dynasties, the island's barbarians could be reached by the

Chinese people who can get a profit, history recorded it and everyone knows it. However, concerning seeing and hearing, all coming from many old books, and there is no personal tour and eyewitness, it is unavailable to get detailed information.

西江汪君煥章，當冠年[1]，嘗兩附舶東西洋[2]，所過輒采錄其山川、風土、物產之詭異，居室、飲食、衣服之好尚，與夫貿易賚用之所宜，非其親見不書，則信乎其可徵也。與予言，海中自多鉅魚，若蛟龍鯨鯢之屬，羣出遊，鼓濤拒風，莫可名數。舟人燔雞毛以觸之，則遠遊而沒。一島嶼間或廣裒數千里，島人浩穰。某君長所居，多明珠、麗玉、犀角、象牙、香木為飾。橋梁或甃以金銀，若珊瑚、琅玕、玳瑁，人不以為奇也。所言尤有可觀，則驪衍皆不誕，焉知是誌之外，煥章之所未歷，不有瑰怪廣大又逾此為國者歟！

白話文(Vernacular)：

西江汪君煥章（即汪大淵），當他二十歲時，曾經兩次搭船前往東西洋，他將經過記錄其山川、風土、物產之詭異，居室、飲食、衣服之偏好，與貿易商品之所宜，不是他親眼看到的不寫，他的記載是可信賴的。他告訴我，海中有很多鉅魚，像蛟龍鯨鯢之類，它們一羣出遊，鼓動浪濤，排拒風，數量多到不可算。船人燒雞毛來碰觸大魚，它們遠遊而沒於水中。有群島連綿數千里，島人人口眾多。某君長所居之處，多明珠、麗玉、犀角、象牙、香木為裝飾。橋梁或井壁以金

---

[1] 冠年是指年滿 20 歲之男子。
　　Crown-year refers to a 20-year-old man.
[2] 東西洋是以婆羅洲為分界線，以東為東洋，以西為西洋。
　　With Borneo as a demarcation point, to the east is called the East Ocean, and to the west is called the West Ocean.

銀裝飾，亦有使用珊瑚、珠玉、玼瑁，人們不以為奇怪。他的說法尤有可觀，騶衍的說法並不荒誕，我們怎能知道該誌之外，汪大淵所未曾經歷的，難道不會有許多珍貴奇怪的事超過這些國家的嗎？

Xijiang Wang Huanzhang(namely Wang Da-yuan), when he was in the crown-year, has twice taking ships to the East Ocean and the West Ocean, and recorded the strangeness of the mountains and rivers, the customs, the products, fondness of the housing, food, and clothes, and the benefit of the trade. If he didn't see it in person will not record it in his book, you can believe what he recorded. He told me, there are many giant fishes in the sea, such as the genus of dragons, whales, and Andrias. They appeared as a group in the sea, arising big waves and wind. It can't be counted for its numbers. If a boatman burns chicken feathers to touch them, they will go far away and dive into the sea. There are archipelagos stretching for thousands of miles, and the islanders have a large population. The residence of a ruler is decorated with pearls, jade, rhino horn, ivory, and fragrant wood. The bridges and walls of well are made of gold and silver, sometimes with coral, jade, and tortoiseshell, which are not surprising to people. What he has said is particularly impressive, then what Zou Yan's saying is not absurd. How can I know that beyond the book, and what Huanzhang has never experienced, is there no one country which has strange things and vast than these countries?

大抵一元之氣，充溢乎天地，其所能融結為人為物。惟中國文明，則得其正氣。環海於外，氣偏於物，而寒燠殊候，材質異賦，固其理也。今乃以耳目弗逮而盡疑之，可乎？莊周有言：「六合之外，聖人存而不論。」然博古君子，求之異書，亦所不廢也。泉修郡乘，既以是誌刊入。煥章將歸，復刊諸西江，以廣其傳，故予序之。至正十年，龍集庚寅二月朔日，翰林修撰河東張翥序。

白話文(Vernacular)：

大抵宇宙一體之氣，充塞於天地之間，它能夠形成人類和萬物。惟中國文明，則得其正氣。它外面環海，氣偏於物，氣候有寒冷、有燠熱，材質異賦，這有其道理所在。今天以耳目未及見聞而給予懷疑，可以這樣嗎？莊周曾說：「六合之外的事，聖人雖知道而不討論。」然通曉古事的君子，尋求奇異書籍，亦沒有停止。泉州府修郡誌，將該誌納入。汪煥章將歸來，又刊行該書於西江，以廣其傳布，故我為之寫序。至正十年，龍集庚寅二月一日，翰林修撰河東張翥序。

Most of the energy of one yuan (referring to the origin of things, or the origin of the world) fills heaven and the earth, and it can form human beings and all things. Only Chinese civilization can get its righteousness. China is surrounded by the sea, the climate is conducive to the growth of all things which have their natural endowments with the change of the cold weather and hot weather. This is the principle of natural change. Now, can I doubt it because my eyes and ears do not reach it? Zhuang Zhou once said, "Beyond the Six Harmonies, even the sages know it but do not discuss it." However, gentleman who knows ancient things asked continuously for a different book. When Quanzhou chronicles were written, they covered this book.

Huanzhang is about to return and again published it in Xijiang for spreading it. Thus I preface it. In the tenth year of Zhì Zhèng (in 1350 A.D.), Longji Gengyin, on the first day of the second month. Preface by the Hanlin compiler, Chang Wengzhu in Hedong.

吳序

Wu's Preface

中國之外，四海維之。海外夷國以萬計，唯北海以風惡不可入，東西南數千萬里，皆得梯航以達其道路，象胥以譯其語言。惟有聖人在乎位，則相率而效朝貢互市。雖天際窮髮不毛之地，無不可通之理焉。

白話文**(Vernacular)**：

中國之外，有四海環繞。海外夷國有一萬多，唯北海以風惡不可進入，東、西、南方數千萬里，皆得航海以到達其國家，由翻譯人員來譯其語言。惟有聖人在乎國家的地位，則相率而建立朝貢進行貿易。雖世界邊陲之地是貧窮不毛之地，沒有不可往來之理。

Outside China, there are four seas. There are tens of thousands of foreign barbarian countries, but the North Sea is inaccessible because of the fierce wind. In the direction of East, West, and South, a distance of tens of thousands of miles, it can be voyaged to reach them, through translators to translate their languages. Only the sages care about the status of the country, and they lead each other to establish tributes for trade. Although the end of the world is a barren place, there is no reason for being unavailable to communicate.

世祖皇帝既平宋氏，始命正奉大夫工部尚書海外諸蕃宣慰使蒲師文，與其副孫勝夫、尤永賢等通道外國，撫宣諸夷。

獨爪哇負固不服，遂命平章[3]高興、史弼等帥舟師以討定之。自時厥後，唐人之商販者，外蕃率待以命使臣之禮，故其國俗、土產、人物、奇怪之事，中土皆得而知。奇珍異寶，流布中外為不少矣。然欲考求其故實，則執事者多祕其說，鑿空者又不得其詳。唯豫章汪君煥章，少負奇氣，為司馬子長[4]之遊，足跡幾半天下矣。顧以海外之風土，國史未盡其蘊，因附舶以浮於海者數年然後歸。其目所及，皆為書以記之。校之五年舊誌，大有逕庭矣。以君傳者其言必可信，故附清源續志之後。不惟使後之圖王會[5]者有足徵，亦以見國家之懷柔百蠻，蓋此道也。至正己丑冬十有二月望日三山吳鑒序。

白話文(Vernacular)：

世祖皇帝既平定宋氏，始命正奉大夫工部尚書海外諸蕃宣慰使蒲師文，與其副使孫勝夫、尤永賢等通使外國，撫宣諸夷。唯獨爪哇固執不肯服從，所以命令平章高興、史弼等率海軍前往討伐。從此時起，中國人到海外做生意的人，外

---

[3] 平章，是位居丞相之下的官名，是平章政事之簡縮詞。

Pingzhang is the official name of the Prime Minister and is an abbreviation for Pingzhang Political Affairs.

[4] 司馬子長，即司馬遷，年輕時曾周遊中國各地。

Sima Zichang. Namely, Sima Qian (145 B.C.-1 century B.C.), had traveled to many places in China when he was young.

[5]「中書侍郎顏師古奏言：『昔周武時，天下太平，遠國歸款，周史乃集其事為王會篇，令萬國來朝至今。如此輩章服，實可圖寫，今請撰為王會圖。』從之。」（李昉編，太平御覽，四夷部九·南蠻四，東謝）

"Yan Shigu, Zhongshu Shilang, said: 'In the period of Zhou Wu, the world was peaceful, and the money was secured from distant countries. The history of the Zhou Dynasty collected this affair as the King's Meeting chapter, which made all countries come to China for a tribute to this day. This kind of subjection can be pictured it. Nowadays suggesting editing the Wang Hui Picture.' Emperor agreed to it." (Li Fang, ed., *Taiping Yulan*, Nine of the Four Barbarians, Four of the Southern Barbarians, Dongxie.)

蕃大都待以皇帝命令的使臣之禮，故其國俗、土產、人物、奇怪之事，中土皆得而知。奇珍異寶，流布中外為數不少。然欲研究其故事是否真實，則執事者多守密不說，憑空想像者又寫不出詳細情況。唯豫章汪君煥章，少有奇才，學司馬遷之遊歷，足跡幾半天下矣。他所記載的海外之風土，國史未盡其詳細，他曾搭船到海外數年然後歸來。他親眼所見，皆寫在書內。比較五年前的舊誌，內容有很大的不同。以他所寫的書，他的話必然可信，故附在清源續志之後。不僅可讓王會所繪的外國使節到中國的圖有充足之證據，亦可以看到國家懷柔百蠻的情形，這是道理所在。至正己丑冬十有二月十五日三山吳鑒序。

Emperor Shìzǔ conquered the Song Dynasty, and first ordered Pu Shiwen, the envoy of Consolation to the Overseas Barbarians, who was serving as the minister of the Ministry of Industry, and his deputy Sun Shengfu, You Yongxian, etc., by voyaging to foreign countries for consolation and declaration [a new dynasty established in China]. Only Java did not accept, so he ordered Pingzhang Gaoxing, Shi Bi, and others to lead navies to attack it. Since then, the Chinese merchants were treated as equivalent envoys of China by foreigners. Therefore, their national customs, local products, people, and strange things can be known in China. There are a few rare and precious treasures that have been circulated in China and abroad. However, if one wants to investigate the truth, the deacons often keep their stories secret and those who imagine do not know the details to write. Only Yuzhang Wang Huanzhang, who has talent, imitates Sima Zichang's travel around China, and his footprints have been around half of the world. Taking into account the customs of overseas countries, the history of China is not a complete record of it, so he took ships going abroad for several years and then return. Everything he sees is recorded in the book. It is quite different from the old book which he published five years ago. The words that he said are certainly credible, so attach the preface to *the Continuation of Qingyuan Chronicles*. Not only did the foreign envoys to China appearing in the picture of Wang Hui have sufficient evidence, but also see the tenderness of China to hundred foreign countries. This is the right way. Zhizhen, Jǐ Chǒu, Winter, 15 December, the preface by San-shan Wu Jian.

附：清源續志序

Attachment: Preface to *the Continuation of Qingyuan Chronicle*

　　古有九丘之書，誌九州之土地，所有風氣之宜，與三墳五典[6]並傳。周列國皆有史，晉有乘輿，楚有檮杌，魯有春秋是也。孔子定書，以黜三墳，衍述職方，以代九丘；筆削春秋，以寓一王法，而乘輿與檮杌遂廢不傳。及秦罷侯置守，廢列國史，西漢司馬遷作史記，關牧守年月不表。郡國記浸無可考，學者病之。厥後，江表「華陽」有誌，汝潁之名士，襄陽之耆舊有傳。隋大業首命學士十八人著十郡誌，凡以補史氏之闕遺也。

　　白話文(Vernacular)：

　　古代有九丘之書，記載九州之土地，所有風氣之事宜，與三墳、五典並傳後世。周朝時各個列國皆有史書，晉國有乘輿，楚國有檮杌，魯國有春秋。孔子刪定各書，廢黜三墳的書，寫四方的史事，以替代九丘的書；他刪改春秋一書，以確立統一王國的法律，像乘輿與檮杌等書遂廢不傳後世。

6　三墳五典，是中國最古老的書籍的總稱。見「三墳五典八索九丘」，維基百科，
　　https://zh.wikipedia.org/wiki/%E4%B8%89%E5%A2%B3%E4%BA%94
　　%E5%85%B8%E5%85%AB%E7%B4%A2%E4%B9%9D%E4%B8%98
　　2022 年 10 月 12 日瀏覽。
　　 The Three Graves and Five Classics is the general term for the oldest books in China. See "Three Graves, Five Classics, Eight Explorations and Nine Hills", *Wikipedia*,
　　https://zh.wikipedia.org/wiki/%E4%B8%89%E5%A2%B3%E4%BA%94
　　%E5%85%B8%E5%85%AB%E7%B4%A2%E4%B9%9D%E4%B8%98
　　October 12, 2022 retrieved.

及秦國罷廢諸侯制度而設置郡守，也廢了列國史，西漢司馬遷作史記，沒有記載牧守及統治年月等。郡國的歷史遂無可考究，學者對此有所批評。此後，江說「華陽」有誌，汝潁之名士，襄陽之耆舊有傳記。隋國大業時期，首命學士十八人著十郡誌，是用來補充史記之缺漏。

In ancient times, there was a book of Jiuchiu that recorded the land of Nine Continentals and all the appropriate customs, which was passed to latter generations along with the *Sān Fén Wǔ Diǎn*. The Zhou Kingdom and surrounding kingdoms all have their histories. The Jin Kingdom has the historic book of *Chengyu* (*Riding*), the Chǔ Kingdom has the historic book of *Táo Wù* (*Monster*), and the Lu Kingdom has the historic book of *The Chūnchiū* (*The Spring and Autumn*). Confucius corrected the book to remove the books of three Ancient kings, to describe the position of four directions, to replace the Jiuchiu; to abridge the *Chūnchiū*, to enact a single law of the kingdom, and the *Chengyu* and *Táo Wù* were abandoned and not passed on. When the Qin Dynasty abolished the vassal states and set up the county system, the history of the kingdoms was abolished, and the Western Han Dynasty Sima Chian wrote the *Historical Records*, but without recording the names and years of chiefs of the county. The history of the county was increasingly to be forgotten, and scholars criticized it. Later, Jiang said that Huayang had its chronicle, Ru Ying's famous person and Xiangyang's old man have their autobiography. In the Daye period of the Sui Dynasty, Emperor ordered 18 scholars to write the *Chronicle on Ten Counties*, all to make up for the deficiencies of Sima Chian's

Historical Records.

　　閩文學始唐，至宋大盛。故家文獻，彬彬可考。時號海濱洙泗[7]，蓋不誣矣。國朝混一區域，至元丙子，郡既內附，繼遭兵寇，郡域之外，莽為戰區。雖值承平，未能盡復舊觀。**清源前誌放失**，後誌止於淳祐庚戌，逮今百有餘年。前政牧守，多文吏武夫，急簿書期會，而不遑於典章文物。比年修宋遼金三史，詔郡國各上其所錄，而泉獨不能具，無稱德意，有識愧焉。

　　白話文(Vernacular)：

　　福建的文學始於唐代，至宋大盛。故各家文獻，斑斑可考。當時號稱住在海濱講學的洙泗，聲望卓著。本朝統一中國，至元丙子年，各郡都內附，仍遭兵寇，郡域之外，變成戰區。雖值承平年代，未能完全恢復舊觀。**清源前誌遺失**，後誌只寫到淳祐庚戌，至今有一百多年。前政府的牧守，多數是文吏和武夫，他們忙於寫公文及開會，而沒有時間注意典章文物。近年修宋、遼、金三史，詔命郡國各呈上其歷史文獻，唯獨泉州沒有這樣做，他們不能稱為有道德的人，他們不會感到慚愧嗎？

　　Fujian literature began in the Tang Dynasty and reached prosperity in the Song Dynasty. And their old documents can be traced. At that time, they are called seaside Zhu-Si (referring to positively pursuing knowledge), it is not a false reputation. Until Yuan reigned over China, the counties were annexed in Zhiyuan

---

[7]洙泗，指孔子在洙水和泗水之間聚徒講學。

　Zhu-Si means that Confucius gathered his disciples to give lectures between Zhu Shui (Zhu River) and Sishui(Si River).

Bingzi Year (in 1276), followed by war and bandits outside the county. Although at present is peace, it cannot fully restore the order as before. *The Qianyuan Former Chronicle* was lost, and the last year of record in the *Later Chronicle* ended at Chunyou Gengxu Year (in 1250), now passing more than one hundred years. The county chiefs of the former government have many civil servants and military men, who were rushed busy with official documents and meetings, with no time to think of ordinances and cultural relics. In recent years the authorities planned to rewrite the history of the Song, Liao, and Jin Dynasties and demanded every county to submit their recorded history, but only Quanzhou can't do it. They can't be called moral people, aren't they ashamed?

　　至正九年，朝以閩海憲使高昌偰侯來守泉。臨政之暇，考求圖誌。顧是邦古今政治、沿革、風土、習尚，變遷不同，太平百年，譜牒猶有遺逸矣。今不紀，後將無徵。遂分命儒士，搜訪舊聞，隨邑編輯成書。鑒時寓泉，辱命與學士君子裁定刪削，為清源續誌二十卷，以補清源故事。然故老漸沒，新學淺於聞見，前朝遺事，蓋十具一二以傳焉。至正十一年暮春修禊日三山吳鑒序。

　　白話文**(Vernacular)**：

　　至正九年，朝庭以閩海憲使高昌偰侯來守泉州府。他在公餘之暇，考求圖誌。蒐集泉州府古今政治、沿革、風土、習尚，變遷歷史，太平百年，有些譜牒猶有遺失。今天不記載，以後將沒有證據。於是分別任命儒士，搜訪舊聞，每個城邑編輯成書。當時我住在泉州，受命與學士君子裁定刪削，

寫成清源續誌二十卷，以補充清源故事。然而老一輩人漸亡
故，新學之見聞還是膚淺，前朝遺事，只有十分之一、二留
傳下來。至正十一年暮春修禊日三山吳鑒序。

  In the ninth year of the Zhì Zhèng (in 1349), the court sent
Gaochang Xiè Hóu, the Official Envoy of the Fujian Sea, to
reign Quanzhou. In the spare time of the administration, he
searched for maps and books, including all of Quanzhou's
ancient and modern politics, evolution, customs, and habits.
Quanzhou experienced change and peace for one hundred years,
and some of the genealogy still has not been collected yet. If it
is not recorded now, it will not be available to trace in the future.
Then he ordered Confucian scholars to search for old news and
edited it into a book. At that time I lived in Quanzhou, receiving
orders to work with some scholars to review it, compiling into
twenty volumes of *the Continuation of Qianyuan Chronicle* to
supplement the story of Qianyuan. However, the old man is gone,
the new one is shallower than hearing and seeing, and the relics
of the previous dynasty are only less than twenty percent of
events to be recorded. In the late spring of the eleventh year of
the Zhì Zhèng (in 1351), the preface by San-shan, Wu Jian.

目次
Contents

譯者之導論
Translator's Introduction

　　元國航海家汪大淵於 1349 年出版島夷志略一書，記錄了他個人從泉州到澎湖、北臺灣到東非甚至地中海的航海經歷，堪稱是一部航海史上的重要著作。汪大淵最早於 1330 年從泉州出海遊歷，1334 年返國。1337 年冬，他第二次由泉州出海遊歷，1339 年夏秋返國。

　　Yuan Dynasty navigator Wang Da-yuan published the book *Dao-yi Chi-lue* in 1349, which recorded his personal voyage experience from Quanzhou, Penghu, and northern Taiwan to East Africa and even the Mediterranean Sea, which can be regarded as an important work in the history of navigation. Wang Da-yuan first traveled from Quanzhou in 1330 and returned to China in 1334. In the winter of 1337, he traveled abroad from Quanzhou for the second time and returned to China in the summer and autumn of 1339.

　　汪大淵的著作晚於宋國趙汝适的諸蕃志 124 年，所描述的國名或地名遠比諸蕃志一書還多，而且更遠。書上所記的國名，都是他親身到過，他將所見所聞記錄下來，因此該書堪稱為他的遊記，其寫作方式迥異於諸蕃志，趙汝适是海關官員，他本人並未出國考察，而是將船員所述記錄下來，猶如口述歷史。

　　Wang Da-yuan's work was 124 years later than Zhao Rugua's *Zhufan Chi* (*Record on Various Barbarians*) in the Song Dynasty, and the country or place names described were far more than *Zhufan Chi*, and the journey farther away. The names of the countries recorded in the book were all he visited in person, and he recorded what he saw and heard, so the book can be called his travelogue. The way of writing is quite different from that of *Zhufan Chi*. Zhao Rugua was a customs official. He did not go abroad to investigate but recorded what the crews said, like an oral history.

　　從島夷誌略一書的安排，略可窺見他的航程。該書第一個論述的地點是澎湖，汪大淵首站從泉州出海到澎湖，他說：「自泉州順風二晝夜可至。」因此，很有可能他是先到澎湖。然後再前往「琉球」，即台灣。在該條最後，他說：「海外諸國蓋由此始」，意即他以後前往其他國家旅行是從台灣為起點。如果此一推論可靠，則當時應有環繞南海周邊國家的航線存在。該書三島條亦提到：「男子常附舶至泉州經紀，罄其資囊，以文其身，既歸其國，則國人以尊長之禮待之，延之上座，雖父老亦不得與爭焉。」據此可知，從菲島中部經由台灣到泉州，已是當時的一條航路。

From the arrangement of *Dao-yi Chi-lue*, we can get a glimpse of his voyage. The first place discussed in the book is Penghu. The first leg of Wang Da-yuan's trip was from Quanzhou to Penghu. He said, "It will take two days and nights to reach Penghu with the wind from Quanzhou." Therefore, it is very likely that he arrived at Penghu first. Then went to Ryukyu, which is Taiwan. At the end of the article, he said: "Overseas countries start from here", which means that his future trips to other countries will start from Taiwan. If this inference is reliable, then there should have been voyage routes around the countries which surround the South China Sea. The entry of Three Islands also is mentioned: "The man often takes a ship to Quanzhou for paying all of his money to tattoo his body. When he returns to his country, the people there treat him with respect, and seat in a prestigious seat. Even the old man or his father's generation will not be able to compete with him." It can be seen from this that the route from the central part of the Philippine Islands to Quanzhou via Taiwan was already a route at that time.

他從臺灣往南前往菲律賓的三島（或三嶼）（今菲律賓中部的民多洛島、班乃島和巴拉望島）、麻逸（菲律賓馬尼拉南部或民多洛）、蘇祿（菲律賓南部）等總共 99 個國家或城市，範圍遍及今天東南亞、南亞和東非地區，甚至到過義大利西西里島（Sicily）。

He went south from Taiwan to the Three Islands of the Philippines (now Mindoro, Panay, and Palawan in the central Philippines), Máyìt (south of Manila, or Mindoro, Philippines), Sulu (south of the Philippines), etc. 99 countries or cities, covering today's Southeast Asia, South Asia and East Africa, and even Sicily, Italy.

他遊歷的最北邊是到北臺灣，東邊是到印尼的文老古（即今印尼的摩鹿加 (Maluku)群島）。南邊到古里地悶（今帝汶島），中間到過淳泥（今汶萊）、爪哇、舊港（印尼蘇門答臘的巴鄰旁）、蘇門答臘島的花面、須文答剌和喃巫里、越南、北蘇門答臘的淡洋、泰國、馬來半島的吉蘭丹、丁家廬（今馬來西亞登嘉樓）、彭坑（今馬來西亞彭亨）、朋加剌（今孟加拉 (Bengal)）、斯里蘭卡、東印度的沙里八丹和土塔，西邊到西印度的曼陀郎（今印度西岸古吉拉特邦卡奇

(Kutch) 南部曼德維 (Mandvi) 東面三十英里的蒙德拉 (Mundra)）、放拜（今印度西岸的孟買 (Bambay)）、北溜（今印度洋中的拉克代夫 (Laccadive) 群島和馬爾地夫 (Maldive) 群島。）、下里（指「鄭和航海圖」中之歇立，今印度西岸卡里庫特 (Calicut) 北部的 Maunt Delly。或謂今科欽 (Cochin) 北二十英里小港阿爾瓦耶 (Alwaye)）、加里那（可能在今波斯灣內伊朗西南部一帶；或謂在今印度沿海，今地不詳。）、古里佛（今印度喀拉拉邦北岸的卡里庫特）、巴南巴西（今印度卡納塔克邦卡爾瓦爾 (Karwar) 東南的 Banavāsi，其西岸的霍納瓦（Honavar）即為其國主要港口。）、以及東非洲的阿思里（位在埃及紅海西岸的 Quseir）、麻那里（位在肯亞的馬林迪 (Malindi)）、層搖羅（位在坦尚尼亞的 Kilwa Kisiwani）、加將門里（位在莫三鼻克的 Quelimane）、伊拉克的波斯離（今伊拉克巴士拉）、麻呵斯離（又作勿斯離，今伊拉克西北部摩蘇爾 (Mosur)）、撻吉那（位在阿拉伯半島南邊的亞丁（Aden）以東的 Tagina 港）、天堂（又作天房，今沙烏地阿拉伯的麥加），義大利西西里島南邊的 （Licata）港。

The far north he traveled was to northern Taiwan, and the east was to Wenlaogu, Indonesia (now the Maluku Islands in Indonesia). From the south to Gulidimen (now Timor Island), in the middle, he went to Bo Ni (now Brunei), Java, Jiu Gang (Palembang) (in Sumatra, Indonesia), Sumatra's Huāmiàn (Flower Face), Xū Wén Dá Lá and Numburi, Vietnam, Dàn Yáng in Northern Sumatra, Thailand, Kelantan on the Malay Peninsula, Dingjialu (now Terengganu, Malaysia), Pengkeng (now Pahang, Malaysia), Penggara (now Bangladesh), Sri Lanka, East India Shālǐ Bā Dān and Tǔtǎ, west to Màn Tuó Láng in West India

(Mundra, thirty miles east of Mandvi, south of Kutch, Gujarat, West Coast, India). Fàng Bài (Bombay, on the west coast of India), Běi Liū (now the Maldives Islands in the Indian Ocean.), Xià Lǐ (referring to Xiē Lì in the *Zheng He Navigational Chart*, today's Maunt Delly to the north of Calicut, West Coast of India., or Alwaye, a small port twenty miles north of Cochin today), Jiālǐ Nà (probably in the southwestern part of Iran in today's Persian Gulf; or in Today's coastal area of India, the present location is unknown.), Gullifo (referring to Calicut on the north coast of Kerala, India), Bā Nán Bāxī (now Banavāsi, southeast of Karwar, Karnataka, India, and Honavar is its major port on the west coast), in East Africa, Ā Sī Lǐ (referring to Quseir on the west coast of the Red Sea in Egypt), Má Nàlǐ (referring to Malindi in Kenya), Céng Yáo Luó (referring to Kilwa Kisiwani, Tanzania), Jiā Jiàngmén Lǐ (referring to Quelimane, Mozambique), Bōsī Lí (now Basra, Iraq)), Má Hē Sī Lí (also known as Musili, present-day Mosur in northwestern Iraq), Tà Jí Nà (the Port of Tagina located in the east of Aden in the southern Arabian Peninsula), Tiāntáng (also known as Kaaba, present-day Mecca, Saudi Arabia), and the port of Licata in the south of Sicily, Italy.

　　汪大淵的旅程中還透露出從中國到勃泥和摩鹿加群島、爪哇和帝汶島的航線。趙汝适的諸蕃志曾記載臺灣南部的毗舍耶人到菲律賓中部的三嶼販售臺灣的土產，也記載了毗舍耶人渡海到泉州。但該書沒有記載中國漢人船隻航行中國、澎湖、臺灣、菲律賓到勃泥的航線。汪大淵的島夷志略則記載了他從泉州到澎湖、臺灣、毗舍耶、蘇祿、勃泥到文老古（即今印尼的摩鹿加群島）的航線。

Wang Da-yuan's journey also revealed routes from China to Boni and the Moluccas, Java, and Timor. Zhao Rugua's *Zhufan Chi* once recorded that the Visaya people in southern Taiwan went to Sanyu (Three Islands) in the central Philippines to sell Taiwan's local products, and also recorded that the Visayan people crossed the sea to Quanzhou. However, the book *Zhufan Chi* does not record the route that Chinese Han people's ships sailed from China, Penghu, Taiwan, and the Philippines to Boni. Wang Da-yuan's *Dao-yi Chi-lue* recorded his route from Quanzhou to Penghu, Taiwan, Visaya, Sulu, Boni to Wén Lǎo Gǔ (now the Moluccas in Indonesia).

在元國，有兩個人物遊歷外國而有專門著作，一位是周達觀，另一位即是汪大淵。周達觀於 1296 年以間諜身份前往真臘（柬埔寨）探查，回國後寫成真臘風土記一書，記錄他在柬埔寨所見所聞。汪大淵是江西南昌人，身份則無從考察，應是單純到海外遊歷的旅遊者。他為何能遊歷多國？除了言語不通外，也涉及攜帶旅費的問題。因此，最大的可能是他搭船當船員換食宿，他去過的港口，可能有華人，可依賴華人協助他搭船或者解決他的食宿問題。

In the Yuan Dynasty, there were two figures who traveled abroad and wrote special works, one is Zhou Da-guan and the other is Wang Da-yuan. Zhou Da-guan went to Zhen-la (Cambodia) as a spy to investigate in 1296. After returning to China, he wrote a book *Record on the Custom and Land of Zhen-la*, recording what he saw and heard in Cambodia. Wang Da-yuan is a native of Nanchang, Jiangxi, but his identity cannot be known. He should be a tourist who simply travels overseas. Why can he travel to many countries? In addition to the language barrier, there is also the issue of carrying travel expenses. Therefore, the biggest possibility is that he took the ship as a crew member for boarding and lodging. There may be Chinese in the ports he has visited, and he can rely on the Chinese to assist him in boarding the ship or solving his boarding and lodging problems.

因為是旅遊所記，故觀察所及的是國家及港口的地理位置、物產、風土民情，有時還加上當地怪誕的傳說，以吸引讀者對外國的奇風異俗之興趣。

Because it is a travel record, the observations are based on the geographical location, products, customs, and folks of the country and port, and sometimes local bizarre legends are added to attract the readers' interest in foreign strange and different customs.

總之，汪大淵的著作還有若干地名無可考，例如，馬魯澗、千里馬、萬年港等，如能清楚知道其位在今天何地，則更可知悉汪大淵整個遊歷的行蹤。如果目前考證出來他遊歷的若干地名確實可靠，則他最遠到過義大利西西里島，也去過東非，因此他應是中國第一個到過上述地方的人。明國鄭和最遠到過東非和阿拉伯半島波斯灣沿岸，可能參考了汪大淵的著作，汪大淵成為鄭和下西洋的先行者，應無問題。這兩人唯一的差別在於，汪大淵是搭乘商船自行旅遊，而鄭和是帶領艦隊巡視各有關港口。

In short, Wang Da-yuan's works still have some place names that cannot be checked, such as Mǎ Lǔ Jiàn, Qiānlǐmǎ,

Wànnián Port, etc. If you can clearly know where those places are today, you can even know the whereabouts of Wang Da-yuan's entire travels. If the current textual research shows that some of the place names he has traveled are reliable, he has traveled to Sicily, Italy, and East Africa at the farthest, so he should be the first person in China to have visited the above-mentioned places. In the Ming Dynasty, Zheng He traveled as far as East Africa and the Persian Gulf coast of the Arabian Peninsula. He may have referred to Wang Da-yuan's writings. Wang Da-yuan became the forerunner of Zheng He's voyages to the West Ocean, and there should be no problem. The only difference between the two is that Wang Da-yuan traveled by himself on a merchant ship, while Zheng He led the fleet to patrol the relevant ports.

正文
Text

1.彭湖
1. Penghu (Pescadores Islands)

島分三十有六，巨細相間，坡隴相望，乃有七澳居其間，各得其名。自泉州順風二晝夜可至。有草無木，土瘠不宜禾稻。泉人結茅為屋居之。氣候常暖，風俗樸野，人多眉壽。男女穿長布杉，繫以土布。

白話文(Vernacular)：

島嶼總數有三十六個，大小不一，彼此相望，中間有七個海灣，各有其名稱。從泉州順風兩個晚上可到。該地有草，沒有樹林，土地貧瘠，不適宜種稻。泉州人結茅草屋居住。氣候常溫暖，風俗樸實，人多長壽。男女穿長布衫，腰圍上土布。

The island has 36 islands, the size is different, and the islands face each other, but there are seven bays among them, each of which has its own name. It can be reached in two days and nights from Quanzhou downwind. There are grasses but no trees, and the soil is not suitable for rice. The people of Quanzhou build thatch huts as houses. The climate is often warm, the customs are simple and wild, and the people are long-lived. Men and women wear long clothes, tied with local cloth.

煮海為鹽，釀秫為酒，採魚、蝦、螺、蛤以佐食，爇牛糞以爨，魚膏為油。地產胡麻、綠豆。山羊之孳生數萬為羣。家以烙毛刻角為記，晝夜不收，各遂其生育。工商興販，以樂其利。

白話文(Vernacular)：

煮海水製鹽，釀高粱製酒，採集魚、蝦、螺、蛤佐餐。燒牛冀煮飯，以魚膏製油。土產有胡麻、綠豆。羊有數萬頭。每家都以烙毛、刻角做記號。白天和晚上都任其在野外，自然生育繁衍。工商繁榮，各蒙其利。

The people boil the sea for salt, brew sorghum for wine, extract fish, shrimp, snails, and clams for food, burn cow dung for cooking and use fish paste for oil. The land produces flax and green beans. Goats breed in groups of tens of thousands. Each family flatirons the goat hair and horns as a mark, and they do not drive them into fenced compounds day and night, let them give birth freely. Industry and commerce prosper with profits accruing.

地隸泉州晉江縣。至元年間立巡檢司，以週歲額辦鹽課中統錢鈔[1]一十錠二十五兩，別無科差。

白話文(Vernacular)：

此地隸屬泉州晉江縣管轄。至元年間設立巡檢司，每年課徵中統錢鈔一十錠二十五兩，此外別無其他課徵。

This land belongs to the jurisdiction of Jinjiang County, Quanzhou. During the Zhì Yuán period, the patrol-inspection

---

[1] 中統錢鈔，是元代中統元年（西元 1260 年）的忽必烈時代發行的紙鈔。參見「中統鈔」，百科知識，
https://www.easyatm.com.tw/wiki/%E4%B8%AD%E7%B5%B1%E9%88%94　2022 年 10 月 11 日瀏覽。

Zhongtong banknotes were issued during the Kublai Khan era in the first year of Zhongtong in the Yuan Dynasty (1260 AD). See "Zhongtong Banknotes", *Encyclopedia Knowledge*,
https://www.easyatm.com.tw/wiki/%E4%B8%AD%E7%B5%B1%E9%88%94　October 11, 2022 retrieved.

department was established, and the Salt Administration annually levies the Zhōng Tǒng qián chāo for 10 ingots and 25 taels, and there were no other taxes.

2. 琉球
2. Ryukyu[2]

　　地勢盤穹，林木合抱。山曰翠麓，曰重曼，曰斧頭，曰大峙。其峙山極高峻，自彭湖望之甚近。余登此山則觀海潮之消長，夜半則望暘谷之出，紅光燭天，山頂為之俱明。土潤田沃，宜稼穡。氣候漸暖，俗與彭湖差異。水無舟楫，以筏濟之。男子婦人拳髮，以花布為衫。

　　白話文(Vernacular)：

　　地勢矗立高聳，林木叢生，山有稱為翠麓、重曼、斧頭和大峙等山。山極高峻，從彭湖看過去，很近。我登上高山觀看海潮的漲落，半夜則看日出之處，紅光照亮了天際，山頂變得很亮。土地濕潤，田地肥沃，適宜種稻。氣候漸漸暖和。其風俗和澎湖不同。人民不使用船，而使用竹筏。男女都髻髮，穿花布衫。

The terrain is like a circling loft, and the trees hug each other. The mountain is called Cuilu, called Chongman, called Fǔtóu, and called Dà Zhì. The mountain is very high and steep, and it is very close to Ryukyu from Penghu watching. When I climbed this mountain, I watched the ebb and flow of the tide, and at midnight, I watched the place of sunrise, the red light

---

[2] 本書的琉球，指的是臺灣。
Ryukyu in this book refers to Taiwan.

flying in the sky, and the top of the mountain was bright. The fields are fertile and suitable for crops. The climate is getting warmer, and the customs are different from Penghu. There is no boat in the water, so a raft is used to supplement it. Men and women wear chignons and wear floral cloth as their shirts.

煮海水為鹽，釀蔗漿為酒。知番主酋長之尊，有父子骨肉之義。他國之人倘有所犯，則生割其肉以啖之，取其頭懸木竿。

白話文(**Vernacular**)：

煮海水製鹽，釀蔗漿製酒。人民知道番主和酋長具有尊嚴，有父子骨肉之義。他國之人如有所侵犯，則生割其肉吃下，砍他的頭臚懸掛在木桿上。

The people boil sea water for salt and brew sugarcane pulp for wine. They know the respect of the chief of the chieftain. The people know the meaning of the flesh and blood of father and son. If they suffered from an attack by another country, they will cut the enemy's flesh to eat it and hang his head on a wooden pole.

地產沙金、黃豆、黍子、硫黃、黃蠟[3]、鹿、豹、麂皮。貿易之貨，用土珠、瑪瑙、珍[4]珠、粗碗、處州[5]磁器之屬。

---

[3]黃蠟，即是蜂蜜。

Yellow wax is honey.

[4] 原文寫為「金」，故改之。

The original text was written as "Gold", so I correct it.

[5] 處州，指浙江處州府，以龍泉縣產的青磁最為有名。參見「龍泉青瓷」，維基百科，https://zh.wikipedia.org/zh-tw/%E9%BE%8D%E6%B3%89%E9%9D%92%E7%93%B7 2022 年

海外諸國蓋由此始。

白話文**(Vernacular)**：

當地生產沙金、黃豆、黍子（黃米）、硫黃、黃蠟、鹿、豹、麂皮。交易使用土珠、瑪瑙、珍珠、粗碗、處州磁器等物品。海外諸國從此地開始

This land produces sand gold, soybean, millet, sulfur, yellow wax, deer, leopard, and chamois. The goods for trade use local beads, agate, pearls, crude bowls, and Chuzhou porcelains. The voyages to overseas countries start from here.

3. 三島[6]

3. Sāndǎo (Three islands)

居大奇山之東，嶼分鼎峙，有疊山層巒，民傍陸居之。田瘠穀少，俗質樸，氣候差暖。男女間有白者。男頂拳髮，婦人椎髻，俱披單衣。男子常附舶至泉州經紀，磬其資囊，以文其身。既歸其國，則國人以尊長之禮待之，延之上坐，雖父老亦不得與爭焉。習俗以其至唐，故貴之也。

白話文**(Vernacular)**：

此地位在大奇山之東方，各島分別矗立，山巒層疊，人民居住在陸地邊。田地貧瘠，穀物少，風俗質樸，氣候暖和。

---

10 月 12 日瀏覽。

Chuzhou refers to the Chuzhou prefecture in Zhejiang Province and is most famous for the green magnets produced in Longquan County. See "Longquan Celadon", *Wikipedia*, https://zh.wikipedia.org/zh-tw/%E9%BE%8D%E6%B3%89%E9%9D%92%E7%93%B7 October 12, 2022 retrieved.

[6] 三島又寫為三嶼，指菲律賓中部民多洛島、班乃島和巴拉望島。
Sāndǎo, also written as San-yu, refers to Mindoro, Panay, and Palawan in the central Philippines.

男女之間皮膚有白者。男頭上盤髮，女則髻髮。都穿單衣。男子常搭乘船舶到泉州做生意，然後傾其所有的錢紋身。他歸國後，國人以尊長之禮待他，請他上座，雖父老也不敢跟他相爭。習俗上以他曾到過中國，所以他就受到尊敬。

This land is located in the east of Dachi Mountain; many islands face each other. There are stacked mountains, and the people live on the land. The fields are barren and have few grains. The customs are vulgar and simple, and the climate is warm. There are some white skin men and women among them. Men wear curly hair, women wear a bun, and a single coat is draped over their shoulders. A man often takes a ship to Quanzhou to do business and pays all of his money to tattoo his body. When he returns to his country, the people of the country treat him with respect and seat him in a prestigious seat. Even the old man or his father's generation will not be able to compete with him. The custom is as long as he has been gone to China, so he is to be respected.

民煮海為鹽，釀蔗漿為酒。有酋長。地產黃臘、木棉、花布。貿易之貨用銅珠、青白花碗、小花印布、鐵塊之屬。

白話文(Vernacular)：

人民煮海製鹽，釀蔗漿製酒。有酋長。當地產黃臘、木棉、花布。貿易之貨品使用銅珠、青白花碗、小花印布和鐵塊等。

The people boil the sea for salt and brew sugarcane pulp for wine. There is a chief. The land produces yellow wax, kapok, and flower cloth. The goods for trade used copper beads, green and white flower bowls, small flower-printed cloth, and iron blocks.

次日答陪，曰海瞻，曰巴弄吉，曰蒲里唠，曰東流里。
無甚異產，故附此耳。

白話文(Vernacular)：

其他地名有答陪、海瞻、巴弄吉、蒲里唠、東流里等。
這些地方沒有特別的出產，故附記在此。

There are other places, called Dá Péi, Hǎi Dàn, Balongji,
Polillo, and Dongliuli. There are no special products, so attached
to record it here.

4. 麻逸[7]

4. Máyìt

山勢平寬，夾溪聚落，田膏腴，氣候稍暖。俗尚節義。
男女椎髻，穿青布衫。凡婦喪夫，則削其髮，絕食七日，與
夫同寢，多瀕於死。七日之外不死，則親戚勸以飲食，或可
全生，則終身不改其節。甚至喪夫而焚屍，則赴火而死。酋
豪之喪則殺奴婢二三十(原文為千字，恐有誤)人以殉葬。

白話文(Vernacular)：

山勢平坦寬廣，聚落沿著溪流兩岸分布，田地膏腴，氣
候稍暖。俗尚節義。男女椎髻，穿青布衫。婦女喪夫，則削
其髮，絕食七日，與夫屍體同寢，多瀕臨死亡。七日之後不
死，則親戚勸她飲食，或可保全生命，她終身不改其節操。

---

[7] 麻逸，指民多洛島（Mindoro）。

Máyìt refers to Mindoro island.　Please see　Eufemio P., Patanñe, *The
Philippines in the 6th to 16th Centuries*, LSA Press Inc., Quezon City, the
Philippines, 1996, p. 66.

甚至在她的丈夫火葬時，她也縱身火堆而殉死。酋長或豪族之喪則殺奴婢二、三十(原文為千字，恐有誤)人以殉葬。

The mountains are flat and wide, the people settle along the river. The fields are fertile. The climate is slightly warm. The customs of people respect human relations. Men and women wear a bun on their heads and wear a green cloth shirt. When a woman loses her husband, she cuts her hair, fasts for seven days, and sleeps with her dead husband, and most of them are on the verge of death. If she does not die beyond seven days, her relatives persuade her to eat something, or she may be able to live, but she will not change her manners for the rest of her life. Even when burning her husband's body, she would even jump into the fire and die. At the funeral of the chieftain, twenty or thirty (The original text is a thousand, may be wrong) slaves and maids were killed for burial.

民煮海為鹽，釀糖水為酒。地產木棉、黃蠟、玳瑁、檳榔、花布。貿易之貨用鼎、鐵塊、五采紅布、紅絹、牙錠之屬。蠻賈議價領去，博易土貨，然後准價，舶商守信，終始不爽約也。

白話文**(Vernacular)**：

人民煮海水製鹽，釀糖水製酒。地產木棉、黃蠟、玳瑁、檳榔、花布。貿易之貨品使用鼎、鐵塊、五采紅布、紅絹和牙錠等。蠻人商人議價後將貨品拿去，換給土產，然後准價，舶商守信，終始不爽約也。

The people boil the sea for salt and brew sugar for wine. The land produces kapok, yellow wax, tortoiseshell, betel nut, and flower cloth. The goods for trade used tripods, iron blocks, five kinds of red cloth, red silk, and silver ingots. The barbarian traders completed the price-bargaining with the Chinese traders and brought the local products to barter with the Chinese goods. Then they comply with the promise to keep their honesty, and never break their promise.

5. 無枝拔[8]
5. Wú Zhī Bá

在闍麻羅華之東南，石山對峙，民墾闢山為田，鮮食多種薯。氣候常熱，獨春有微寒。俗直。男女褊髮纏頭，繫細紅布。極以婚姻為重，往往指腹成親。通國守義，如有失信者，罰金二兩重，以納其主。

白話文(Vernacular)：

在闍麻羅華之東南方，有石山對峙，人民墾闢山地為田地，多種蕃薯食用。氣候常熱，春天時有點寒冷。風俗純樸。男女將頭髮紮在頭上，繫一塊細紅布。他們很重視婚姻，往往指腹成親。人民很守信義，如有失信者，罰金二兩重，繳納給其酋長。

This place is located in the southeast of Kanma Luohua, the stone mountains face each other, and the people reclaim the mountains as fields and eat a variety of sweet potatoes. The climate is often hot, with a slight chill in spring. The customs are

---

[8]日本藤田豐八認為無枝拔是滿剌加（馬六甲）。參見藤田豐八校註，島夷志略校註，文殿閣書莊，北平，1936年，頁12。

Japanese Fujita Toyohachi believes that Wú Zhī Bá is Melaka. See Fujita Toyohachi notes, *Notes on Dao-yi Chi-lue*, Wendian Pavilion Bookstore, Peiping, 1936, p. 12.

quite simple. Men and women have their hair tied around their heads and tied with fine red cloth. The people attach great importance to marriage. Often pointing to the big belly, two children grow up and get married. Everyone keeps righteousness; if someone didn't keep up a promise, he will be fined gold two taels by the chief.

.

民煮海為鹽，釀椰漿、蕨粉為酒。有酋長。產花斗錫、鉛。綠毛狗。貿易之貨，用西洋布、青白處州磁器、瓦壜和鐵鼎之屬。

白話文**(Vernacular)**：

人民煮海水製鹽，釀椰漿、蕨粉製酒。有酋長。生產花斗錫、鉛。綠毛狗。貿易之貨品使用西洋布、青白處州磁器、瓦壜和鐵鼎等。

The people boil the seawater for salt and brew coconut milk and fern powder for wine. There is a chief. Natural tin and lead are produced there. A green hair dog exists there. The goods for trade use the West Ocean cloth, green and white Chuzhou porcelains, earthen jars, and iron tripods.

6. 龍涎嶼[9]

---

[9] 龍涎嶼，位在蘇門答臘島東北邊的 Bulas Island。參見 Ulrich Theobald, "Xingcha shenglan 星槎勝覽," *ChinaKnowledge.de -An Encyclopaedia on Chinese History, Literature and Art,* http://www.chinaknowledge.de/Literature/Science/xingchashenglan.html 2022 年 10 月 16 日瀏覽。藤田豐八亦認為是 Bulas Island，參見藤田豐八校註，前引書，頁 16。

Lóng Xián Yǔ is located on Bulas Island in the northeast of Sumatra Island. See Ulrich Theobald, "Xīng Chá Shèng Lǎn," China Knowledge.de -An Encyclopaedia on Chinese History, Literature and Art,

6. Lóng Xián Yǔ

嶼方而平,延袤荒野,上如雲塢之盤,絕無田產之利。每值天清氣和,風作浪湧,羣龍游戲,出沒海濱,時吐涎沫於其嶼之上,故以得名。涎之色或黑于烏香,或數于浮石,聞之微有腥氣。然用之合諸香,則味尤清遠,雖茄藍木、梅花腦、檀、麝、梔子花[10]、沉速木、薔薇水衆香,必待此以發之。

白話文(Vernacular):

龍涎嶼地形方正而平坦,多處是荒野,島上多雲霧,絕無田產之利。每值天清氣和,風作浪湧,有許多鯨魚游戲,出沒海濱,經常吐涎沫於該島上,故以得名。涎沫之色澤比烏香還黑,散佈在浮石之間,聞之微有腥氣。然將它與其他各種香料混合,則味尤清遠,雖茄藍木、梅花腦、檀、麝、梔子花 、沉速木、薔薇水衆香,必待此香來啟發香氣。

The island is square and flat, extending into the wilderness, with cloudy and fog on it, and there is absolutely no benefit for land production. When it is a clear day, the wind is surging, and the dragons (referring to whales) play games and haunt the seashore. They spit on the island, hence the name. The color of

---

http://www.chinaknowledge.de/Literature/Science/xingchashenglan.html, October 16, 2022 retrieved.

　Fujita Toyohachi also thinks it is Bulas Island, See Fujita Toyohachi, *op.cit.*, p. 16.

[10]梔子花之功用是做黃色的染料。參見 Willem Pieter Groeneveldt, *Notes on the Malay Archipelago and Malacca, compiled from Chinese Sources*, W. Bruining, Batavia, 1876, p.134.

　The function of gardenia is to make a yellow dye. See Willem Pieter Groeneveldt, *Notes on the Malay Archipelago and Malacca, compiled from Chinese Sources*, W. Bruining, Batavia, 1876, p.134.

the saliva may be as black as black incense or spread on the pumice, and it smells slightly fishy. However, when used in combination with various incense, the smell is fragrant. Although Jiā Lán wood, Méihuā Nǎo, sandalwood, musk, gardenia, agarwood, fast incense wood, and rose water are all incense, they must wait for this dragon saliva incense to initiate it.

此地前代無人居之，間有他番之人，用完木鑿舟，駕使以拾之，轉鬻於他國。貨用金、銀之屬博之。

白話文(**Vernacular**)：

此地從前沒有人居住，偶有他處之人，用整塊木頭鑿舟，駕駛到該島採集海物，轉賣到他國。貨品交易使用金、銀等。

This place was uninhabited in previous generations, and there were people from other countries who hewed a boat out of a single piece of wood. They drive the boat to pick up local products and sell them to other countries. They use gold and silver to do business.

7. 交趾

7. Jiāozhǐ (Cochin)

古交州之地，今為安南大越國。山環而險，溪道互布。外有三十六庄，地廣人稠，氣候常熱。田多沃饒，俗尚禮義，有中國之風。男女面白而齒黑，戴冠，穿唐衣、皂褶，絲襪方履。凡民間俊秀子弟，八歲入小學，十五入大學，其誦詩讀書、談性理、為文章，皆與中國同，惟言語差異耳。古今歲貢中國，已載諸史。

白話文(**Vernacular**)：

此地為古交州之地方，今為安南大越國。有山環繞，相當危險，河流密佈。外有三十六個村莊，地廣人稠，氣候常熱。田地肥沃，俗尚禮義，有中國之風。男女臉面是白的而牙齒是黑的，戴帽子，穿中國式衣服、黑色便服，穿絲織襪子、方型的鞋子。凡民間俊秀子弟，八歲入小學，十五歲入大學，其誦詩讀書、談性理、寫文章，皆與中國相同，不過言語有所差異。從古到今都對中國進貢，史書都有記載。

The land is of the ancient Jiaozhou, now the Annan Da-Viet Kingdom. This country is surrounded by mountains and dangerous with many rivers. There are thirty-six villages outside, vast lands, and a dense population, and the climate is often hot. Most of the fields are fertile. The custom advocates etiquette and has a Chinese style. Men and women have white faces and black teeth. They wear crowns, Chinese clothes, black casual clothes, silk stockings, and square shoes. All the sparkish children of the folk entered elementary school at the age of eight and entered university at fifteen. They recited poetry, read books, talked about nature and reason, and wrote essays, which are all the same as China, but the language is different. They pay tribute to China in ancient and modern years which has been recorded in history.

民煮海為鹽，釀秫為酒。酋長以同姓女為妻。地產沙金、白銀、銅、錫、鉛、象牙、翠毛、肉桂、檳榔。貿易之貨，用諸色綾羅、匹帛、青布、牙梳、紙紮、青銅、鐵之類。流通使用銅錢。民間以六十七錢折中統銀壹兩。官用止七十為率。舶人不販其地。惟偷販之舟，止於斷山上下，不得至其官場，恐中國人窺見其國之虛實也。[11]

白話文(**Vernacular**)：

人民煮海水製鹽，釀高粱製酒。酋長娶同姓女為妻。該地產沙金、白銀、銅、錫、鉛、象牙、翠毛、肉桂和檳榔。貿易之貨品使用各種綾羅、匹帛、青布、牙梳、紙紮、青銅和鐵等。流通使用銅錢。民間以六十七錢折中統銀壹兩。官方則以七十為兌換率。船商不到該地做生意。那些偷偷到該地做生意的船隻，是到斷山登岸，不可至其官署所在地港口做生意，恐中國人窺見該國之虛實也。

The people boil the seawater for salt and brew rice for wine. The chief marries a woman who has the same surname as him. The land produces sand gold, silver, copper, tin, lead, ivory, kingfisher feathers, cinnamon, and betel nut. The goods for trade use various colors of silk, textiles, green cloth, ivory comb, paper, green copper, iron, etc. Circulation uses copper coins. The folks use sixty-seven coins as a discount for one tael of Zhōng Tǒng silver. But officials use seventy as the rate. The boatmen do not sell their goods over there. But the boats land secretly at the Duàn Shān (a steep mountain), and cannot reach its official port, lest the Chinese see the reality of their country.

8. 占城

8. Zhàn Chéng (Champa)

---

[11] 當時越南和元國有戰爭，越南禁止中國船隻進入其港口，以防其刺探軍情。

　　At that time, Vietnam and Yuan State were at war, and Vietnam banned Chinese ships from entering its ports to prevent them from spying on military conditions.

地據海衝，與新、舊州為鄰。氣候乍熱。田中上等，宜種穀。俗喜侵掠。歲以上、下元日縱諸人採生人膽，以鬻官家。官家以銀售之，以膽調酒與家人同飲，云通身是膽，使人畏之，亦不生疿癗也。

白話文(**Vernacular**)：

此地控制海洋要衝，與新、舊州為鄰。氣候會突然炎熱。田地屬中上等肥沃，適宜種穀。俗喜侵掠。每年在上、下元節日，讓大家採活人的膽，賣給政府。政府再賣出，收取銀錢。膽是用來調酒與家人同飲，傳說喝過膽酒的人會通身是膽，使人害怕，也可預防疾病。

The land is located in the pivotal of the sea shipping route, adjacent to New Zhōu and Old Zhōu. The climate is hot. The field is the second best, suitable for planting grains. The vulgar like to plunder. On the days of 15th January and October respectively, permit the people to excise the guts of the living person, and sell them to officials. The officials sell it to general people for silver. The people blend the guts with wine and then drink with their family. It is said that it can increase his courage and make other people scared of him. It can also prevent disease.

城之下，水多洄旋，舶往復數日，止舟，載婦人登舶，與舶人為偶。及去，則垂涕而別。明年，舶人至，則偶合如故。或有遭難流落於其地者，則婦人推舊情以飲食衣服供其身，歸則又重贐以送之，蓋有此情義如此。仍禁服半[12]，似

---

[12] 服半，可能為「半服」之倒寫，是中國山東南部的方言，指不正經。參見「半服」，百度百科，
https://baike.baidu.hk/item/%E5%8D%8A%E6%9C%8D/2275649

唐人。日三四浴。以腦、麝合油塗體。以白字寫黑皮為文書。

白話文**(Vernacular)**：

在新州城的下方，水多迴旋，使得船隻在此迴旋數日，船停在岸外，有小船載婦人登上大船，與船人相會（共宿）。她們要離去時，則流淚告別。明年，船人再到，則與這些女人相會如故。或有遭難流落於該地者，則婦人念舊情以飲食衣服供其吃穿，當落難者歸國時，這些婦女又贈給財物，因為有此情義的關係。但仍禁止不正經的行為，這一點跟中國人相似。每日洗澡三、四次。以腦、麝合油塗抹身體。寫作是以白色筆跡寫在黑色皮革上。

Under the New Zhōu city, the water is swirling, and the ships go back and forth for several days. The ship finally stops off the coast, and the women were loaded onto the ship, and they meet(slept with) the people on the ship. When these women leave the ships, they weep and say goodbye. Next year, when the ships arrive, the meet affairs remain the same. Or if there are unfortunate people distressed in this country, the woman will provide food and clothes with old affection for them. When the distressed people return to their country, these women will give them great gifts that are because of this affection. But here Fú Bàn (referring to misbehaving) still is banned, like Chinese people. The people take baths three or four times a day and mix Dipterocarpaceae and musk oil to smear their bodies. The

2022 年 10 月 12 日瀏覽。

Fú Bàn, which may be the reverse of " Bàn Fú", is a dialect in southern Shandong, China, which means not serious. See " Bàn Fú ", *Baidu Encyclopedia*,
https://baike.baidu.hk/item/%E5%8D%8A%E6%9C%8D/2275649
October 12, 2022 retrieved.

writing is with white handwriting on black leather.

煮海為鹽，釀小米為酒。地產紅柴、茄藍木、打布。貨用青磁、花碗、金銀首飾、酒、厄布、燒珠之屬。

白話文(Vernacular)：

煮海水製鹽，釀小米製酒。當地產紅柴、茄藍木、打布。貨品使用青磁、花碗、金銀首飾、酒、厄布和燒珠等。

The people boil the sea for salt and brew millet for wine. The land produced red firewood, Jiā Lán wood, and beat cloth. The goods for trade used green porcelains, flower bowls, gold and silver jewelry, wine, Gardenia-dyed fabric, and burning beads.

9. 民多朗[13]

9. Mindorang

臨海要津，溪通海。水不鹹。田沃饒，米穀廣。氣候熱，俗尚儉。男女椎髻，穿短皂衫，下繫青布短裙。民鑿井而飲，煮海為鹽，釀小米為酒。

白話文(Vernacular)：

該地靠近海上的重要航道，溪流通向大海。水不鹹。田地肥沃，到處生產米穀。氣候熱，風俗崇尚節儉。男女椎髻，穿短的黑布衫，下半身繫青布短裙。民鑿井而飲，

This place faces important ocean waterways; the streams

---

[13]藤田豐八認為民多朗是指越南東南部的潘郎（Phanrang）港。參見藤田豐八校註，前引書，頁25。

Fujita Toyohachi refers to Mindorang as the port of Phanrang in southeastern Vietnam. See Fujita Toyohachi notes, *op. cit.*, p. 25.

connect to the sea. The water is not salty. The fields are fertile, and everywhere grains are planted. The climate is hot and vulgar is still frugal. Men and women wear a bun on their heads, short black shirts on the upper body, and green short skirts on the lower body. The people dig wells and drink water, boil the sea for salt, and brew millet for wine.

有酋長。禁盜，盜則戮及一家。地產烏梨木、麝、檀、木棉花、牛䴢皮。貨用漆器、銅鼎、闍婆布、紅絹、青布、斗錫、酒之屬。

白話文(Vernacular)：

有酋長。禁止偷盜，犯強盜罪者，殺其全家人。地產烏梨木、麝、檀、木棉花和牛䴢皮。貨品使用漆器、銅鼎、闍婆布、紅絹、青布、斗錫和酒等。

There is a chief. Prohibition of robbery: if one commits robbery, then his family members are killed. The land produces ebony, musk, sandalwood, kapok, and cow suede. The goods for trade use lacquerware, copper tripods, Java cloth, red silk, green cloth, natural tin, and wine.

10. 賓童龍[14]
10. Bintonglong

賓童龍隸占城，土骨與占城相連，有雙溪以間之，佛書

---

[14]藤田豐八認為賓童龍是越南慶和省（Khan-hoa）之婆那加（Po-nagar）。參見藤田豐八校註，前引書，頁 25。

Fujita Toyohachi believed that Bintonglong was the Po-nagar of Khan-hoa province, Vietnam. See Fujita Toyohachi notes, *op. cit.*, p. 25.

所稱王舍城是也。或云目連屋基猶存。田土、人物、風俗、氣候與占城略同。人死則持孝服，設佛，擇僻地以葬之。國主騎象或馬，打紅傘，從者百餘人，執盾讚唱曰亞或僕（番語也）。

白話文(Vernacular)：

賓童龍隸屬占城，領土與占城相連，有兩條河流隔開，佛書所稱的王舍城，就是此地。或者傳說目連屋基還存在這裡。田地、人物、風俗、氣候與占城約略相同。人死了，家人要穿孝服，設立佛壇，擇偏僻的地方加以埋葬。國主出門騎象或馬，打著紅傘，隨從有百餘人，執盾牌，口裡唱著「亞」或「僕」（番語也）。

Bintonglong belongs to the Zhàn Chéng, and the land is connected to the Zhàn Chéng. There are two rivers to separate both countries. Here the Buddhist books call it King's City. It is said that the house base of the Maudgalyayana still exists. The fields, figures, customs, and climate are similar to those of Zhàn Chéng. When a person dies, his relatives should wear filial garments, set up a Buddha hall, and bury him in a secluded place. The lord of the country rides on an elephant or a horse carries a red umbrella, and more than a hundred followers hold shields and sing praises of "Ya" or "Pu" (barbarian language).

其屍頭蠻女子害人甚於占城，故民多廟事而血祭之。蠻亦父母胎生，與女子不異，特眼中無瞳人。遇夜，則飛頭食人糞尖。頭飛去，若人以紙或布掩其項，則頭歸不接而死。凡人居其地大便後，必用水淨浣，否則蠻食其糞，卽逐臭與人同睡。倘有所犯，則腸肚皆為所食，精神盡為所奪而死矣。

白話文(Vernacular)：

該地傳說有屍頭蠻女子，其害人的程度超過占城，所以當地人民多在廟裡用血祭拜它。屍頭蠻也是父母所生，與一般女子相同，唯一不同的是她的眼中無瞳仁。一到晚上，她的頭會飛起來去吃人的糞便。當她的頭飛出去後，若使用紙或布遮蓋她的脖子，使得她的頭飛回後無法與脖子相接，她就會死去。凡住在當地的人，在大便後，必用水清洗乾淨，否則屍頭蠻會來吃大便，她逐臭與人同睡。如果對她有所侵犯，她就會吃掉侵犯者的腸肚，精神被她所奪，最後死去。

The female Shī Tóu Mán harmed people more than in Zhàn Chéng (Champa), so the people sacrificed with blood in the temple for worship. This Shī Tóu Mán is also born to their parents, and she is no different from a woman, but she has no pupils in her eyes. In the night, her head flies to eat the tip of a man's dung. When her head flies, if one with paper or cloth blanks her neck, her head can't connect to her neck, and she will die. After feces are on the ground, people must wash them with water; otherwise, Shī Tóu Mán will eat the dung and sleep with them. If one encroaches her, the man's intestines and stomach will be eaten by her, and the spirit will be taken away and die.

地產茄藍木、象牙。貨用銀、印花布。次曰胡麻、沙曼、頭羅、沙犢、寶毗齊。新故、越州諸番，無所產，舶亦不至。

白話文(Vernacular)：
當地生產茄藍木、象牙。貨品使用銀、印花布。其次還有胡麻、沙曼、頭羅、沙犢和寶毗齊。新故、越州等地，無所產，船舶也不去。

The land produces Jiā lán wood and ivory. The goods for trade used silver and printed cloth. The next ones are flax, shaman, tuluo, shaan, baopiqi. Xingu and Yuezhou, etc.; all the barbarians have nothing to produce, and ships do not go there.

11. 眞臘[15]
11. Zhen-la (Cambodia)

　　州南之門，實為都會，有城週圍七十餘里，石河周圍廣二十丈，戰象幾四十餘萬。殿宇凡三十餘所，極其壯麗。飾以金壁，舖銀為磚，置七寶椅，以待其主。貴人貴戚所坐，坐皆金机。歲一會，則以玉猿、金孔雀、六牙白象、三角銀蹄牛羅獻於前。列金獅子十隻於銅臺上，列十二銀塔，鎮以銅象。人凡飲食，必以金茶盤、籩豆金碗貯物用之。外名百塔州，作為金浮屠百座。一座為狗所觸，則造塔頂不成。次曰馬司錄池，復建五浮屠，黃金為尖。次曰桑香佛舍，造裹金石橋四十餘丈。諺云：「富貴眞臘」者也。

　　白話文(Vernacular)：

　　該國南方的大門，實為都會，該城市週圍七十餘里，石河周圍廣二十丈，戰象幾乎有四十餘萬。殿宇有三十餘所，極其壯麗。都裝飾有金壁，磚上舖銀，置七寶椅，俾讓其國主坐。貴人、貴戚所坐的也都是小金椅。貴族每年會見國主一次，會獻上玉猿、金孔雀、六牙白象、三角銀蹄牛羅給國主。列金獅子十隻於銅臺上，列十二銀塔，旁邊還有銅象矗立。他們在飲食時，必使用金茶盤、籩豆金碗貯物。城外有個名叫百塔州的地方，有金浮屠百座。一座若被狗所碰觸，那麼造塔頂就不成。其次，有叫馬司錄水池，建有五座浮屠，

---

[15] 眞臘是柬埔寨在第七世紀到十七世紀時的國名。
　　Zhen-la is the name of Cambodia from the seventh century to the seventeenth century.

其尖頂鑲有黃金。其次叫桑香佛舍，造裹金石橋四十餘丈。
俗諺說：「眞臘眞是富貴」的地方。

The entrance of the south of the state is actually a
metropolis. There are more than 70 miles around the city, 20 feet
around the Shihe (Stone River), and more than 400,000 war
elephants. There are more than thirty palace buildings,
extremely magnificent. It is decorated with gold and jades,
paved silver as bricks, and one seven-treasure chair, waiting for
its Lord. The nobles and their relatives are sitting on the small
golden chairs. The nobles meet with their Lord once a year, the
jade apes, gold peacocks, six-tooth white elephants, and triangle
silver hoof cattle are presented. Ten Golden Lions are on the
bronze platform, the twelve silver towers are set out, and the
bronze elephant. People use golden tea trays and cowpea golden
bowls to store the food. Out of the city, there is a 100-Tower
county, having a hundred golden Buddha towers. If it is touched
by a dog, then the top of the tower can't be completed. Next is
Mǎ Sī Lù Pond, upon which are built five Buddha towers
decorated with gold on the top of the tower. Next is the
Sangxiang Buddha House; there is a more than four hundred feet
stone bridge wrapped in gold. It is said: "What a Rich and
precious Zhen-la."

氣候常暖，俗尚華侈，田產富饒。民煮海為鹽，釀小米
為酒。男女椎髻。生女九歲，請僧作梵法，以指挑童身，取
紅點女額及母額，名為「利市」，云如此則他日嫁人，宜其
室家也。滿十歲卽嫁。若其妻與客淫，其夫甚喜，誇於人：
「我妻巧慧，得人愛之也」。以錦圍身，眉額施朱。酉出入，

用金車羽儀，體披瓔珞，右手持劍，左手持麈尾。法則劓、刖、刺配之刑。國人犯盜，則斷手足、烙胸背、鯨額，殺唐人則死。唐人殺番人至死，亦重罰金，如無金，以賣身取贖。

白話文(**Vernacular**)：

氣候常是暖和的，風俗崇尚華麗奢侈，田產富饒。人民煮海水製鹽，釀小米製酒。男女椎髻。生女兒九歲時，請僧侶作佛法，用手指挑破其處女膜，取血點在該女孩額頭及母親的額頭，稱為「利市」，傳說這樣做。他日嫁人的話，有益於其家庭也。年滿十歲就嫁人。若其妻子與客人做愛，其夫甚為高興，誇口對人說：「我妻巧慧，得到別人的喜愛」。以錦布包裹身體，眉額點上紅點。酋長出入，乘坐金車，還有穿戴羽毛儀隊跟從，上身披著珍珠帶子，右手持劍，左手持麈的尾毛。刑法則有割鼻子、砍斷雙腳、臉上刺青及發配邊疆。國人犯強盜罪，則斷手足、烙胸背、額頭刺青。若殺中國人則處死。中國人殺死番人，亦處重罰金，如無金錢，就賣身以贖罪。

The climate is often warm, the vulgar is very luxurious, and the fields are fertile. The people boil the sea for salt and brew millet for wine. Men and women wear a bun on their heads. When a girl reaches being nine-years-old, her parents ask the monk to make a Buddhist ritual; the monk uses his finger to break the girl's hymen and takes the blood dotting on the girl and her mother's forehead, naming it "Li Shi (good sign)". It is said that it will be good for her family when she gets married. Generally, girls get married at the age of ten. If one's wife sleeps with guests, her husband is very happy, and he exaggerates: "My wife is ingenious, and she is loved by others." The women wear brocade and dotted red points on their eyebrows. The chief enters and goes out, taking the golden car followed by the ceremonial team wearing feathers, putting jade strings on the upper body, holding the sword in the right hand, and holding the Zhǔ wěi (Elk's tail) in the left hand. The criminal penalty includes cutting off the nose, and feet, tattooing the face, and exile far away. If the nationals commit a crime of theft, they will have their hands or feet cut off, with a hot iron burn on the chest and back, and a tattooed forehead. If the nationals kill the Chinese, they will be punished with the death penalty. If the Chinese killed the local nationals, he will be fined a great sum of money. If he has no money, then sells himself for paying.

地產黃蠟、犀角、孔雀、沉速香、蘇木、大楓子[16]、翠羽，冠於各番。貨用金銀、黃紅燒珠、龍緞、建寧錦、絲布之屬。

白話文(**Vernacular**)：

當地生產黃蠟（蜂蜜）、犀角、孔雀、沉速香、蘇木、大楓子和翠羽，冠於各地。貨品使用金銀、黃紅燒珠、龍緞、建寧錦和絲布等。

The land produces yellow wax, rhino horn, peacock, agarwood, fast incense, Biancaea sappan, big maple, and kingfisher feathers; these products are the best among barbarian

---

[16]大楓子，是大楓子 (Hydnocarpus anthelmintica Pier) 的成熟種子，主要功效是治療疥癬，楊梅瘡，酒齄鼻，粉刺，黃褐斑。參見「大楓子」，醫砭，http://yibian.hopto.org/db/?yno=294 　2022 年 10 月 16 日瀏覽。

Dafengzi, the mature seed of Hydnocarpus anthelmintica Pier, is mainly used to treat mange, bayberry sores, rosacea, acne, and chloasma. See "Da Fengzi", *Yibian*, http://yibian.hopto.org/db/?yno=294 　October 16, 2022 retrieved.

countries. The goods for trade use gold and silver, yellow and red braised beads, dragon satin, Jianning brocade, and silk cloth.

12. 丹馬令[17]
12. Thammarak

地與沙里[18]、佛來安[19]為鄰國。山平互,田多,食粟有餘,新收者復留以待陳。俗節儉。氣候溫和。男女椎髻,衣白衣衫,繫青布縵。定婚用緞、錦、白錫若干塊。

白話文(**Vernacular**):

該地與沙里、佛來安為鄰國。山不高,田地多,食用的粟有剩餘,新收成的留待以後食用。風俗節儉。氣候溫和。男女椎髻,穿白衣衫,繫青布縵。定婚用緞、錦和白錫若干塊。

The land is neighbors with Shali and Folai'an. The mountains are flat, and there are many fields, with more than enough millet to eat. The new harvesters will be kept waiting until the old one is finished. The custom is frugal. The climate is moderately warm. Men and women wear a bun on their heads, are dressed in white clothes, and are tied with a green cloth

---

[17]丹馬令是位在泰南半島泰國的一個港口。

Thammarak is a port in Thailand on the southern peninsula of Thailand.

[18] 沙里,可能為泰國的蘇叻他尼(Surat Thani)。

Shali refers probably to Surat Thani, Thailand.

[19] 佛來安,又寫為佛羅安,是位在北大年和關丹之間的登嘉樓州的龍運(Dungun)。參考許雲樵,馬來亞史(上冊),新嘉坡青年書局,新加坡,1961頁192、194。

Folai'an, also written as Fó Luó An, refers to the Terengganu State's Dungun between Pattani and Kuantan. See Xu Yunqiao, *History of Malaya* (Volume 1), Singapore Youth Bookstore, Singapore, 1961, pp.192, 194.

mantle. Several pieces of satin, brocade, and white tin are used for engagement.

民煮海為鹽，釀小米為酒。有酋長。產上等白錫、米腦[20]、龜筒[21]、鶴頂[22]、降眞香[23]及黃熟香頭。貿易之貨，用甘

---

[20] 米腦，為龍腦之一種，狀如米粒的碎顆粒。

Small-grained borneol, a kind of borneol, is shaped like broken grains of rice.

[21] 龜筒，是龜殼，有兩種功用。第一，用於貼飾。參見「龜筒」，百度百科，https://baike.baidu.hk/item/%E9%BE%9C%E7%AD%92/4774903 2022 年 9 月 24 日瀏覽。

第二，用於清熱解毒。參見「蠵龜筒」，醫學百科，http://cht.a-hospital.com/w/%E8%A0%B5%E9%BE%9F%E7%AD%92 2022 年 9 月 24 日瀏覽。

Guī Tǒng is a turtle shell, that has two functions. First, for stickers. See " Guī Tǒng ", *Baidu Encyclopedia*, https://baike.baidu.hk/item/%E9%BE%9C%E7%AD%92/4774903 September 24, 2022   retrieved.

Second, Guī Tǒng is used for reducing heat and detoxifying. See " Xī Guī Tǒng (The loggerhead turtle shell)", *Medical Encyclopedia*, http://cht.a-hospital.com/w/%E8%A0%B5%E9%BE%9F%E7%AD%92 September 24, 2022 retrieved.

[22] 鶴頂，不是鶴，而是一種角犀鳥屬（buceros），有大鳥喙，頭頂上有贅肉，中間是空的，有些物種則是實心的，通常被切下當作胸針或其他裝飾品。參見 Willem Pieter Groeneveldt, *op.cit.*, p.74.

Heding, not cranes, but a species of hornbill (Buceros), have large beaks, and dewlaps on top of their heads, inside is hollow, or solid in some species, often cut out for brooches or other ornaments. See Willem Pieter Groeneveldt, *op.cit.*, p.74.

[23] 降眞香木材有濃郁的香氣，可做中藥，具有止血鎮痛、消腫等功效。參見「降眞香」，教育部重編國語辭典修訂本，https://dict.revised.moe.edu.tw/dictView.jsp?ID=95395&la=0&powerMode=0 2022 年 10 月 19 日瀏覽。

Jiangzhenxiang wood has a strong aroma, can be used as traditional Chinese medicine, and has the functions of hemostasis, analgesia, and swelling. See " Jiangzhenxiang ", *Ministry of Education Re-edited the Revised Version of the Mandarin Dictionary*, https://dict.revised.moe.edu.tw/dictView.jsp?ID=95395&la=0&powerMod

埋里布[24]、紅布、青白花碗和鼓之屬。

白話文**(Vernacular)**：

人民煮海水製鹽，釀小米製酒。有酋長。產上等白錫、米腦、龜筒、鶴頂、降眞香及黃熟香頭[25]。貿易之貨品使用甘埋里布、紅布、青白花碗和鼓等。

The people boil the sea for salt, and brew millet for wine. There is a chief. The land produces high-quality white tin, small-grained borneol, Guī Tǒng, Heding, Jiangzhen incense, and head of Huáng Shú incense. The goods for trade use the Gān Mái Lǐ cloth, red cloth, green-white flower bowls, and drums.

13.日麗[26]
13. Rì Lì

---

e=0   October 19, 2022 retrieved.

[24]原文寫為「甘理」，應是「甘埋里」之誤，故改之。

The original text was written as "Gan Li", which should be a mistake of " Gān Mái Lǐ ", so correct it.

[25] 黃熟香，是埋在土中非常久的熟香，所有的木質纖維組織結構熟爛，只剩下蜂窩狀的香腺組織留存，色黃，因為在土中的緣故，又稱為土沉香。見「黃熟香」，華人百科，https://www.itsfun.com.tw/%E9%BB%83%E7%86%9F%E9%A6%99/wiki-6722022-7481802 2023 年 5 月 17 日瀏覽。

Huáng Shú incense is ripe incense that has been buried in the soil for a very long time. All the woody fibrous tissue structure is ripe and rotten, leaving only the honeycomb-shaped scent gland tissue. It is yellow in color because it is in the soil, it is called earth agarwood. See "Huang Shuxiang," *Chinese Encyclopedia*,

https://www.itsfun.com.tw/%E9%BB%83%E7%86%9F%E9%A6%99/wiki-6722022-7481802 May 17, 2023 retrieved.

[26]藤田豐八認為日麗是位在蘇門答臘島北岸的日裏（Delli）。參見藤田豐八校註，前引書，頁 37。

Fujita Toyohachi believed that Rili was Delli on the north coast of Sumatra. See Fujita Toyohachi notes, *op. cit.*, p. 37.

介兩山之間，立一關之市。田雖平曠，春乾而夏雨，種植常違其時，故歲少稔，仰食於他國。氣候冬暖。風俗尚節義。男女椎髻，白縵纏頭，繫小黃布。男喪，女不嫁。

白話文(Vernacular)：

該地介於兩山之間，設有一個海關收稅。田地雖然平曠，春天乾燥而夏天多雨，種植常常不按時序，故每年產量少，仰賴他國進口食物。氣候冬暖。風俗尚節義。男女椎髻，白縵纏頭，繫小黃布。男子若去世，其妻不改嫁。

The place is located between two mountains and sets up customs to levy tax. Although the fields are flat and wide, the spring is dry, and the summer rains and the planting often go against the season time. As a result, food production is insufficient and needs to rely on imports. The climate is warm in winter. The customs are still righteous. Men and women wear a bun on their heads. They use white mandrels wrapped around their heads and tie a small yellow cloth on their lower body. When a husband dies, the wife does not remarry.

煮海為鹽，釀漿為酒。有酋長。土產龜筒、鶴頂、降眞、錫。貿易之貨，用青磁器、花布、粗碗、鐵塊、小印花布、五色布之屬。

白話文(Vernacular)：

煮海水製鹽，釀漿製酒。有酋長。土產龜筒、鶴頂、降眞和錫。貿易之貨品使用青磁器、花布、粗碗、鐵塊、小印花布和五色布等。

The people boil the sea for salt and brew the pulp for wine. There is a chief. The local products include Guī Tǒng, Heding,

Jiangzhen incense, and tin. The goods for trade use green porcelains, floral cloth, crude bowls, iron blocks, small printed cloth, and five-color cloth.

14. 麻里魯[27]
14. Málǐ Lǔ

小港迢遞，入於其地。山隆而水多鹵股石，林少，田高而瘠。民多種薯芋。地氣熱。俗尚義。若番官沒，其婦再不嫁於凡夫；必有他國番官之子孫，閥閱相稱者，方可擇配，否則削髮看經，以終其身。男女拳髮，穿青布短衫，繫紅布縵。

白話文(Vernacular)：

經過很遠的航行，才抵達這個小港地方，山高而水中多鹵股石，林少，田地位在高處而貧瘠。人民多種蕃薯和芋頭。地氣熱。風俗尚義。若番官死亡了，其妻不嫁給一般人；必嫁給他國番官之子孫，地位相稱者，方可擇配，否則削髮唸經，以終其身。男女將髮盤在頭上，穿青布短衫，繫紅布縵。

Through a long distant voyage, one arrives at this small port. The mountains are high and the waters are full of bittern stones. The forests are few, and the fields are high and barren. The people plant various sweet potatoes and taros. The climate is hot. The custom is righteous. If local officers die, their wives will not marry an ordinary man; the widows might choose the

---

[27]藤田豐八認為麻里魯是指馬尼拉（Manila）。參見藤田豐八校註，前引書，頁39。

　　Fujita Toyohachi believed that Málǐ Lǔ refers to Manila. See Fujita Toyohachi notes, *op. cit.*, p. 39.

descendants of the officers in other countries, and those who match the noble clan, otherwise they will cut their hair and chant the scriptures, until the end of their life. Men and women have curly hair and wear green shorts shirts, and ties with red cloth.

民煮海為鹽，釀蔗漿為酒，編竹片為床，燃生蠟為燈。地產玳瑁、黃蠟、降香、竹布、木棉花。貿易之貨，用牙錠、青布、磁器盤、處州磁、水壜、大甕、鐵鼎之屬。

白話文**(Vernacular)**：

人民煮海水製鹽，釀蔗漿製酒，編竹片為床，燃生蠟為燈。當地生產玳瑁、黃蠟、降香、竹布和木棉花。貿易之貨品使用牙錠、青布、磁器盤、處州磁、水壜、大甕和鐵鼎等。

The people boil the sea for salt, brew sugarcane pulp for wine, weave bamboo pieces for beds, and burn raw wax for lamps. The land produces tortoiseshell, yellow wax, fragrance, bamboo cloth, and kapok. The goods for trade used silver ingots, green cloth, porcelain dishes, Chuzhou porcelain, water jars, large urns, and iron tripods.

15. 遐來物[28]

15. Xiá Lái Wù

古淚[29]之下，山盤數百里，厥田中下。俗尚妖怪。氣候

---

[28]遐來物，或寫為遐來勿，藤田豐八認為是指吉利問（Karimun）、吉里門之異譯。參見藤田豐八校註，前引書，頁 41。

Xiá Lái Wù, or written as Xialaiwu, Fujita Toyohachi believed that it refers to the different translations of Karimun and Gilliman. See Fujita Toyohachi notes, *op. cit.*, p. 41.

[29]藤田豐八認為古淚是指勾欄山或交欄山（Gelam 島）。參見藤田豐八校

春夏秋熱，冬微冷，則人無病；反此則瘴生，人畜死。男女挽髻，纏紅布，繫青棉布捎。凡人死，則研生腦調水灌之，以養其屍，欲葬而不腐。

白話文(Vernacular)：

在古淚的下方，山延展數百里，該地的田地屬中下等。俗尚妖怪。氣候春夏秋熱，冬微冷，人很少生病；若氣候跟此反常不同，那麼就會有瘴癘，人畜會死亡。男女挽髻，纏紅布，繫青棉布巾。凡人死了，研究用水灌入死者的腦中，以養其屍，目的是葬後屍體不腐爛。

Under the Gǔ Lèi, the mountains extend hundreds of miles, and the fields are of the middle and low grades. The customs of people are fond of monsters. The climate is hot in spring, summer, and autumn, and mildly cold in winter, so people will be free from disease. On the contrary, miasma will be produced, and people and animals will die. Men and women wear a bun on their heads, wrapped in red cloth, and tied with a green cotton cloth towel. When a person dies, people study to put water into the dead's brain, keeping up the corpse, which could make the corpse not rot after it is buried into the ground.

民煮海為鹽，釀椰漿為酒。有酋長。地產蘇木、玳瑁、木棉花、檳榔。貿易之貨，用占城海南布、鐵線、銅鼎、紅絹、五色布、木梳、篦子、青器、粗碗之屬。

白話文(Vernacular)：

註，前引書，頁40。

Fujita Toyohachi believed that Gǔ Lèi refers to Gelam Mountain or Jiaolan Mountain (Gelam Island). See Fujita Toyohachi remarks, *op. cit.*, p.40.

人民煮海水製鹽，釀椰漿製酒。有酋長。當地生產蘇木、玳瑁、木棉花、檳榔。貿易之貨品使用占城海南布、鐵線、銅鼎、紅絹、五色布、木梳、篦子、青器和粗碗等。

The people boil the sea for salt and brew coconut milk for wine. There is a chief. The land produces Biancaea sappan, tortoiseshell, kapok, and betel nut. The goods for trade used Hainan cloth of Zhàn Chéng, iron wire, copper tripods, red silk, five-color cloth, wooden comb, grates, utensils, and crude bowls.

16. 彭坑

16. Péng Kēng (Pahang)

石崖週匝崎嶇，遠如平塞，田沃，谷稍登。氣候半熱。風俗與丁家盧小異。男女椎髻，穿長布衫，繫單布捎。富貴女頂帶金圈數回。常人以五色焇珠為圈以束之。凡講婚姻，互造換白銀五錢重為准。

白話文(**Vernacular**)：

該地有陡峭的山崖，周邊山區崎嶇，遠處則是平坦的地方，田土肥沃，谷物生產豐富。氣候半熱。風俗與丁家盧稍有不同。男女椎髻，穿長布衫，繫單布巾。富貴女孩頭上戴著數個金圈。一般人以五色焇珠為圈戴在頭上。凡講婚姻，互相交換白銀五錢重為禮物。

This place has steep cliffs and the surrounding mountains are rugged. A little farther is flat. The fields are fertile, and grain growth is booming. The climate is semi-hot. The customs are slightly different from those of Terengganu. Men and women wear a bun on their heads, long cloth shirts, and single cloth towel. The noble and wealthy women wear several gold circles on their heads. Ordinary people use five-colored beads as a circle on their heads. When talking about marriage, the two sides exchange gifts of five maces in silver

民煮海為鹽，釀椰漿為酒。有酋長。地產黃熟香頭、沉速、打白香、腦子、花錫、粗降眞。貿易之貨，用諸色絹、闍婆布、銅鐵器、漆磁器、鼓、板之屬。

白話文(Vernacular)：

人民煮海水製鹽，釀椰漿製酒。有酋長。當地生產黃熟香頭、沉香、速香、打白香、腦子、花錫和粗降眞香。貿易之貨品使用諸色絹、闍婆布、銅鐵器、漆磁器、鼓和板等。

The people boil the sea for salt and brew coconut milk for wine. There is a chief. The land produced the head of Huáng Shú incense, agarwood, fast incense wood, white incense, Borneol, natural tin, and crude Jiangzhen incense. The goods for trade used various colors of silk, Java cloth, copper and ironware, lacquer and porcelain ware, drums, and boards.

17. 吉蘭丹
17. Kelantan

地勢博大，山瘠而田少，夏熱而倍收。氣候平熱，風俗尚禮。男女束髮，繫短衫布皂縵。每遇四時節序、生辰、婚嫁之類，衣紅布長衫為慶。

白話文(Vernacular)：

該地廣大，山地貧瘠，田地少，夏天熱，收穫增加一倍。氣候溫暖，風俗尚禮。男女束髮，繫短衫，穿黑色布衣服。每遇四時節序、生辰、婚嫁等節日，穿紅布長衫慶祝。

The terrain is broad, the mountains are barren and the fields are few, and the summer is hot, but the harvest is doubled. The climate is warm and the customs are polite. Men and women have their hair tied together and wear short shirts and black cloth. Whenever they meet four seasons' festivals, birthdays, weddings, etc., they wear red gowns to celebrate.

民煮海為鹽，織木棉為業。有酋長。地產上等沉速、粗降眞香、黃蠟、龜筒、鶴頂、檳榔。外有小港，索遷極深，水鹹魚美。出花錫，貨用塘頭市[30]布、占城布、靑盤、花碗、紅綠烧珠、琴阮、鼓、板之屬。

白話文**(Vernacular)**：

人民煮海水製鹽，織木棉為業。有酋長。當地生產上等沉香、速香、粗降眞香、黃蠟、龜筒、鶴頂和檳榔。外有小港，用繩索探查，水極深。水鹹魚美。出花錫。貨品使用塘頭市布、占城布、靑盤、花碗、紅綠烧珠、琴阮、鼓和板等。

The people boil the sea for salt and weave kapok for the cloth. There is a chief. The land produces high-quality agarwood, fast incense wood, crude Jiangzhen incense, yellow wax, Guī Tǒng, Heding, and betel nut. There is a small port outside, probing with a rope, the water is very deep. The water is salty

---

[30] 塘頭市，是今天貴州省銅仁市的一個行政單位。參見「塘頭鎮」，百度百科，
https://baike.baidu.hk/item/%E5%A1%98%E9%A0%AD%E9%8E%AE/8535116 2022 年 10 月 12 日瀏覽。

Tangtou City is an administrative unit in Tongren City, Guizhou Province of China today. See "Tangtou Town", *Baidu Encyclopedia*, https://baike.baidu.hk/item/%E5%A1%98%E9%A0%AD%E9%8E%AE/8535116 October 12, 2022 retrieved.

and the fish is beautiful. Here produce tin. The goods for trade used Tangtou City cloth, Zhancheng cloth, green pans, flower bowls, red and green beads, qín ruǎn (musical instrument), drums, and boards.

18. 丁家盧
18. Terengganu

三角嶼對境港，已通其津要。山高曠，田中下，民食足。春多雨，氣候微熱。風俗尚怪。男女椎髻，穿綠頡布短衫，繫遮里絹。刻木為神，殺人血和酒祭之。每水旱疫癘，禱之則立應。及婚姻病喪，則卜其吉凶，亦驗。今酋長主事貪禁，勤儉守土。

白話文(Vernacular)：

三角嶼面對著境港，可通到它的重要港口。山很廣大，田地屬於中下等，人民糧食夠吃。春多雨，氣候微熱。風俗喜歡怪誕。男女椎髻，穿綠頡布短衫，繫遮里絹。在木頭上刻上神明，殺人後以血和酒祭拜。每遇水災、旱災、疫癘，對該神明禱告，立可應驗。婚姻病喪，則卜其吉凶，亦極為靈驗。今酋長主事禁止貪污，勤儉守土。

The Triangle Islet is opposite Jìnggǎng (port) and the boats can reach its important harbor. The mountains are high and the fields are of the middle and low fertile, and the people have enough food. Spring is rainy and the climate is slightly hot. Customs are fond of weird. Men and women wear a bun on their heads and wear green short shirts of Jie cloth, and tied with Zhē Lǐ silk. God's statue is carved on wood, and the people worship with human blood and wine. Whenever there is a flood or drought, or plague, the people pray to this log god for blessing and get an immediate response. Even if forecasting whether marriage, illness, and death are good or bad luck, it is also proven true. Today, the chief is in charge of anti-corruption and is diligent, thrifty, and guarding the territory.

地產降眞、腦子、黃蠟、玳瑁。貨用青白花磁器、占城布、小紅絹、斗錫、酒之屬。

白話文**(Vernacular)**：

當地生產降眞香、腦子、黃蠟和玳瑁。貨品使用青白花磁器、占城布、小紅絹、斗錫和酒等。

The land produces Jiangzhen incense, Borneol, yellow wax, and tortoiseshell. The goods for trade used green and white-flowered porcelain, Zhancheng cloth, small red silk, natural tin, and wine.

19. 戎[31]
19. Rong

---

[31] 戎，指泰國南部半島東岸，即克拉地峽附近的春蓬（Chumpon），亦譯尖噴。（參見藤田豐八校註，前引書，頁 46。）蘇繼卿推測汪大淵可能是從該地走路越過克拉（Kra）地峽，然後到緬甸的「針路」，即墨吉。（參見蘇繼卿，*南海鉤沈錄*，臺灣商務印書館，臺北市，民國 78 年，頁 253。）

Rong refers to the east coast of the southern peninsula of Thailand, namely Chumpon near the Isthmus of Kra, also translated as Jiān Pēn. (See Fujita Toyohachi notes, *op. cit.*, p. 46.) Su Jiqing speculates that Wang Da-yuan may go on foot across the Isthmus of Kra from there, and then to "Zhēnlù " in Burma, namely Mergi. (See Su Jiqing, *Records on Hook Out Hidden Stories in Nanhai*, Taiwan Commercial Press, Taipei, 1989, p. 253.)

山邐溪環，部落坦夷，田畬連成片，土膏腴。氣候不正，春夏苦雨。俗陋，男女方頭，兒生之後，以木板四方夾之，二周後，去其板。四季祝髮，以布縵遶身。

白話文(Vernacular)：

溪流繞著山，部落位在平坦的地方，田地連成一片，土地肥沃。氣候不穩定，春夏雨過多。風俗淺陋，男女的頭形是方的，小孩出生後，以木板四方夾之，二周後，把板拿開。四季要剃短頭髮，以布縵包著身體。

This place is surrounded by mountains and streams. The tribes are located on a plain, the fields are connected, and the soil is fertile. The climate is not stable, and the spring and summer are rainy. The customs are vulgar and the male and female heads are square. Because after a baby is born, the head is sandwiched with wooden boards. After two weeks, the boards are removed. The children need to cut short their hair in the four seasons and wrap it around the body with cloth.

以椰水浸秫米，半月方成酒，味極苦辣而味長。二月海榴結實，復釀榴實酒，味甘酸，宜解渴。地產白荳蔻、象牙、翠毛、黃蠟、木棉紗。貿易之貨，用銅、漆器、青白花碗、磁壺、瓶、花銀、紫燒珠、巫崙布之屬。

白話文(Vernacular)：

以椰子水浸泡高粱，半月可製成酒，味極苦辣而味道留存久。二月，海榴結實，又釀製榴實酒，味甘酸，宜解渴。當地生產白荳蔻、象牙、翠毛、黃蠟和木棉紗。貿易之貨品使用銅、漆器、青白花碗、磁壺、瓶、花銀、紫燒珠和巫崙布等。

The rice is soaked in coconut juice, and it is made into wine for half a month, which is extremely bitter and spicy and has a strong taste. In February, the Hǎi Liú gets fruit, and brews the pomegranate wine which tastes sweet and sour, and is suitable for quenching thirst. The land produces white cardamom, ivory, kingfisher feathers, yellow wax, and kapok yarn. The goods for trade used copper, lacquerware, green and white flower bowls, porcelain pots, bottles, flower silver, purple burnt beads, and Wu Lun cloth.

20. 羅衞[32]
20. Luo Wei

南眞駱[33]之南，實加羅山卽故名也。山瘠田美，等為中

---

[32]羅衞，指泰國的叻丕（Rajaburi），又訛作 Rajburi，梵語意為王城。古又稱金鄰。參見「Rajaburi」，古代南海地名匯釋 Part II(R)，南溟網，http://www.world10k.com/blog/?p=2256　2022 年 10 月 12 日瀏覽。
藤田豐八則認為羅衞乃羅越之異寫。（參見藤田豐八校註，前引書，頁 48。）而羅越就是今馬來西亞之柔佛。

    Luo Wei refers to Ratburi in Thailand, also falsely called Rajburi. It means King City in Sanskrit. In ancient times, it was also called Jinlin. See "Rajaburi", *Interpretation of Ancient South China Sea Place Names Part II(R)*, *Nanming Net*, http://www.world10k.com/blog/?p=2256　October 12, 2022 retrieved.

    Fujita Toyohachi believed that Luo Wei is a different writing from Luo Yue. (See Fujita Toyohachi notes, *op.cit*., p. 48.) And Luo Yue is Johor in present-day Malaysia.

[33]南眞駱，指泰國的夜功（Samut Song Khram）。見「Samut Song Khram」或「實加羅山」，南溟網，
　http://www.world10k.com/blog/index.php?s=%E5%AF%A6%E5%8A%A0%E7%BE%85%E5%B1%B1　2022 年 10 月 12 日瀏覽。
藤田豐八則認為南眞駱，應是南眞臘之誤寫。參見藤田豐八校註，前引書，頁 46。

    Nanzhenluo refers Samut Song Khram in Thailand. See "Samut Song Khram" or "Sikalo Mountain", *Nanming Net*,

上。春末則禾登，民有餘蓄，以移他國。氣候不齊，風俗勤儉。男女文身為禮。以紫縵纏頭，繫溜布。以竹筒實生蠟為燭。織木棉為業。

白話文(Vernacular)：

南眞駱的南邊，實加羅山是它的舊名。山地貧瘠，但田地肥沃，屬於中上等。春末則收穫稻米，人民有多餘的米，就賣到外國。氣候不穩定，風俗勤儉。男女紋身是一種禮節。以紫縵包住頭，繫溜布。以竹筒裝生蠟做成蠟燭。織木棉為業。

This place is located in the south of Nanzhenluo, its former name is Shí Jiā Luóshān. The mountains are barren and the fields are beautiful; it belongs to a middle-upper grade. At the end of the spring, the season is for harvesting rice. The people's harvests have a surplus, to export to other countries. The climate is unstable. The customs are diligent and thrifty. Men's and women's tattoos are decorous. They wrap the head with purple mandarin and tie it with a slippery cloth. They put wax into the bamboo tube as a candle and weave kapok for the cloth.

煮海為鹽，以葛根浸水釀酒，味甘軟，竟日飲之不醉。有酋長。地產粗降眞、玳瑁、黃蠟、棉花。雖有珍樹，無能割。貿易之貨，用棊子、手巾、狗跡絹、五花燒珠、花銀、靑白碗、鐵條之屬。

白話文(Vernacular)：

---

http://www.world10k.com/blog/index.php?s=%E5%AF%A6%E5%8A%A0%E7%BE%85%E5%B1%B1　October 12, 2022 retrieved.
Fujita Toyohachi believed that Nanzhenluo should be a mistaken writing of Nanzhenla. See Fujita Toyohachi notes, *op. cit.*, p. 46.

煮海水製鹽，以葛根浸水釀酒，味甘軟，喝一整天也不會醉。有酋長。當地生產粗降眞香、玳瑁、黃蠟和棉花。雖有珍貴的樹，但不會割樹取脂。貿易之貨品使用旗幟、手巾、狗跡絹、五花燒珠、花銀、青白碗和鐵條等。

The people boil the sea for salt and soak the Pueraria in water to make wine that tastes sweet and soft, and it is not drunk after a long day of drinking. There is a chief. The land produces crude Jiangzhen incense, tortoiseshell, yellow wax, and cotton. Although there are precious trees, no one can cut them for producing resin. The goods for trade used flags, handkerchiefs, dog trace silk, five-flower burnt beads, flower silver, green and white bowls, and iron bars.

21. 羅斛

21. Luó Hú (Lopburi)

山形如城郭，白石峭厲。其田平衍而多稼，暹人仰之。氣候常暖如春。風俗勁悍。男女椎髻，白布纏頭，穿長布衫。每有議刑法錢穀出人之事，並決之於婦人，其志量常過於男子。

白話文(Vernacular)：

山的形狀像城郭一樣，有陡峭白石。其田地平坦廣大而產量多，暹人仰賴該種作物。氣候常暖如春。風俗強悍。男女椎髻，白布纏頭，穿長布衫。每有討論刑法、錢穀出人等事情，多是由婦女決定，其處事能力常超過男子。

The shape of the mountain is like a castle, and the white rocks are steep and sharp. Its fields are flat and produce plentiful grains and the Siamese rely on it. The climate is always warm like spring. The customs are strong and tough. Men and women wear a bun on their heads, white cloth wrapping around their heads, and long cloth shirts. Whenever there is a discussion about criminal affairs, one can use money and grains to atone for their crime, and the decision is made by a woman; her ambition is often higher than that of a man.

煮海為鹽，釀秫米為酒。有酋長。法以𧈅子[34]代錢，流通行使，每一萬準中統鈔二十四兩，甚便民。

白話文(Vernacular)：

煮海水製鹽，釀高粱製酒。有酋長。法律規定以𧈅子[35]代錢，流通使用，每一萬𧈅子約值中統鈔二十四兩，甚便民。

The people boil the sea for salt and brew rice for wine. There is a chief. The law regulates using Pazi (shell money) to take the place of money, and it is circulated. 10,000 quasi- Zhōng Tǒng banknotes are equivalent to twenty-four taels which is very convenient for the people.

此地產羅斛香，味極清遠，亞於沉香。次蘇木、犀角、象牙、翠羽、黃蠟。貨用青器、花印布、金、錫、海南檳榔口、𧈅子。

白話文(Vernacular)：

此地生產羅斛香，味極清香，次於沉香。其他還有蘇木、犀角、象牙、翠羽和黃蠟。貨品使用青器、花印布、金、錫、

---

[34] 𧈅子，是指貝殼做的貨幣。
Pazi refers to the currency made of shells.
[35] 𧈅子，是指貝殼做的貨幣。
Pazi refers to the currency made of shells.

海南檳榔口和肌子等。

The place produced Luó Hú incense and the smell is clean and fresh, but inferior to agarwood. The next products are Biancaea sappan, rhino horn, ivory, kingfisher feather, and yellow wax. The goods for trade use utensils, flower-printed cloth, gold, tin, Hainan betel nut, and Pazi.

次曰彌勒佛，曰忽南圭[36]，曰善司坂，曰蘇剌司坪，曰吉頓力。地無所產，用附於此。

白話文(Vernacular)：

其他地名還有彌勒佛、忽南圭、善司坂、蘇剌司坪和吉頓力。這些地方沒有什麼生產，附記在此。

The next places are Maitreya Buddha, Hu Nangui, Shansiban, Sulasiping, and Jidunli. These lands yield nothing, attaching their situations here.

22. 東沖古剌[37]
22. Dōng Chōng Gǔ Lá（Songkhla）

巖崿豐林，下臨淡港[38]，外堞為之限界。田美穀秀，氣

---

[36] 蘇繼卿認為忽南圭位在泰國南部的巴蜀（Prachuab）。參見蘇繼卿，前引書，頁 254。

　Su Jiqing believed that Hu Nangui is located in Prachuab in southern Thailand. See Su Jiqing, *op. cit.*, p.254.

[37] 藤田豐八認為東沖古剌是位在泰國南部的宋卡（Songkhla）。參見藤田豐八校註，前引書，頁 52。

　Fujita Toyohachi believed that Dōng Chōng Gǔ Lá is located in Songkhla in southern Thailand. See Fujita Toyohachi notes, *op. cit.*, p. 52.

[38] 淡港，指今泰國的宋卡（Songkhla）港。參見「淡港」，南溟網，http://www.world10k.com/blog/?p=1131　2022 年 10 月 14 日瀏覽。

候驟熱，雨下則微冷。風俗輕剽。男女斷髮，紅手帕纏頭，穿黃棉布短衫，繫越里布。凡有人喪亡者，不焚化，聚其骨撒於海中，謂之種植法，使子孫復有生意。持孝之人，齋戒數月而後已。

白話文(Vernacular)：

山高，林木茂盛，下臨淡港，外面有牆作為界限。田地肥沃，穀物生長良好，氣候會突然炎熱，下雨就會微冷。風俗不喜歡掠奪。男女剪短髮，用紅手帕纏頭，穿黃棉布短衫，繫越里布。凡有人喪亡者，不焚化，將其骨骸拋入海中，謂之種植法，可使子孫生生不息。守孝之人，會齋戒數月。

The mountains are high and have lush forests, and the south is neighboring Dangang. There is a wall for its scope. The fields are fertile and the grains are plentiful. The climate is hot and cold when it rains. The customs do not like robbery. Men and women have their hair cut, wrapping red handkerchiefs around their heads, wearing yellow cotton short blouses, and tied with Yuè Lǐ cloth. When the people die, they are not incinerated, but their bones are gathered and thrown into the sea. This is called the planting method, to make their descendants proliferate. Those who hold filial piety must fast for several months.

民不善煮海為鹽，釀蔗漿為酒。有酋長。地產沙金、黃蠟、粗降眞香、龜筒、沉香。貿易之貨，用花銀、鹽、青白花碗、大小水埕、青緞、銅鼎之屬。

白話文(Vernacular)：

Dangang refers to the port of Songkhla, Thailand. See "Dangang", *Nanming Net*, http://www.world10k.com/blog/?p=1131　October 14, 2022 retrieved.

人民不善於煮海水製鹽，釀蔗漿製酒。有酋長。當地生產沙金、黃蠟、粗降眞香、龜筒和沉香。貿易之貨品使用花銀、鹽、靑白花碗、大小水埕、靑緞和銅鼎等。

The people are not good at boiling the sea for salt and brewing sugarcane pulp for wine. There is a chief. The land produces sand gold, yellow wax, crude Jiangzhen incense, Guī Tǒng, and agarwood. The goods for trade used silver, salt, green and white flower bowls, large and small water jars, satin, and copper tripods.

23. 蘇洛鬲[39]
23. Srokam (Kedah)

洛山如關，幷溪如帶，互有聚落。田瘠穀少，氣候少暖。風俗勇悍。男女椎髻，穿靑布短衫，繫木棉白縵。凡生育後，惡露不下，汲井水澆頭卽下。有害熱症者，亦皆用水沃數四則愈。[40]

白話文(Vernacular)：

洛山像關口一樣，溪流像帶子一樣，中間散落著聚落。田地貧瘠，穀物生長少，氣候不很暖和。風俗勇悍。男女椎髻，穿靑布短衫，繫木棉白縵。婦女生育後，身上的髒血沒

---

[39] 藤田豐八認為吉打之舊名為 Srokam，故蘇洛鬲即是其對音。而洛山是指 Gunong Geriang 河。參見藤田豐八校註，前引書，頁 52。.

Fujita Toyohachi believed that Kedah's old name is Srokam, so Srokam is its counterpart sound. And Loksan refers to the Gunong Geriang River. See Fujita Toyohachi notes, *op. cit.*, p. 52.

[40] 此一風俗習慣至今還保留在東南亞國家，每天洗澡要用水洗頭數次，可免生熱病。

This custom is still preserved in Southeast Asian countries. It is necessary to wash your head with water several times a day to avoid fever.

有排出，汲井水澆頭卽可將它排出。有得熱症者，亦可用水澆頭四次卽可痊癒。

Luosan is like a pass, and the stream is like a belt, and there are settlements among them. The fields are barren and the grains are few, and the climate is a little warm. The customs are brave and tough. Men and women wear a bun on their heads, wear green short shirts, and tie them with white kapok cloth. After a woman gives birth, her lochia can't excrete from the body, so she must use well water to drizzle down her head, and lochia can be excreted immediately. Those who are infected with fever disease are also cured with water drizzling down the head four times.

民煮海為鹽。有酋長。地產上等降眞、片腦、鶴頂、沉速、玳瑁。貿易之貨用靑白花器、海南巫崙布、銀、鐵、水埕小罐、銅鼎之屬。

白話文(Vernacular)：

人民煮海水製鹽。有酋長。當地生產上等降眞香、片腦、鶴頂、沉香、速香和玳瑁。貿易之貨品使用靑白花器、海南巫崙布、銀、鐵、水埕小罐和銅鼎等。

The people boil the sea for salt. There is a chief. The land produces first-class Jiangzhen incense, Borneol, Heding, agarwood, fast incense wood, and Tortoiseshell. The goods for trade use green white flower utensils, Hainan Wulun cloth, silver, iron, small water jars, and copper tripods.

24.針路[41]
24. Zhēnlù

自馬軍山水路，由麻來墳[42]至此地，則山多鹵股，田下下等，少耕植。民種薯及葫蘆、西瓜，兼採海螺、螃蛤、蝦食之。內坪下小溪，有魚蟹極美。民間臨溪每一舉網，輒食數日而有餘。氣候差熱。俗惡。男女以紅棉布纏頭，皂縵繫身。

白話文(Vernacular)：

自馬軍山走水路，由麻來墳到此地，山區多鹵股石，田地屬於下下等，很少耕種。人民種蕃薯及葫蘆、西瓜，兼採海螺、螃蛤和蝦食用。內坪下有條小溪，有魚蟹極美。老百姓在河裡每下網，其魚貨可吃好幾天還有剩。氣候有點熱。風俗不好。男女以紅棉布纏頭，黑布縵繫身。

From Mǎjūnshān (mountain) sailing through Má Lái Fén to this place, there are more coral stones, the fields are inferior and there is less farming. People plant sweet potatoes, gourds, and watermelons, and eat conch, clams, and shrimp. There is a creek below the flat, there are good fish and crabs. Every time the people in the stream lift a net, they get a rich harvest and will eat for more than a few days. The climate is a little hot. The customs

---

[41] 蘇繼卿認為針路為丹荖或丹老，即是泰語所稱的 Tanau 或 Tanaos，指今緬甸的墨吉（Mergi）。參見蘇繼卿，前引書，頁 252-253。

　Su Jiqing believed that Zhēnlù is Danao or Danlao, which is called Tanau or Tanaos in the Thai language, referring to Mergi in present-day Myanmar. See Su Jiqing, *op. cit.*, pp. 252-253.

[42] 蘇繼卿認為麻來墳為 Packchan 河口西岸之 Maliwan。參見蘇繼卿，前引書，頁 253。

　Su Jiqing believed that Má Lái Fén is Maliwan on the west bank of the Packchan Estuary. See Su Jiqing, *op. cit.*, p. 253.

are vulgar. Men and women wrap their heads with a red cotton cloth and tie their bodies with black fabric.

民煮海為鹽，織竹絲布為業。有酋長。地產苧蕉。贝子通暹，准錢使用。貿易之貨，用銅條、鐵鼎、銅珠、五色焇珠、大小埕、花布、鼓、青布之屬。

白話文(Vernacular)：

人民煮海水製鹽，織竹絲布為業。有酋長。當地生產苧蕉。跟暹國做生意，可使用贝子當錢使用。貿易之貨品使用銅條、鐵鼎、銅珠、五色焇珠、大小埕、花布、鼓和青布等。

The people boil the sea for salt and weave bamboo silk cloth. There is a chief. The land produces bananas. The people can use Pazi as a quasi-money to trade with Sien. The goods for trade used copper bars, iron tripods, copper beads, five-color beads, large and small water jars, flower cloths, drums, and green cloth.

25. 八都馬[43]

25. Baduma(Martaban)

闤市廣陽，山茂田少，民力齊，常足食。氣候暖，俗尚樸。男女椎髻，纏青布縵，繫甘埋里[44]布。酋長守土安民樂

---

[43]藤田豐八認為八都馬是位在緬甸薩爾溫江口的馬達班（Martaban，Mottama）。參見藤田豐八校註，前引書，頁54。

　Fujita Toyohachi believed that Baduma is Martaban (Mottama) at the mouth of the Salween River in Myanmar. See Fujita Toyohachi notes, *op. cit.*, p. 54.

[44]原文寫為「甘理」，應是「甘埋里」之誤，故改之。

　The original text was written as "Gan Li", which should be a mistake of "

其生。親沒，必沐浴齋戒，號泣半月而葬之，日奉桑香佛惟謹。有犯奸盜者，梟之以示戒。有遵蠻法者，賞之以示勸。俗稍稍近理。

白話文**(Vernacular)**：

該地有一個類似廣陽的鬧市，山多田地少，但人民勤奮，糧食夠吃。氣候暖，風俗儉樸。男女椎髻，纏青布縵，繫甘埋里布。酋長守土安民，人民生活快樂。雙親死亡，必沐浴齋戒，號泣半月才加以埋葬，每天要祭拜桑香佛，非常尊敬。有犯奸盜者，砍頭以警告勿犯。有遵守當地法律者，給予獎賞，以示典範。俗稍稍近情理。

The city is as lively as Guangyang. There are more mountains and few fields. The people are hardworking, and there is always enough food. The climate is warm and custom is still simple. Men and women wear a bun on their heads, wrap a cloth mantle, and tie it with the Gān Mái Lǐ cloth. The chief guards the land well and the people live happily. If the parents die, children must bathe and fast, crying for half a month, and bury their parents. People burned piously mulberry incense every day to worship Buddha. If adultery or robbery is committed, the perpetrator should be sentenced to beheading. Those who follow the barbarous laws will be rewarded as a model. The custom is a little closer to rationality.

地產象牙，重者百餘斤，輕者七、八十斤。胡椒亞於闍婆。貿易之貨，用南北絲、花銀、赤金、銅、鐵鼎、絲布、草金緞、丹山錦、山紅絹、白礬之屬。

Gān Mái Lǐ ", so I correct it.

白話文(**Vernacular**)：

當地生產象牙，重者百餘斤，輕者七、八十斤。胡椒的品質次於闍婆。貿易之貨品使用南北絲、花銀、赤金、銅、鐵鼎、絲布、草金緞、丹山錦、山紅絹和白礬等。

The land produces ivory which is more than 100 catties in weight and 70 to 80 catties in light. Pepper is inferior to that of Java. The goods for trade used north-south silk, flower silver, red gold, copper, iron tripods, silk cloth, grass gold satin, Danshan brocade, Shān Hóng silk, and alum.

26. 淡邈[45]
26. Dàn Miǎo (Dawei, Tavoy)

小港去海口數里，山如鐵筆，迤邐如長蛇，民傍緣而居。田地平，宜穀粟，食有餘。氣候暖，風俗儉。男女椎髻，穿白布短衫，繫竹布捎。民多識山中草藥，有疪癘之疾，服之其效如神。

白話文(**Vernacular**)：

小港距離海口數里遠，山像鐵筆一樣高聳，延展像一條長蛇，人民沿著山腳居住。田地平坦，適宜種穀和粟，糧食有剩餘。氣候溫暖，風俗儉樸。男女椎髻，穿白布短衫，繫竹布巾。人民多認識山中草藥，生病服用，效力像神一樣。

Dàn Miǎo is a small port that is distant from the seaside by several miles. The mountains are like a stylus pen, continuous

---

[45] 藤田豐八認為淡邈是位在今緬甸南部的土瓦（Dawei, Tavoy）。參見藤田豐八校註，前引書，頁55。

Fujita Toyohachi believed that Danmiao is Dawei (Tavoy) in southern Myanmar. See Fujita Toyohachi notes, *op. cit.*, p. 55.

like a serpent, and the people live on the edge of a mountain. The fields are flat, suitable for grain and millet, and there is more than enough food. There are a warm climate and frugal customs. Men and women wear a bun on their heads, wearing white short shirts tied with bamboo cloth towel. Many people know the herbal medicine grown in the mountains, and if there is a disease or plague, eating it has a magical effect.

煮海為鹽，事網罟為業。地產胡椒，亞於八都馬。貨用黃硝珠、麒麟粒、西洋絲布、粗碗、青器、銅鼎之屬。

白話文(Vernacular)：

煮海水製鹽，編織漁網為業。當地生產胡椒，品質次於八都馬。貨品使用黃硝珠、麒麟粒、西洋絲布、粗碗、青器和銅鼎等。

The people boil the sea for salt and weave fishing nets for fishing. The land produced pepper, but it is inferior to Baduma. The goods for trade used yellow nitrate beads, unicorn grains, West Ocean silk cloth, crude bowls, green utensils, and copper tripods.

27. 尖山[46]

27. Jianshan (Steep Mountain)

自有宇宙，茲山盤據於小東洋，卓然如文筆插霄漢，雖懸隔數百里，望之儼然。田地少，多種薯，炊以代飯。氣候

---

[46] 尖山，應是沙巴的神山（Kinabalu）。
Jianshan refers to the sacred mountain (Kinabalu) of Sabah.

頓熱，風俗纖嗇。男女斷髮，以紅絹纏頭，以佛南圭布纏身。

白話文**(Vernacular)**：

自有宇宙開始，此山就座落在小東洋，卓然像一枝筆一樣矗立天空，雖然遠隔數百里，仍可看到它直立。田地少，多種蕃薯，煮熟後可代替米飯。氣候會突然炎熱，風俗吝嗇。男女剪短髮，以紅絹包裹頭，以佛南圭布包裹身體。

Since the universe begins, this mountain is located in the Little East Ocean, and it looks like a pen in the sky. Although it is looked at from hundreds of miles away, it looks tall. A few fields plant a variety of sweet potatoes. The people cook sweet potatoes to replace rice. The climate is hot and the customs are stingy. Men and women have their hair cut, wrap their heads with red silk, and wrap their bodies with Fernangue's cloth.

煮海為鹽，釀蔗漿水、米為酒。地產木棉花、竹布、黃臘。粗降眞沙地所生，故不結實。貿易之貨，用牙錠、銅鐵鼎、靑碗、大小埕甕、靑皮[47]、單錦、鼓樂之屬。

白話文**(Vernacular)**：

煮海水製鹽，釀蔗漿水、米製酒。當地生產木棉花、竹布和黃臘。粗降眞香因為是沙地所生，故不結果實。貿易之貨品使用牙錠、銅鐵鼎、靑碗、大小埕甕、靑皮 、單錦和鼓樂等。

---

[47] 青皮，是一種柑橘果皮之中藥，用以治療腹痛、脹氣和胸悶。參見「青皮」，醫砭，https://yibian.hopto.org/db/?yno=313 2022 年 9 月 25 日瀏覽。

Qingpi, a traditional Chinese medicine for citrus peel, is used to treat abdominal pain, gas, and chest tightness. See "Qingpi", *Medical Bianstone*, https://yibian.hopto.org/db/?yno=313 September 25, 2022 retrieved.

The people boil the sea for salt and brew sugarcane pulp water and rice for wine. The land produces kapok, bamboo cloth, and yellow wax. Crude Jiangzhen wood is produced from sandy ground, so it can't fruit. The goods for trade use silver ingots, copper and iron tripods, green bowls, urns of different sizes, Citrus Reticulata Blanco, single brocade, and drums.

28.八節那間[48]
28.Bā Jié Nà Jiān（Surabaya, Surabaja）

其邑臨海，嶺方木瘦，田地瘠，宜種粟、麥。俗尚邪，與湖北道澧州風俗同。男女椎髻，披白布縵，繫以土布。一歲之間，三月內，民採生以祭鬼酬願，信不生災害。

白話文(Vernacular)：
該城市臨海，山嶺是方形，生長的樹木枝幹瘦小，田地貧瘠，適宜種粟、麥。風俗崇尚邪惡，與湖北道澧州鬼城風俗同。男女椎髻，披白布縵，繫以土布。一年之內有三個月，人民會抓活人祭鬼以祈願，他們相信這樣可不生災害。

The town is facing the sea and the mountainous areas have a few trees. The fields are barren and suitable for planting millet and wheat. The customs are fond of the forces of evil, which is the same as the customs of Fengzhou, Hubei Province, China. Men and women wear a bun on their heads, covered with white cloth, and tied with crude cloth. People spend three months

---

[48]八節那間，又寫為八節澗，印尼文寫為 Surabaya 或 Surabaja，指今之泗水。

Bā Jié Nà Jiān is also written as Bā Jié Jiàn, and in Indonesian it is written as Surabaya or Surabaja.

within a year, collecting live men to sacrifice to ghosts in return for their wishes. They believe that no disaster will occur in that way.

民煮海為鹽。有酋長。地產單莢、花印布不退色、木棉花、檳榔。貿易之貨，用青器、紫鑛、土粉、青絲布、埕甕、鐵器之屬。

白話文(Vernacular)：

人民煮海水製鹽。有酋長。當地生產單面蒙皮的小鼓、花印布不退色、木棉花和檳榔。貿易之貨品使用青器、紫鑛、土粉、青絲布、埕甕和鐵器等。

The people boil the sea for salt. There is a chief. The land produces small drums, flower printing cloth (not fade), kapok, and betel nut. The goods for trade used green utensils, purple ore, soil powder, green silk cloth, jars, and iron utensils.

29. 三佛齊[49]
29. Sanfoqi (Sri-Vijaya)

自龍牙門去五晝夜至其國。人多姓蒲。習水陸戰，官兵服藥，刀兵不能傷，以此雄諸國。其地人煙稠密，田土沃美。氣候暖，春夏常雨。俗淳。男女椎髻，穿青棉布短衫，繫東沖布。喜潔淨，故於水上架屋。

白話文(Vernacular)：

---

[49]三佛齊，又稱室利佛逝(Sri-Vijaya)，其首府在印尼蘇門答臘島的巴鄰旁（Palembang）。

Sanfoqi, also known as Sri-Vijaya, has its capital in Palembang, Sumatra, Indonesia.

自龍牙門航行經過五晝夜到該國。人多姓蒲。習水陸戰，官兵吃一種草藥，可刀槍不傷其身體，因此成為該一地區的強國。其地人煙稠密，田土肥沃。氣候暖和，春夏常下雨。風俗純樸。男女椎髻，穿青棉布短衫，繫東沖布。喜歡潔淨，所以都是在水上架屋居住。

From the Lingga Islands to this country takes five days and nights. Most people have the surname Pu. The people learn to fight on land and water, officers and soldiers take medicine, and swordsmen and soldiers cannot be injured, so this country becomes the strongest one among neighboring countries. The land is densely populated and the land is fertile and beautiful. The climate is warm, with frequent rains in spring and summer. The customs are vulgar. Men and women wear a bun on their heads, wearing green cotton blouses, tied with Dongchong's cloth. People like to be clean, so they build their houses on the rivers.

採蚌蛤為鮓，煮海為鹽，釀秫為酒。有酋長。地產梅花片腦[50]、中等降眞香、檳榔、木棉布、細花木。貿易之貨，

---

[50] 片腦，又稱龍腦（camphor dragonsbrain perfume）、腦子、梅花腦子（prune-blossoms）、梅花片腦，即是樟腦。主治開竅醒神，散熱止痛，明目去翳。參見「片腦」，中醫百科，https://zhongyibaike.com/wiki/%E7%89%87%E8%84%91　2022 年 10 月 25 日瀏覽。

　　Pian Nao, also known as camphor dragonsbrain perfume, brain, prune-blossoms, plum-blossoms, is camphor. Its functions are refreshing the mind, dissipating heat and relieving pain, improving eyesight, and removing nebula. See "Pian Nao", *Chinese Medicine Encyclopedia*, https://zhongyibaike.com/wiki/%E7%89%87%E8%84%91　October 25, 2022 retrieved.

用色絹、紅焇珠、絲布、花布、銅鐵鍋之屬。舊傳其國地忽穴出牛數萬，人取食之，後用竹木塞之，乃絕。

白話文(Vernacular)：

採蚌蛤醃製食用，煮海水製鹽，釀高梁製酒。有酋長。當地生產梅花片腦、中等降眞香、檳榔、木棉布、細花木。貿易之貨品使用色絹、紅焇珠、絲布、花布和銅鐵鍋等。過去傳說該國地面突然凹陷，從洞中跑出數萬頭牛，人民宰牛食用，後用竹木把該洞口塞住，就沒有牛跑出來了。

The clams are collected as pickles. The people boil the sea for salt and brew rice for wine. There is a chief. The land produces Borneol, medium-grade Jiangzhen incense, betel nut, kapok cloth, and fine flower wood. The goods for trade used colored silk, red beads, silk cloth, flower cloth, and copper and iron pots. According to old legends, tens of thousands of cattle came out of the cave in the country, people took them for food and then stuffed the cave with bamboo and wood, and it disappeared.

30. 嘯噴[51]

30. Xiào Pēn

絲監毗[52]、吉陀以東，其山陂延袤數千里。結茅而居，

---

[51]嘯噴，在今印尼蘇門答臘島東岸哈里河(Hari R.)北岸的新邦(Simpang)一帶。參見藤田豐八校註，前引書，頁 63。

Xiào Pēn is located in the Simpang area on the north bank of the Hari River on the east coast of Sumatra, Indonesia. See Fujita Toyohachi notes, *op. cit.*, p. 63.

[52]監毗，又寫為監篦(Kampei, Kampar)， 今蘇門答臘島東部的甘巴(Kampar) 河流域。參見「監篦」，南溟網，

田沃，宜種粟。氣候常暖。俗陋。男女椎髻。以藤皮煮軟，織粗布為短衫。以生布為捎。

白話文(**Vernacular**)：

從監毗、吉陀[53]向東，其山嶺延展數千里。老百姓築茅屋居住，田地肥沃，適宜種粟。氣候常暖。風俗淺陋。男女椎髻。將藤皮煮軟後，編織成粗布，做短衫。以生布做手巾。

This country is located to the east of Kampei and Jí Tuó (Kedah); the mountains extend for thousands of miles. People lived in thatched houses. The fields are fertile and suited for planting millet. The climate is usually warm. The customs are vulgar. Men and women wear a bun on their heads. People cook the rattan skin for softness and use it to weave into the short shirts and they take raw clothes as towel.

地產惟蘇木盈山，他物不見。每歲與前網國[54]相通，貿易通舶人。貨用五色硝珠、磁器、銅鐵鍋、牙錠、瓦甕、粗碗之屬。

白話文(**Vernacular**)：

當地只有蘇木一樣生長得滿山都是，其他的作物都不見蹤影。每年與以前的網國相往來貿易和船人交流。貨品使用五色硝珠、磁器、銅鐵鍋、牙錠、瓦甕和粗碗等。

---

http://www.world10k.com/blog/?p=1189　　2022 年 10 月 25 日瀏覽。

　　Kampei, also written as Kampar, is located in the Kampar River Basin in the eastern part of Sumatra Island. See " Kampei ", *Nanming Net*, http://www.world10k.com/blog/?p=1189　　October 25, 2022 retrieved.

[53]吉陀，即今馬來西亞的吉打（Kedah）。

Jí Tuó is now Kedah in Malaysia.

[54] 網國，如以閩南語解之，則可能為曼谷（Bangkok）。

Wǎng Guó, if it is interpreted in Hokkien dialectic, may refer to Bangkok.

The land produces only Biancaea sappan in a whole mountain, with no other trees in sight. Every year, it is traded by boat people with the former friendly country. The goods for trade used five-color nitrate beads, porcelains, copper and iron pots, silver ingots, tile urns, and crude bowls.

31.淳泥[55]
31.Bó Ní (Borneo)

龍山礠碑於其右。基宇雄敞，源田獲利。夏月稍冷，冬乃極熱。俗尚侈。男女椎髻，以五采帛繫腰，花錦為衫。崇奉佛像唯嚴。尤敬愛唐人，醉也則扶之以歸歇處。

白話文(Vernacular)：

由黑色大石頭構成的龍山位在該國右邊。山的氣勢雄偉廣大，水田種植獲利良多。夏月稍冷，冬乃極熱。風俗崇尚奢侈。男女椎髻，以五采帛繫腰，花錦為衣衫。篤信佛陀。尤敬愛中國人，中國人喝醉了，會扶他回去休息。

Longshan (Long Mountain) of big black stones is on this country's right. The momentum of the mountain is majestic and vast, and the paddy fields are very profitable.The summer months are slightly cold, and the winter is extremely hot. The customs are fond of extravagance. Men and women wear a bun on their heads, with five pieces of silk cloth tied at the waist, and flower brocade as the shirt. Worship of Buddha statues is strict.

---

[55]淳泥，指古代的婆羅洲。明國張燮認為淳泥是指北大年，此說不甚可靠。

Bó Ní refers to ancient Borneo. Zhang Xie of the Ming Dynasty believed that Bó Ní was Pattani. But this is not very reliable.

In particular, the local people love the Chinese people, if the Chinese are drunk, local people will help to take them home for a rest.

　　民煮海為鹽，釀秫為酒。有酋長，仍選其國能算者一人掌文簿，計其出納，收稅，無纖毫之差焉。地產降眞、黃蠟、玳瑁、梅花片腦。其樹如杉檜，劈裂而取之，必齋浴而後往。貨用白銀、赤金、色緞、牙箱錠[56]、鐵器之屬。

白話文(Vernacular)：

　　人民煮海水製鹽，釀高粱製酒。有酋長，選擇該國會算術的一個人掌文簿，由其負責出納和收稅，計算絲毫不差。當地生產降眞香、黃蠟、玳瑁、梅花片腦。梅花片腦之樹形類似杉木和檜木，劈裂而取之，而且必需齋戒沐浴後才前往採取。貨品使用白銀、赤金、色緞、牙箱錠和鐵器等。

The people boil the sea for salt and brew rice for wine. There is a chief, who is chosen from a person who can count in his country to hold the book, count the cashiers, collect taxes, and make no slight difference. The land produces Jiangzhen incense, yellow wax, tortoiseshell, and Borneol. The Borneol tree is like cedar and juniper, must be split and taken, and the people must fast and bathe before going to take it. The goods for trade used white silver, red gold, colored satin, silver ingots, and iron utensils.

---

[56]原文寫為「牙箱」，故改之。牙箱錠，是指銀錠或銀塊。

The original text was " Yá Xiāng ", so I correct it. Yá Xiāng ingot refers to silver ingot or silver nugget.

32. 朋家羅[57]
32. Péng Jiā Luó

故臨國[58]之西，山而三島；中島桑香佛所居，珍寶而前人莫能取；一島虎豹蛇虺縱橫，人莫敢入；一島土中紅石，握而取之，其色紅活，名鴉鶻也。舶人興販，往往金銀與之貿易。

白話文(Vernacular)：

該國位在故臨國之西邊，有三個島；中島是桑香佛所居地，有珍寶而以前人不能取得；第二個島則有許多虎、豹、蛇和虺，人不敢進入；第三個島是土中有紅石，用手握取，

---

[57]藤田豐八認為朋家羅即是斯里蘭卡的 Pingalla(Pangala)。（參見藤田豐八校註，前引書，頁 67。）然而根據該條目，朋家羅位在故臨以西，有三個小島。Pingalla 則是位在斯里蘭卡中北部內陸省分，不靠海。而較為可能的地點是故臨以西印度洋中印度的拉克沙群島（Lakshadweep）的 Bangaram 島。據傳說西元前第 6 世記印度的佛教經典本生經(Jataka)書中有個故事曾提及該群島。參見" Lakshadweep," *Wikipedia*, https://en.wikipedia.org/wiki/Lakshadweep 2022 年 10 月 18 日瀏覽。

Fujita Toyohachi believes that Péng Jiā Luó is Pingalla (Pangala) of Sri Lanka. (See Fujita Toyohachi note, *op. cit.*, p. 67.) However, according to this entry, Péng Jiā Luó is located in the west of Gù Lín Guó (Quilon), with three small islands. Pingalla is located in the north-central inland province of Sri Lanka, not by the sea. The more likely location is Bangaram Island in the Lakshadweep of India in the west of the Indian Ocean. According to legend, the archipelago is mentioned in a story in the Indian Buddhist classic Jataka in the sixth century BC. See " Lakshadweep," *Wikipedia*, https://en.wikipedia.org/wiki/Lakshadweep October 18, 2022

[58]故臨，位在印度西南部的奎隆（Quilon, Kollam）。「奎隆」，維基百科，https://zh.wikipedia.org/wiki/%E5%A5%8E%E9%9A%86 2022 年 10 月 15 日瀏覽。

Gù Lín is located in Quilon(Kollam) in southwestern India. "Quilon", *Wikipedia*, https://zh.wikipedia.org/wiki/%E5%A5%8E%E9%9A%86 October 15, 2022 retrieved.

它的顏色鮮紅，叫著鴉鶻。船人到該地做生意，往往用金銀跟它貿易。

This country is located to the west of the Gù Lín Guó (Quilon), there are three islands; on the middle island where Sangxiang Buddha lives, there are treasures that none of the predecessors could take; on the second island, there are tigers, leopards, and snakes crawling around, and no one dares to enter; the third island which has red stones in the soil can be taken by hand; its red color is also named as Crow Falcon. The boatmen go to trade them with gold and silver.

土瘠宜種粟，氣候大熱。俗朴。男女衣青單被。民煮海為鹽。有酋長。惟產紅石之外，別物不見。

白話文(Vernacular)：

土地貧瘠，適宜種粟，氣候炎熱。風俗純樸。男女穿青色單衣。人民煮海水製鹽。有酋長。除了產紅石之外，其他作物都沒有。

Its soil is barren and suitable for planting millet, and the climate is very hot. The customs are vulgar. Men and women wear single quilt cloth. The people boil the sea for salt. There is a chief. Except for the production of Redstone, no other products are seen.

33. 暹[59]

33. Sien (Sukhothai)

---

[59]暹，指 1238 年成立的素可泰（Sukhothai）王國。
Sien refers to the Sukhothai kingdom established in 1238.

自新門臺[60]入港[61]，外山崎嶇，內嶺深邃。土瘠，不宜耕種，穀米歲仰羅斛。氣候不正。俗尚侵掠。每他國亂，輒駕百十艘以沙糊[62]滿載，捨生而往，務在必取。近年以七十餘艘來侵單馬錫[63]，攻打城池，一月不下。本處閉關而守，不敢與爭。遇爪哇使臣經過，暹人聞之乃遁，遂掠昔里[64]而歸。

---

[60] 新門台，指泰國湄南（Menam）河口港口 Samut Prakan 之省譯，俗稱北欖（Paknam）。參見「Samut Prakan」，南溟網，http://www.world10k.com/blog/index.php?s=%E6%96%B0%E9%96%80 2022 年 10 月 15 日瀏覽。

Xinmentai refers to Samut Prakan port at the mouth of the Menam River in Thailand, commonly known as Paknam. See "Samut Prakan", *Nanming Net*,
http://www.world10k.com/blog/index.php?s=%E6%96%B0%E9%96%80 October 15, 2022 retrieved.

[61] 該港應是指阿瑜陀耶（Ayudhaya）。

The port should refer to Ayudhaya.

[62] 沙糊，又稱為西米（sago, sagu），通過用水洗滌搗碎的沙糊棕櫚樹幹，將其中的澱粉粒從樹幹中洗滌出來，故西米是一種澱粉，主要用於烹飪布丁、麵條、麵包和作為增稠劑。在新幾內亞的塞皮克河（Sepik River）地區，由西米製成的煎餅是主食，通常與新鮮的魚一起食用。參見"Metroxylon sagu," *Wikipedia*,
https://en.wikipedia.org/wiki/Metroxylon_sagu 2022 年 10 月 17 日瀏覽。

Shā Hú, also known as sago (sagu), is a kind of starch, mainly used for cooking pudding, noodles, and bread, and as a thickener. In the Sepik River region of New Guinea, pancakes made from sago are a staple, usually served with fresh fish. See "Metroxylon sagu," *Wikipedia*, https://en.wikipedia.org/wiki/Metroxylon_sagu October 17, 2022 retrieved.

[63] 單馬錫，或寫為淡馬錫（Tamusik），都是馬來文「Temasek」的對音，指今天的新加坡。

Tan Masek, or Tamusik, is the antiphon of the Malay word "Temasek", referring to today's Singapore.

[64] 藤田八豐認為昔里即實叻。實叻，又寫為石叻，即馬來語的 selat，海峽之意。參見饒宗頤，新加坡古事記，中文大學出版社，香港，1993 年，頁 310。筆者認為是指柔佛的新山（Johore Bahru）一帶。

Fujita Toyohachi believed that Xī Lǐ is selat. Shila, which means strait.

至正己丑夏五月，降於羅斛。

白話文(**Vernacular**)：

從新門臺入港，外圍的山崎嶇，裡面的山嶺深邃。土地貧瘠，不適宜耕種，穀米每年都要仰賴羅斛進口。氣候不穩定。風俗崇尚侵掠。每次他國有亂事，就會駕一百多艘船，上面滿載沙糊，奮不顧生前往，志在奪取。近年以七十餘艘船來侵略單馬錫，攻打城池，一個月未能攻下。單馬錫閉關而守，不敢與他戰爭。剛好爪哇使臣經過，暹人聽到此一消息才逃遁，遂掠奪昔里而歸。至正己丑夏五月，該國向羅斛投降。

Entering the port (Ayudhaya) from Xinmentai, the outer mountains are rugged and the inner ridges are deep. The fields are barren and unsuitable for cultivation. The grain needed depends on Lopburi's supply annually. The climate is unstable. The customs are fond of plundering. Every time another country is in chaos, they will drive a hundred or more ten ships loaded with Shā Hú (a kind of sago food), and sacrifice their life intending to take it. In recent years, they dispatched more than 70 ships to invade Temasek, attacking the city, but couldn't conquer it for one month. Temasek closed and guarded by itself, not daring to fight. When the Javanese envoys passed by, the Sien people fled when they heard it, so they plunder Xī Lǐ and returned. In May, Zhì Zhèng Jǐ Chǒu (1349), Xiān State surrendered to Lopburi.

凡人死，則灌水銀以養其身。男女衣著與羅斛同。仍以

See Ráo Zōngyí, *Chronicles of Singapore*, Chinese University Press, Hong Kong, 1993, p. 310. I think it refers to the area of Johore Bahru in Johor.

肞子權錢使用。

白話文(Vernacular)：

凡人死了，則灌水銀以培養其身體（目的在使其不腐爛）。男女衣著與羅斛相同。仍以肞子代替錢使用。

When people die, mercury is poured on them to nourish their bodies. (The purpose is to keep it from rotting) Men and women dress the same as Lopburi. They still use Pazi to replace the money.

地產蘇木、花錫、大楓子、象牙、翠羽。貿易之貨，用硝珠、水銀、青布、銅、鐵之屬。

白話文(Vernacular)：

當地生產蘇木、花錫、大楓子、象牙和翠羽。貿易之貨品使用硝珠、水銀、青布、銅和鐵等。

The land produces Biancaea sappan, tin, big maple, ivory, and Kingfisher feathers. The goods for trade used nitrate beads, mercury, green cloth, copper, and iron.

34. 爪哇
34. Java

爪哇卽古闍婆國。門遮把逸[65]山係官場所居，宮室壯麗，地廣人稠，實甲東洋諸番。舊傳國王係雷震石中而出，令女子為酋以長之。其田膏沃，地平衍，穀米富饒，倍於他國。民不為盜，道不拾遺。諺云：「太平闍婆者，此也。」俗朴，

---

[65]門遮把逸，又寫為滿者伯夷、麻喏巴歇。

Mén Zhē Bǎ Yì is also written as Majapahit or Mazao Paxie

男子椎髻，裹打布。惟酋長留髮。

白話文(**Vernacular**)：

爪哇卽是古闍婆國。門遮把逸山係官署所在地，宮室壯麗，地廣人稠，實為東洋諸番國第一大國。古代傳說國王係雷打到石頭後蹦出來的，令女子為酋長。其田地肥沃，土地平坦，穀米富饒，比他國多一倍。人民不當強盜，路上不拾遺。諺云：「太平闍婆者，就是此地。」風俗純樸，男子椎髻，上頭裹著布。但酋長留著頭髮。

Java is namely the ancient Jay Po country. The Majapahit Mountain is the official residence. The palace is magnificent, the land is vast and the people are dense. It is really the number one country in the East Ocean area. According to the old legend, the king came out of stone which was split by thunder. The woman was commanded as the chief to raise him. The fields are fertile, the land is flat, and the grain is plentiful, double that in other countries. The people are not fond of thievery, and no one picks up something which is left on the road. The proverb goes: "There is no more peace than Jay Po. Here it is." The customs are vulgar and simple; men wear a bun on their heads, wrapped in cloth. But the chief keeps his hair.

大德年間，亦黑迷失、平章史弼、高興曾往其地，令臣屬納稅貢，立衙門，振綱紀，設鋪兵，以遞文書。守常刑，重鹽法，使銅錢。俗以銀、錫、鉛、銅雜鑄如螺甲大，名為銀錢，以權銅錢使用。

白話文(**Vernacular**)：

大德年間，亦黑迷失、平章史弼、高興曾到過該地，要求該地官署納稅貢，並設立衙門，振綱紀，設立驛站軍隊，來傳遞文書。制訂刑法,頒佈鹽法,使用銅錢。市面上以銀、錫、鉛和銅一起混合鑄錢,大小如螺甲,名為銀錢,以代替銅錢使用。

During the Dade years, Yì hēi Míshī, Pingzhang Shibi, and Gāoxìng went to this country, ordered those Javanese subjects to pay tribute, set up a government, revived the rules, and set up post station soldiers to deliver documents. They practiced criminal regulation, enacted a salt law, and used copper coins. Silver, tin, lead, and copper are as large as a snail cast, and it is called silver coin and is used to replace copper coin.

地產青鹽,係曬成。胡椒每歲萬斤。極細堅耐色印布及鸚鵡之類。藥物皆自他國來也。貨用硝珠、金、銀、青緞、色絹、青白花碗、鐵器之屬。

白話文**(Vernacular)**:

當地生產青鹽,係日曬而成。胡椒每年產量為一萬斤。亦生產極細堅耐色印布及鸚鵡之類。藥物皆自他國進口。貨品使用硝珠、金、銀、青緞、色絹、青白花碗和鐵器等。

The land produces green salt which is made from sun-drying. It produces thousands of catties of peppers per year. It also produces very fine durable printed cloth, parrots, and the like. Medicines come from other countries. The goods for trade used nitrate beads, gold, silver, satin, colored silk, green and white flower bowls, and ironware.

次曰巫崙，曰希苓，曰三打板[66]，曰吉丹[67]，曰孫剌[68]等。
地無異產，故附此耳。

白話文(Vernacular)：

其他地名有巫崙、希苓、三打板、吉丹和孫剌等。這些
地方都沒有特別出產，故附記在此。

The next place is called Wu Lun, Xiling, San Daban, Jidan,
Sun La, etc. There are no different products in this land, so it is
attached here.

35. 重迦羅[69]

35. Janggala

---

[66] 三打板，應是打板，指杜並（Tuban）或稱廚閩。參見馮承鈞校注，
諸蕃志校注，台灣商務印書館，台北市，民國 75 年，頁 28-29，註一
至註三。

　San Daban should be Daban, referring to Du Bing (Tuban). See Annotated
by Feng Chengjun, *Zhu Fanzhi*, Taiwan Commercial Press, Taipei, 1986,
pp. 28-29, note 1 to note 3.

[67] 吉丹，可能是蘇吉丹或斯吉丹，指吉力石（Gressie, Gresik）（即錦石）。
參見藤田豐八校註，前引書，頁 73。

　Gidan, possibly Sujidan or Sjidan, refers to Gressie (Gresik). See Fujita
Toyohachi notes, *op. cit.*, p. 73.

[68] 藤田豐八認為孫剌是梭羅（Solo）。參見藤田豐八校註，前引書，頁 74。

　Fujita Toyohachi believed that Sun La is Solo. See Fujita Toyohachi notes,
op. cit., p. 74.

[69] 重迦羅，又譯戎牙路、重迦盧、重伽蘆。首都在卡胡利班（今之錦石），
又稱章加拉（Karajan Janggala）。根據薩努西•巴尼的說法，戎牙路，
即唐朝的訶陵，其首都位在今東爪哇錦石地區。（參見薩努西•巴尼
(Sanusi Pane)著，印度尼西亞史(*Sedjarah Indonesia*)（上冊），商務印書
館香港分館，香港，1980 年，頁 52-53、89。）

　Janggala is also translated to Róng Yá Lù, Chongjialu. Its capital is
Kahuliban (now Gresik), also known as Karajan Janggala. According to
Sanusi Pane, Róng Yá Lù is Kalinga of the Tang Dynasty, its capital is in
Gresik of present-day East Java. (See Sanusi Pane, *Sedjarah Indonesia*,
Volume 1, Commercial Press Hong Kong Branch, Hong Kong, 1980, pp.52-
53,89.)

杜瓶[70]之東曰重迦羅，與爪哇界相接。間有高山奇秀，不產他木，滿山皆鹽敷樹及楠樹。一石洞，前後三門，可容一、二萬人。田土亞於闍婆。氣候熱，俗淳。男女撮髻，衣長衫。

白話文(Vernacular)：

杜瓶之東邊有重迦羅，與爪哇界相接。中間有高山奇秀，不產其他樹木，滿山皆是鹽敷樹及楠樹。有一個石洞，前後有三個門，可容一、二萬人。田土肥沃程度次於闍婆。氣候熱，風俗純樸。男女撮髻，穿長衫。

The east of Tuban is called Janggala, which is connected to Java. There are beautiful mountains, grows many Yán Fū trees and Nan trees. No other trees are produced. There is one stone cave, with three doors in the front and back, which can accommodate 10,000 - 20,000 people. The land is inferior to Jay Po. The climate is hot and the customs are pure vulgar. Men and women wear a bun on their heads and long gowns.

地產綿羊、鸚鵡、細花木棉單、椰子、木棉花紗。貿易之貨，用花銀、花宣絹、諸色布。煮海為鹽，釀秫為酒。無酋長，年尊者統攝。

白話文(Vernacular)：

當地生產綿羊、鸚鵡、細花木棉單、椰子和木棉花紗。貿易之貨品使用花銀、花宣絹和諸色布。煮海水製鹽，釀高粱製酒。沒有酋長，由年長者統治。

---

[70]杜瓶，又寫為杜並或杜並足，即今天東爪哇北岸的杜板，或廚閩。

　　Tu Pingm also written as Tu Bing or Tu Bing Zu, is today's Tuban on the north shore of East Java.

The land produces sheep, parrots, fine flower kapok cloth, coconuts, and kapok yarn. The goods for trade used silver, flower Xuan silk, and various colors of cloth. The people boil the sea for salt and brew rice for wine. There is no chief, and the senior old man is in charge.

次曰諸番，相去約數日水程，曰孫陀、曰琵琶、曰丹重、曰負嶠、曰彭里。不事耕種，專尚寇掠。與吉陀、亞崎諸國相通交易，舶人所不及也。

白話文(**Vernacular**)：

其他各部落，相去約數日水程，其名稱有孫陀、琵琶、丹重、負嶠和彭里。他們不事耕種，專門寇掠。與吉陀、亞崎諸國相互交易，一般船人的船隻追趕不上他們。

The next various barbarian countries are at a distance of about a few days' water journey. They are called Sun Tuo, Pipa, Danzhong, Fù jiào, and Pengli. They do not farm but specialize in plundering. They are trading with Kedah and Aceh countries. The boats of ordinary boatmen can't catch up with them.

36. 都督岸[71]

---

[71]都督岸，可能位在卡里曼丹島西北部一帶。參見「都督岸」，南溟網，http://www.world10k.com/blog/?p=1144　2022 年 10 月 15 日瀏覽。

藤田豐八認為都督岸位在婆羅洲西南部有一岬名稱為 Tanjang Datu，其音義同都督岸，從該岬入即為砂拉越。參見藤田豐八校註，前引書，頁 79。

Dūdū Àn is probably located in the northwest area of Kalimantan. See " Dūdū Àn," *Nanming Net*, http://www.world10k.com/blog/?p=1144 October 15, 2022 retrieved.

Fujita Toyohachi believed that there is a cape to the southwest of Borneo named Tanjang Datu; its name and pronunciation are the same as "Tanjang

36. Dūdū Àn

自海腰平原，津通淡港[72]。土薄地肥，宜種穀，廣栽薯芋。氣候夏涼多淫雨，春與秋冬皆熱。俗尚節序。男女椎髻，穿綠布短衫，繫白布捎。民間每以正月三日，長幼焚香拜天，以酒牲祭山神之後，長幼皆羅拜於庭，名為慶節序。

白話文(Vernacular)：

從海灣的平原可通到淡港。土地不多，但田地肥沃，宜種穀，廣栽蕃薯和芋頭。氣候夏涼雨多，春與秋冬皆熱。風俗尊重節氣的順序。男女椎髻，穿綠布短衫，繫白布巾。民間每在正月三日，長幼焚香拜天，以酒和三牲祭山神，長幼皆在庭院祭拜，名為慶祝節序。

The boat can sail from the sea gulf plain to Dàn Gǎng port. The land is not much, but the fields are fertile and suitable for planting grains and yams. The climate is cool and rainy in summer, hot in spring and autumn and winter. The customs are in respect to the season's order. Men and women wear a bun on their heads, wearing a green cloth short shirt, tied with a white cloth towel. On the third day of the first lunar month, the elders and the younger people burn incense to worship the sky, and after offering sacrifices of wine and animals to the mountain gods, the elders and the younger people all worship in the courtyard, which is called the season's order festival.

Datu". Entering from this cape is Sarawak. See Fujita Toyohach notes, *op. cit.*, p. 79.

[72] 藤田豐八認為淡港指的是古晉（Kuching）。參見藤田豐八校註，前引書，頁79。

Fujita Toyohachi believed that Tamgang refers to Kuching. See Fujita Toyohachi notes, *op. cit.*, p. 79.

不喜煮鹽，釀蜜水為酒。有酋長。地產片腦、粗速香、
玳瑁、龜筒。貿易之貨，用海南占城布、紅綠絹、鹽、鐵、
銅鼎、色緞之屬。

白話文(Vernacular)：

不喜歡煮海水製鹽，但釀蜜水製酒。有酋長。當地生產
片腦、粗速香、玳瑁和龜筒。貿易之貨品使用海南占城布、
紅綠絹、鹽、鐵、銅鼎和色緞等。

The people do not like to boil salt, and brew honey water
as wine. There is a chief. The land produces Borneol, crude fast
incense, tortoiseshell, and Guī Tǒng. The goods for trade used
Hainan Champa cloth, red and green silk, salt, iron, copper
tripods, and colored satin.

37. 文誕[73]

37. Wén Dàn

渤山高環，溪水若淡，田地瘠。民半食沙糊、椰子。氣
候苦熱。俗淫。男女椎髻，露體，繫青皮布捎。日間畏熱，
不事布種。月夕耕鋤、漁獵、採薪、取水。山無蛇虎之患，
家無盜賊之虞。

白話文(Vernacular)：

渤山很高，環繞周邊，溪水是淡味，田地貧瘠。人民一

---

[73]藤田豐八認為文誕乃 Bândan 之對音，即今印尼之班達（Banda）島。
（參見藤田豐八校註，前引書，頁 80。）然而，爪哇島西端之萬丹之
發音是 Banten，亦可能是文誕之所在地。

　　Fujita Toyohachi believed that Wén Dàn's pronunciation is the same as
Bândan, namely the Banda Island, Indonesia. (See Fujita Toyohachi notes,
op. cit., p. 80.) However, Banten at the western end of Java Island has its
pronunciation the same as Bândan, and may also be the location of Wén
Dàn.

半食沙糊和椰子。氣候苦熱。風俗淫亂。男女椎髻，裸體，繫青皮布巾。日間怕熱，不事耕種。晚上月亮出來時下田耕鋤、漁獵、採薪和取水。山裡沒有蛇、虎為患，家無盜賊之虞。

Boshan (Bo Mountain) is high and around this country. The streams are a very light taste. The fields are barren. The people eat Shā Hú (a kind of sago food) in half and coconuts in half. The climate is very hot. The customs are licentious. Men and women wear a bun on their heads, and their naked bodies are tied with green cloth towel. The people are afraid of heat during the day and do not weave and cultivate. On the moon night, there is plowing and hoeing, fishing and hunting, collecting fuelwood, and fetching water. Mountains are free from snakes and tigers, and homes are free from thieves intruding.

煮海為鹽，釀椰漿為酒。婦織木棉為業。有酋長。地產肉荳蔻、黑小廝、荳蔻花、小丁皮。貨用水綾絲布、花印布、烏瓶、鼓瑟、青磁器之屬。

白話文(**Vernacular**)：

煮海水製鹽，釀椰漿製酒。婦女織木棉為業。有酋長。當地生產肉荳蔻、小黑人、荳蔻花和小丁皮。貨品使用水綾絲布、花印布、烏瓶、鼓瑟和青磁器等。

The people boil the sea for salt and brew coconut milk for wine. Women weave kapok. There is a chief. The land produces nutmeg, Negritos, cardamom flower, and diced peel. The goods for trade use the genus of water silk cloth, flower printing cloth, black bottles, zither, and green porcelains.

38. 蘇祿
38. Sulu

其地以石倚山為保障，山畬田瘠，宜種粟、麥。民食沙糊、魚、蝦、螺、蛤。氣候半熱。俗鄙薄。男女斷髮，纏皂縵，繫小印花布。

白話文(**Vernacular**)：

該地環繞著石倚山，山裡的田地貧瘠，適宜種粟、麥。人民食用沙糊、魚、蝦、螺和蛤。氣候半熱。風俗鄙薄。男女剪短髮，包著黑色布縵，繫小印花布。

The land is surrounded by Shí Yǐ Mountain, and the fields in the mountains are barren and are suited for planting millet and wheat. People eat Shā Hú (a kind of sago food), fish, shrimp, snails, and clams. The climate is semi-hot. The customs are vulgar. Men and women have their hair cut, wrapped in black fabric, and tied with small prints cloth.

煮海為鹽，釀蔗漿為酒，織竹布為業。有酋長。地產中等降眞條、黃蠟、玳瑁、珍珠，較之沙里八丹[74]、第三港等

---

[74] 沙里八丹，即印度東南部的納格伯蒂訥姆（Nagapattinam）港口，大唐西域求法高僧傳中譯作那伽鉢亶那，明朝稱之為小瑣里。參見「納加帕蒂南」，維基百科，
https://zh.wikipedia.org/wiki/%E7%BA%B3%E5%8A%A0%E5%B8%95%E8%92%82%E5%8D%97 2022 年 9 月 28 日瀏覽。「沙里八丹」，百度百科，
https://baike.baidu.com/item/%E6%B2%99%E9%87%8C%E5%85%AB%E4%B8%B9/10144350 2022 年 9 月 28 日瀏覽。
　　藤田豐八認為沙里八丹位在納加帕蒂南，而不在馬蘇利派特南。（參見藤田豐八校註，前引書，頁 121-122。）蘇繼卿認為沙里八丹為古代的注輦。（參見蘇繼卿，前引書，頁 216。）

處所產，此蘇祿之珠，色青白而圓，其價甚昂。中國人首飾用之，其色不退，號為絕品。有徑寸者，其出產之地，大者已值七、八百餘錠，中者二、三百錠，小者一、二十錠。其餘小珠一萬上兩重者，或一千至三、四百兩重者，出於西洋之第三港，此地無之。貿易之貨，用赤金、花銀、八都剌布、青珠、處器、鐵條之屬。

白話文(Vernacular)：

煮海水製鹽，釀蔗漿製酒，織竹布為業。有酋長。當地生產中等降眞香、黃蠟、玳瑁和珍珠。較之沙里八丹、第三港等處所產，此蘇祿之珠，色青白而圓，其價甚昂。中國人首飾用之，其顏色不退，號為絕品。有徑長一寸者，其出產之地，大者已值七、八百餘錠，中者二、三百錠，小者一、二十錠。其餘小珠一萬多兩重者，或一千至三、四百兩重者，此出於西洋之第三港，這裡則不生產。貿易之貨品使用赤金、花銀、八都剌布、青珠、處器和鐵條等。

The people boil the sea for salt, brew sugarcane pulp for wine, and weave bamboo cloth. There is a chief. The land produces medium-sized Jiangzhen incense, yellow wax,

---

Shalibatan refers to the port of Nagapattinam in southeast India. It was translated as Nagabotan in the *Biography of the Dharma-seeking Monks in the Western Regions of the Tang Dynasty*, and it was called Xiaosuoli in the Ming Dynasty. See "Nagapatinan", *Wikipedia*,
https://zh.wikipedia.org/wiki/%E7%BA%B3%E5%8A%A0%E5%B8%95%E8%92%82%E5%8D%97   September 28, 2022 retrieved.

"Shalibatan," *Baidu Encyclopedia*,
https://zh.wikipedia.org/wiki/%E7%BA%B3%E5%8A%A0%E5%B8%95%E8%92%82%E5%8D%97   September 28, 2022 retrieved.

Fujita Toyohachi believed that Sharibatan is located in Nagapatinan, not in Masuripatnam. (See Fujita Toyohachi notes, *op. cit.*, pp. 121-122.) Su Jiqing believed that Shalibatan is an ancient Chola. (See Su Jiqing, *op. cit.*, p. 216.)

tortoiseshell, and pearls. Compared with those products in Shalibatan and Third Port, this pearl of Sulu is white in color and round, and its price is very high. The Chinese use it for jewelry, its color does not fade, and it is called excellent. For those with a diameter of 1 inch, the large ones have a value of more than seven or eight hundred ingots, the medium ones are two or three hundred ingots, and the small ones are ten or twenty ingots. The rest of the small beads are 10,000 or over ounces in weight, or 1,000 to 3 hundred or 4 hundred ounces, which originate from the Third Port of the West Ocean, which is not found here. The goods for trade use red gold, silver, Badulla cloth, green pearls, Chuzhou utensils, and iron bars.

39. 龍牙犀角[75]
39. Lóng Yá Xījiǎo

峯嶺內平而外聳，民環居之，如蟻附坡。厥田下等。氣候半熱。俗厚。男女椎髻，齒白，繫麻逸布。俗以結親為重。親戚之長者一日不見面，必攜酒持物以問勞之。為長夜之飲，不見其醉。

白話文(Vernacular)：

峯嶺內平坦，而外圍高聳，人民圍繞四周居住，像螞蟻附在山坡一般。該地的田地屬於下等。氣候半熱。風俗純厚。

---

[75]藤田豐八認為龍牙犀角又寫為狼牙修（Langkasuka）、朗迦戍、凌牙斯加、凌牙蘇加，地當在北大年到吉打之間。參見藤田豐八校註，前引書，頁82-83。

Fujita Toyohachi believed that Lóng Yá Xījiǎo is also written as Langkasuka, Langkashu, Lingyaska, and Lingyasuga, which is located between Pattani and Kedah. See Fujita Toyohachi notes, *op. cit.*, pp. 82-83.

男女椎髻，牙齒白，繫麻逸布。風俗重視親屬關係。親戚之長者一日不見面，必攜酒持禮物去問候。飲酒一整夜，不見其醉。

The land within the peaks is flat and towering on the outside, and the people live around the mountain, like ants attached to the slope. The fields are inferior. The climate is semi-hot. The customs have a lot of local etiquette. Men and women wear a bun on their heads. The people have white teeth, tied with Mayit cloth. It is custom to attach importance to marriage. If the elders of relatives do not meet in a day, they will bring wine and gifts to visit them. They drink wine for the long night, I don't see them drunk.

民煮海為鹽，釀秫為酒。有酋長。地產沈香，冠於諸番。次鶴頂、降眞、蜜糖、黃熟香頭。貿易之貨，用土印布、八都剌布、靑白花碗之屬。

白話文(Vernacular)：

人民煮海水製鹽，釀高粱製酒。有酋長。當地生產沈香，冠於諸番。其次生產鶴頂、降眞香、蜜糖和黃熟香頭。貿易之貨品使用土印布、八都剌布和靑白花碗等。

The people boil the sea for salt and brew rice for wine. There is a chief. The land produced agarwood which is number one among barbarian countries. The next products are Heding, Jiangzhen incense, honey, and the head of Huáng Shú incense. The goods for trade use locally printed cloth, Badura cloth, and green and white-flowered bowls.

40. 蘇門傍[76]

40. Sumen Pang

　　山如屏而石峭,中有窩藏平坦。地瘠田少,多種麥而食。氣候常暖。俗鄙薄,藉他番以足其食,賴商賈以資其國。男女披長髮,短衫為衣,繫斯吉丹[77]布。

白話文(Vernacular):

　　山如屏障,而石頭陡峭,中間有平坦的地方。土地貧瘠,田地少,多種麥食用。氣候常暖。風俗鄙薄,藉仰賴他國進口糧食,賴商賈將它的產品賣到外國,以獲取資金。男女披長髮,穿短衫,繫斯吉丹布。

　　The mountain is like a barrier wall and the rock is steep, and there is a flat part within it. The land is barren and the fields are few, and wheat is grown on most land. The climate is usually warm. The customs are vulgar and contemptible. Businessmen

---

[76]蘇門傍,可能位在泰國素攀武裏(Suphan Buri)一帶,或印尼馬都拉島南岸城市 Sampang。參見「蘇門傍」,百度百科,
　https://baike.baidu.hk/item/%E8%98%87%E9%96%80%E5%82%8D/10046708　2022 年 10 月 15 日瀏覽。

　　Sumen Pang may be located in the area of Suphan Buri in Thailand, or Sampang, a city on the south coast of Madura Island, Indonesia. See "Sumen Pang", *Baidu Encyclopedia*,
　https://baike.baidu.hk/item/%E8%98%87%E9%96%80%E5%82%8D/10046708　October 15, 2022 retrieved.

[77]斯吉丹,又寫為蘇吉丹。其地點有二種說法,一說認為在今印尼爪哇島中部,位布格(Bugel)角南面。另一說在卡里曼丹島西南岸蘇卡丹那(Sukadana)。參見「蘇吉丹」,南溟網,
　http://www.world10k.com/blog/?p=1320　2022 年 10 月 15 日瀏覽。

　　Sī Jí Dān, also written as Sujidan. There are two versions of its location. One is that it is located in the central part of Java Island, Indonesia, to the south of Cape Bugel. Another said in Sukadana on the southwest coast of Kalimantan Island. See "Su Jidan", *Nanming Net*,
　http://www.world10k.com/blog/?p=1320　October 15, 2022 retrieved.

import foods from foreign countries to finance this country. Men and women wear long hair, and short shirts for clothing, which are tied with Sī Jí Dān cloth.

煮海為鹽。有酋長。地產翠羽、蘇木、黃蠟、檳榔。貿易之貨，用白糖、巫崙布、紬絹衣、花色宣絹、塗油、大小水埕之屬。塗油出於東埕塗，熱曬而成。

白話文(Vernacular)：

煮海水製鹽。有酋長。當地生產翠羽、蘇木、黃蠟和檳榔。貿易之貨品使用白糖、巫崙布、紬絹衣、花色宣絹、塗油和大小水甕等。塗油是產自東埕塗，經過熱曬而成。

The people boil the sea for salt. There is a chief. The land produces Kingfisher feathers, Biancaea sappan, yellow wax, and betel nut. The goods for trade used white sugar, Wu Lun cloth, silk garments, colored silk, painting oil, and large and small water jars. The oil comes out of Dongcheng paint materials which were made by heating and drying in the sun.

41. 舊港
41. Jiu Gang(Old Port) (Palembang)

自淡港入彭家門[78]，民以竹代舟。道多磚塔。田利倍於他壤。云：一年種穀，三年生金，言其穀變而為金也。後西

---

[78] 彭家，是指邦加島（Bangka），門是指海峽，故彭家門指邦加海峽。指竹筏從邦加海峽進入穆西河（Musi River），溯河前往巴鄰旁。

Pengjia refers to Bangka Island, and the gate refers to the strait, so Pengjiamen refers to the Bangka Strait. It refers to taking the bamboo raft entering the Musi River from the Bangka Strait and going up the river to Palembang.

洋人聞其田美，故造舟來取田內之土骨，以歸，彼田為之脈
而種穀。舊港之田金不復生，亦怪事也。

白話文(Vernacular)：

從淡港入彭家門，人民以竹筏代替舟。路上多磚塔。田
地的產量比其他田地多一倍。傳說：一年種穀，三年生金，
言其穀子變成黃金也。後西洋人聽到它的田地肥沃，故造舟
來取田內之土壤回去，他們的田地就可以種穀子。舊港之田
不再產金，真是怪事一椿。

From Dangang to Pengjiamen, the people replace the boat
with bamboo rafts. There are many bricked towers along the
road. The benefit of the fields is double the price of other places.
It is said that: "One year to plant grain, passing through three
years, it produces gold. That means the grain is transformed into
gold." Later, the people of the West Ocean heard the beauty of
the fields, so they built boats to fetch back the soil in the fields
and to make their fields grow grains. After then, it results in
strange things that the fields of Jiu Gang do not produce gold.

氣候稍熱。男女椎髻，以白布為捎。煮海為鹽，釀椰漿
為酒。有酋長。地產黃熟香頭、金顏香，木棉花冠於諸蕃，
黃蠟、粗降眞、絕高鶴頂、中等沈速。貿易之貨，用門邦丸
珠、四色燒珠、麒麟粒、處甆、銅鼎、五色布、大小水埕甕
之屬。

白話文(Vernacular)：

氣候稍熱。男女椎髻，以白布做手巾。煮海水製鹽，釀
椰漿製酒。有酋長。當地生產黃熟香頭和金顏香，木棉花是
各蕃國最好的，此外還生產黃蠟、粗降眞香、絕高鶴頂、中
等沈香和速香。貿易之貨品使用門邦丸珠、四色燒珠、麒麟

粒、處甕、銅鼎、五色布和大小水埕甕等。

The climate is slightly warmer. Men and women wear a bun on their heads and white cloth towel. The people boil the sea for salt and brew coconut milk for wine. There is a chief. The land produces the head of Huáng Shú incense, golden face incense, Kapok (which is the best one among various countries), yellow wax, crude Jiangzhen incense, high-quality Heding, medium class agarwood, and fast incense wood. The goods for trade used Mengbang ball beads, four-color burnt beads, unicorn pills, Chuzhou porcelains, copper tripods, five-color cloth, and large and small water jars.

42. 龍牙菩提[79]
42. Lóng Yá Pútí

　　環宇皆山，石排類門。無田耕種，但栽薯芋，蒸以代糧。當收之時，番家必堆貯數屋，如中原人積糧，以供歲用，食餘則存下年之不熟也。園種菓，採蛤、蚌、魚、蝦而食，倍於薯芋。氣候倍熱，俗朴。男女椎髻，披絲木棉花單被。

　　白話文(Vernacular)：
　　該國四周都是山環繞，有石排像門一樣。無田可耕種，但栽種蕃薯和芋頭，蒸煮來食以代替糧食。當收成時，番家必堆貯在好幾個屋間，像中國中原人積存糧食一樣，以供一年食用，吃剩下的則保存以準備下年可能收成不好時食用。

---

[79]龍牙菩提，指馬來西亞北海上的蘭卡威島（Lankawi）。參見藤田豐八校註，前引書，頁87。

　　Lóng Yá Pútí refers to Langkawi Island in the north of Malacca Strait, Malaysia. See Fujita Toyohachi notes, *op. cit.*, p. 87.

園子裡種水菓，採蛤、蚌、魚和蝦而食，其數量比蕃薯和芋頭多一倍。氣候倍熱，風俗純樸。男女椎髻，穿絲木棉花單衣。

There are mountains all around the country, and stones are scattered everywhere. A stonewall looks like a gate. No field can be cultivated, only planting sweet potatoes and taro steaming for eating to replace grain. When it is harvested, the families will store it in several rooms, just like the Chinese people in the Central Plains accumulate grain for the next year, and the leftovers will be stored for the next year's famine. The garden grows fruit, picks clams, mussels, fish, and shrimp, and eats it, which is twice as much as sweet potato and taro. The climate is hot and the customs are vulgar. Men and women wear a bun on their heads and cover them with silk, kapok single quilt cloth.

煮海為鹽，浸葛根汁以釀酒。地產速香、檳榔、椰子。貿易之貨，用紅綠燒珠、牙箱錠、鐵鼎、青白土印布之屬。

白話文(Vernacular)：

煮海水製鹽，浸葛根汁以釀酒。當地生產速香、檳榔和椰子。貿易之貨品使用紅綠燒珠、牙箱錠、鐵鼎和青白土印布等。

The people boil the sea for salt and soak Gě Gēn (Pueraria Root) juice to make wine. The land produces fast incense, betel nut, and coconut. The goods for trade used red and green burning beads, silver ingots, iron tripods, and green and white clay printed cloth.

43. 毗舍耶[80]

43. Pi-sir-ya (Visaya)

僻居海東之一隅，山平曠，田地少，不多種植。氣候倍熱。俗尚虜掠。男女撮髻，以墨汁刺身至疏頸項。頭纏紅絹，繫黃布為捎。

白話文(Vernacular)：

僻居海東的一個角落，山不高但廣大，田地少，種植不多。氣候炎熱。風俗崇尚虜掠。男女撮髻，從身上到脖子都用墨汁刺青。頭包著紅絹，繫黃布巾。

Pi-sir-ya is secluded in the east corner of the South China Sea; the mountains are flat, the fields are few, and there are not many plantings. The climate is hotter. The customs are fond of plundering. Men and women wear a bun on their heads and tattoos from their bodies to their necks with ink. The head is wrapped in red silk and tied with yellow cloth towel.

國無酋長，地無出產。時常裹乾糧，棹小舟，遇外番。伏荒山窮谷無人之境，遇捕魚採薪者，輒生擒以歸，鬻於他國。每人易金二兩重。蓋彼國之人遞相倣傚，習以為業。故東洋聞毗舍耶之名，皆畏而逃焉。

白話文(Vernacular)：

該國沒有酋長，土地上也沒有出產。時常裹乾糧，駕小舟，遇到外番。埋伏荒山窮谷沒有人之地方，遇捕魚採木材的人，常常活捉回去，賣給其他國家。每人可賣得黃金二兩

---

[80]毗舍耶，指位在菲律賓中部的米賽亞（Visaya）。

Pi-sir-ya refers to Visaya, in the central part of the Philippines.

重。該國之人競相倣傚，習以為業。故東洋聽說毗舍耶之名字，都害怕就逃走了。

This country has no chief, and the land has no products. The people always wrap dry food by taking a boat to ambush in the desolate mountains and valleys, where they meet foreigners, or fishermen and timber gatherers; they often captured them and sell them to other countries. Each person is sold for two ounces of gold. The people of the countries imitate each other, and they are accustomed to it. Therefore, when the people of the East Ocean hear the name of Pi-sir-ya, all are afraid and fled.

44.班卒[81]
44.Bān Zú

地勢連龍牙門後山，若纏若斷，起凹峯而盤結，故民環居焉。田瘠，穀少登。氣候不齊，夏則多雨而微寒。俗質，披短髮，緞錦纏頭，紅紬布繫身。

白話文(Vernacular)：
該國地形連接到龍牙門島後面的島，中間有島嶼斷斷續

---

[81]班卒（Panchor），是馬來西亞麻坡（Muar）縣的一個小鎮，位於麻坡河旁。參見「班卒」，維基百科，https://zh.m.wikipedia.org/zh-tw/%E7%8F%AD%E5%8D%92　2022 年 10 月 15 日瀏覽。

但 Willem Pieter Groeneveldt 認為班卒位在蘇門答臘島西岸的 Fansur 或 Fantsur。參見 Willem Pieter Groeneveldt, *op.cit.*, p.37.

Bān Zú is a town in Muar County, Malaysia, located beside the Muar River. See " Panchor ", *Wikipedia*, https://zh.m.wikipedia.org/zh-tw/%E7%8F%AD%E5%8D%92　October 15, 2022 retrieved.

But Willem Pieter Groeneveldt believed that Panchu is located in Fansur or Fantsur on the west coast of Sumatra. See Willem Pieter Groeneveldt, *op.cit.*, p.37.

續，山峯和山谷盤錯在一起，所以老百姓是環繞山邊居住。田地貧瘠，穀物收成不好。氣候不穩定，夏天多雨而微寒。風俗質樸，剪短髮，用緞錦包著頭，紅紬布繫身。

The terrain is connected to the islands behind Longyamen (Lingga Islands), and it looks entangled and broken, and peaks and valleys come together, so the people live around the mountain. The fields are barren, and the harvests of grains are few. The climate is unstable, and the summer is rainy and slightly cold. The customs are vulgar. The people have short hair, satin brocade wrapped around their heads, and red cloth tied around their bodies.

煮海為鹽，釀米為酒，名明家。有酋長。地產上等鶴頂、中等降眞、木棉花。貿易之貨，用絲布、鐵條、土印布、赤金、甆器、鐵鼎之屬。

白話文(Vernacular)：

煮海水製鹽，釀米製酒，叫明家。有酋長。當地生產上等鶴頂、中等降眞香和木棉花。貿易之貨品使用絲布、鐵條、土印布、赤金、甆器和鐵鼎等。

The people boil the sea for salt and brew rice for wine which is named Mingjia. There is a chief. The land produces top-grade Heding, medium-grade Jiangzhen incense, and kapok. The goods for trade used silk cloth, iron bars, local cloth, red gold, porcelains, and iron tripods.

45. 蒲奔[82]

---

[82]蒲奔，位在馬都拉島（Madura）南邊的大海。參見 Willem Pieter

45. Pu Ben

地控海濱，山蹲白石，不宜耕種，歲仰食於他國。氣候乍熱而微冷。風俗果決。男女青黑，男垂髻，女拳髻，繫白縵。

白話文(Vernacular)：

該地控制海濱，山區丘陵地有白色石塊，不宜耕種，每年要仰賴外國進口糧食。氣候會突然炎熱而微冷。風俗果決。男女穿青黑色衣服，男子頭髮紮起來後頭垂下，女子則頭髮盤髻，繫白色布。

The country controls the seashore, and the hills have white stones, which are not suitable for farming. The people have to import food from other countries every year. The climate is suddenly hot and sometimes slightly cold. The custom is resolute and acts fast. Men and women wear green and black cloth. Men do not have curly hair, and women wear a bun on their heads and tie their heads with white cloth.

民煮海為鹽，採蠏黃為鮓。以木板造舟，藤篾固之，以棉花塞縫底，甚柔軟，隨波上下蕩，以木而為槳，未嘗見有損壞。有酋長。地產白藤、浮留藤、檳榔。貿易之貨，用青甆器、粗碗、海南布、鐵線、大小埕甕之屬。

白話文(Vernacular)：

人民煮海水製鹽，採蟹黃醃製。以木板造舟，用藤條綁固，以棉花塞縫底，舟甚柔軟，隨波上下起伏，以木頭做槳，

Groeneveldt, *op.cit.*, p. 23.

Puben is located in the sea on the south side of Madura Island. See Willem Pieter Groeneveldt, op.cit., p.23.

不容易損壞。有酋長。當地生產白藤、浮留藤和檳榔。貿易之貨品使用青甖器、粗碗、海南布、鐵線和大小埕甕等。

The people boil the sea for salt and pick the crab eggs for pickles. The boats are made of wooden boards and use rattan strips to fasten them, and the seams are stuffed with cotton. It is very soft and swayed up and down with the waves. The oars are made of wood, and there is no damage to be seen. There is a chief. The land produces white rattan, Fu Liu rattan, and betel nut. The goods for trade use green porcelains, crude bowls, Hainan cloth, iron wires, and large and small water jars.

46. 假里馬打[83]
46. Jiǎ Lǐ Mǎ Dǎ

山列翠屏,闤闠臨溪,田下,穀不收。氣候熱。俗澆薄。男女髡頭,以竹布為桶樣穿之,仍繫以捎。罔知廉恥。

白話文(Vernacular):

群山排列得像綠色的屏風,店鋪靠近河邊,田地屬於下等,穀物收成不佳。氣候熱。風俗澆薄。男女都剃髮留辮子,穿以竹布做成桶樣的衣服,仍繫以手巾。不知廉恥。

The mountains are arranged like a green screen; the shops

---

[83]假里馬打,又寫為假里馬荅,為婆羅洲西邊的卡利馬達島(Karimata Is.)。參見李則芬,元史新講(二),黎明文化事業公司,台北市,民國78年3月再版,頁493-494;Willem Pieter Groeneveldt, *op.cit.*, 1876, p.26.

　Jiǎ Lǐ Mǎ Dǎ is Karimata Is. to the west of Borneo. See Li Zefen, *New Lectures on the History of the Yuan Dynasty* (2), Le Ming Cultural Enterprise Company, Taipei, reprinted in March 1978, pp. 493-494; Will[ ]m Pieter Groeneveldt, *op.cit.*, 1876, p.26.

are close to the river. The fields are inferior and grains grow few. The climate is hot. The customs are vulgar. Both men and women shave their hair and keep their braids, wearing bamboo cloth like a barrel. They are still wearing towel. But without knowing shame.

採蕉實為食。煮海為鹽，以適他國易米。每鹽一斤易米一斗。地產番羊，高大者可騎，日行五六十里，及玳瑁。貿易之貨，用硫磺、珊瑚珠、闍婆布、青色燒珠、小花印布之屬。

白話文**(Vernacular)**：

採蕉實食用。煮海水製鹽，以交換他國的米。每鹽一斤可易米一斗。當地生產番羊，高大者可騎，日行五、六十里，另有玳瑁。貿易之貨品使用硫磺、珊瑚珠、闍婆布、青色燒珠和小花印布等。

The people pick bananas for food. The people boil the sea for salt which is used to exchange for rice from other countries. One pound of salt is exchanged for rice per bucket. The land produces tortoiseshell and sheep, of which the tall ones can be ridden and can travel fifty or sixty miles a day. The goods for trade use sulfur, coral beads, Java cloth, green and yellow-colored burnt beads, and small flower-printed cloth.

47. 文老古[84]

---

[84] 文老古，即今印尼的摩鹿加（Maluku）群島。「文老古」，古代南海地名匯釋，
http://mall.cnki.net/Reference/ref_search.aspx?bid=R200809105&inputText=%E6%96%87%E8%80%81%E5%8F%A4　2022 年 10 月 9 日瀏覽。

47. Wén Lǎo Gǔ

益溪通津，地勢卑窄。山林茂密，田瘠稻少。氣候熱，俗薄。男女椎髻，繫花竹布為捎。以象齒樹之內室，為供養之具。

白話文(Vernacular)：

有一條益溪通到港口，地勢低窄。山林茂密，田地貧瘠，稻作收成少。氣候熱，風俗淺薄。男女椎髻，繫花竹布巾。以象牙掛在內室，做為一種供奉之物品。

A Yi River is flowing into the port. The terrain is low and narrow. The mountains have dense forests. The fields are barren and have few grains. The climate is hot. The customs are vulgar. Men and women wear a bun on their heads. They are tied with flower bamboo cloth towel. Ivory was hung on the wall in their inner chamber as an offering.

民煮海為鹽，取沙糊為食。地產丁香，其樹滿山，然多不常生，三年中間或二年熟。有酋長。地每歲望唐舶販其地，往往以五梅雞雛出，必唐船一隻來；二雞雛出，必有二隻，以此占之，如響斯應。貿易之貨，用銀、鐵、水綾、絲布、巫崙八節那潤布、土印布、象齒、燒珠、青甆器、埕器之屬。

白話文(Vernacular)：

人民煮海水製鹽，取沙糊食用。當地生產丁香，其樹種了滿山，然多不常生丁香，三年中間或二年才收成一次。有

Wén Lǎo Gǔ is the Maluku archipelago in Indonesia.　See "Wen Laogu", *An Interpretation of Ancient South China Sea Place Names*, http://mall.cnki.net/Reference/ref_search.aspx?bid=R200809105&inputText=%E6%96%87%E8%80%81%E5%8F%A4　October 9, 2022 retrieved.

酋長。當地每年盼望中國船隻到來做生意，他們占卜以五梅雞孵出小雞一隻，中國船必有一艘來；孵出兩隻小雞，必有二艘來，非常靈驗。貿易之貨品使用銀、鐵、水綾、絲布、巫崙八節那澗布、土印布、象牙、燒珠、靑甆器和甕器等。

The people boil the sea for salt and take the Shā Hú (a kind of food) for food. The land grows cloves, and their mountains are full of trees. However, they are not often grown and mature in three years or two years. There is a chief. Every year, the people hope the Chinese ship sells their goods here. They foretell that when the Wǔ Méi chicks are born, a Chinese ship will come here. If the two chicks are born, there must be two Chinese ships. This divination is very effective. The goods for trade used silver, iron, water velvet, silk cloth, Wulun Bā Jié Nà Jiàn cloth, locally printed cloth, ivory, burnt beads, green porcelains, and water jars.

48. 古里地悶[85]
48. Gǔlǐ De Mèn (Timor)

居加羅之東北，山無異木，唯檀樹為最盛。以銀、鐵、碗、西洋絲布、色絹之屬為之貿易也。地謂之馬頭，凡十有二所。有酋長。田宜穀粟。氣候不齊，朝熱而夜冷。

白話文(Vernacular)：

人民居住在加羅之東北，山沒有奇特的樹木，唯檀樹最多。以銀、鐵、碗、西洋絲布和色絹等作為貿易商品。當地稱為碼頭的，總數有十二處。有酋長。田地適宜種穀粟。氣

---

[85]古里地悶，指帝汶島。

Gǔlǐ De Mèn refers to Timor Island.

候不穩定，早上熱而夜晚冷。

This place is located to the northeast of Garo. There are no different trees in the mountains, but sandalwood is the most prosperous. The goods for trade used silver, iron, bowls, West Ocean silk cloth, and colored silk. The ground is called Mătóu, and there are twelve places in total. There is a chief. The fields are suitable for planting grains and millet. The climate is unstable, hot in the morning and cold at night.

風俗淫濫。男女斷髮，穿木棉短衫，繫占城布。市所酒肉價廉。婦不知恥。部領目縱食而貪酒色之餘，臥不覆被，至染疾者多死，倘在番苟免。回舟之期，櫛風沐雨，其疾發而為狂熱，謂之陰陽交，交則必死。昔泉之吳宅，發舶梢眾百有餘人，到彼貿易，既畢，死者十八九，間存一二，而多羸弱乏力，駕舟隨風回舶。或時風恬浪息，黃昏之際，則狂蕩唱歌。搖櫓夜半，則添炬輝燿，使人魂遊而膽寒。吁！良可畏哉！然則其地互市雖有萬倍之利，何益！昔柳子厚謂海賈以利易生，觀此有甚者乎！

白話文(Vernacular)：

風俗淫濫。男女剪短髮，穿木棉短衫，繫占城布。市面上賣的酒和肉價格便宜。婦女不知羞恥。部領頭目縱食而貪酒色，睡覺不蓋被，以至染疾者多死亡，中國人在此勉強可免除此種疾病。中國人在回國時，在外奔走辛勞，其疾發而為狂熱，謂之陰陽交，交則必死。從前泉州有姓吳的，帶了一百多人搭船到此做貿易，生意完成後，死了十之八、九人，存活的有十之一、二人，而多羸弱乏力，駕舟隨風回國。或遇到風平浪靜，黃昏之際，則瘋狂唱歌。在半夜搖櫓，則添火炬照燿，使人魂遊而膽寒。吁！真是讓人害怕啊！然則其

地互市雖有萬倍之利益，有什麼益處嗎！從前柳子厚說，海
外貿易以利益換取生命，就此來看，有什麼比這個更壞的嗎！

The customs are licentious. Men and women have their hair cut and wear kapok shirts and Champa cloth. The price of wine and meat in the market is cheap. Women have no shame. In addition to gluttonous food and alcohol, the ministers lie down without covering up, until many people who contract the disease die. If a Chinese who lived here can be freed from this disease, when he returns to his home country and runs outside and does very hard work, he will be prone to major diseases, which are called yin and yang copulation. If there is copulation, then he will die. In ancient times, there was a Wu family in Quanzhou, and he brought several hundred people to take ships to go to do business there; eighty or ninety persons died, and ten or twenty survived and were weak. When those weak men drove the ship back following with wind to China, sometimes they met calm and peaceful waves. At dusk, they sing wildly. Shaking the scull at midnight, they add the brilliance of the torch, which will make people spiritually wander and be terrified. Oh! Awesome! However, although the overseas market has ten thousand times the benefits, what are the benefits? In the past time, Liu Zihou said that oversea businessmen are to earn benefits to exchange for their life. With that in mind, is there anything worse than this?

49. 龍牙門[86]

---

[86]龍牙門，指位在新加坡和林伽（或譯為龍牙）群島（Lingga Islands）
之間的新加坡海峽。

Lóng Yá Mén refers to the Singapore Strait between Singapore and the

49. Lóng Yá Mén (Lingga Island)

門以單馬錫番兩山相交，若龍牙狀，中有水道以間之。田瘠稻少。天氣候熱，四五月多淫雨。俗好劫掠。昔酋長掘地而得玉冠。歲之始，以見月為正初，酋長戴冠披服受賀，今亦遞相傳授。男女兼中國人居之。多椎髻，穿短布衫，繫青布捎。

白話文(Vernacular)：

屬於單馬錫番的兩個島相交形成一個門，像龍牙狀，中間有水道隔開。田地貧瘠，稻作收成少。天氣炎熱，四、五月多下雨。俗好劫掠。從前酋長掘地而得玉冠。一年之始，以看見月亮為正月初一，酋長戴該玉冠穿上禮服受拜賀，今亦延續此一傳統。有中國的男人和女人住在這裡。當地男人和女人多椎髻，穿短布衫，繫青布巾。

The two islands belonging to Temasek barbarians intersect to form a gate, shaped like a dragon's tooth, with a water channel in between. The fields are barren and have few grains. The weather is hot and rainy in April and May. The customs are fond of looting. In the past, the chief dug the ground to get the jade crown. At the beginning of the year, seeing the moon as the first day of January, the chief wears the crown and robes to receive congratulations, and now they continue this practice. Some Chinese people, men, and women, are living there. The local men and women wear a bun on their heads, wearing a short cloth shirt, and tie it with a green cloth towel.

Lingga Islands

地產粗降眞、斗錫。貿易之貨，用赤金、靑緞、花布、處甆器、鐵鼎之類。蓋以山無美材，貢無異貨。以通泉州之貨易，皆剽竊之物也。

白話文**(Vernacular)**：

當地生產粗降眞香、斗錫。貿易之貨品使用赤金、靑緞、花布、處甆器和鐵鼎之類。由於該島沒有出產好產品，進貢沒有特異貨物。它運至泉州之貨物，都是劫掠來的。

The land produced crude Jiangzhen incense and natural tin. The goods for trade use red gold, green satin, floral cloth, Chuzhou porcelains, iron tripods, and the like. There are no beautiful materials on the islands, and there are no precious goods in tribute. The goods of trade to Quanzhou are all plundered goods.

舶往西洋，本番置之不問。回船之際，至吉利門[87]，舶人須駕箭棚，張布幕，利器械以防之。賊舟二三百隻必然來迎敵數日。若僥倖順風，或不遇之。否則人為所戮，貨為所有，則人死係乎頃刻之間也。

白話文**(Vernacular)**：

船開往西洋，本島番人置之不問。但船回航到吉利門時，船人須架好檔箭棚子，張開布幕，並準備武器以防備。賊匪駕舟二、三百隻必然來劫掠數日。若僥倖順風，或者沒有遇到該賊匪，就可逃脫。否則人被該賊匪殺害，貨物為其所奪，人死是頃刻之間的事。

When the ships are going to the West Ocean, the people of

---

[87] 吉利門，位在爪哇的 Karimon。參見 W. P. Groeneveldt, *op.cit.*, p.22.
Jílì Mén is located in Karimon, Java. See W. P. Groeneveldt, *op.cit.*, p.22.

this island do not care. When it returns, entering Jílì Mén, the boatmen must construct an arrows shelf, put up a curtain, and sharpen weapons to inhibit them. Two or three hundred pirates' boats will surely come to meet them, and fighting by both sides will continue for a few days. If they are lucky, they may not encounter this island's pirates. Otherwise, people will be killed and the goods will be plundered, and people will die in an instant.

50. 崑崙
50. Kūnlún

　　古者崑崙山，又名軍屯山[88]。山高而方，根盤幾百里，截然乎瀛海之中，與占城、東西竺[89]鼎峙而相望。下有崑崙洋，因是名也。舶泛西洋者，必掠之。順風七晝夜可渡。諺云：「上有七州，下有崑崙，針迷舵失，人船孰存。」
　　　白話文(Vernacular)：
　　在古代，崑崙山又稱軍屯山 。山高而呈方形，根盤幾百里，矗立在大海中，與占城、東西竺鼎峙而相望。它的南邊有崑崙洋，因此得名。船航行到西洋者，必然被它劫掠。順風七晝夜可渡過該島。俗諺說：「上有七州，下有崑崙，

---

[88] 軍屯山，又寫為軍突弄山、軍徒弄山。指越南湄公河出海口外之崑崙島（Poulo Condore），越南語寫為 Con Lon。參見「軍屯山」，南溟網，http://www.world10k.com/blog/?p=1209　2022 年 10 月 14 日瀏覽。
　　Juntun Mountain is also written as Juntunong Mountain and Jūn Tú Nòng Mountain. It refers to Poulo Condore outside the mouth of the Mekong River in Vietnam. It is written as Con Lon in Vietnamese. See "Juntun Mountain", *Nanming Net*, http://www.world10k.com/blog/?p=1209 October 14, 2022 retrieved.
[89] 東西竺，指馬來西亞的 Aur Island。Ulrich Theobald, *op.cit.*
　Dongxi Zhu refers to Aur Island in Malaysia. Ulrich Theobald, *op.cit.*

針路和舵失去方向，人和船怎能存活呢。」

The ancient Kūnlún Mountain is also known as Juntun Mountain. The mountain is high and square, extending hundreds of miles, and it is independently in the middle of the big ocean. It faces Champa and Donxizhu. To its south is the Kunlun Ocean, so it gets the name. Those ships that sail to the West Ocean will surely be plundered by them. The ships with downwind can cross it from Qī Zhōu (seven islands) to Kūnlún for seven days and nights. The proverb goes: "There are Qī Zhōu above, and Kūnlún below, the needle and the rudder are lost, can the people and ships survive?"

雖則地無異產，人無居室，山之窩有男女數十人，怪形而異狀，穴居而野處。旣無衣褐，日食山菓、魚蝦，夜則宿於樹巢，仿摽技野鹿之世，何以知其然也。凡舶阻惡風灣泊其山之下，男女羣聚而覘，撫掌而笑，良久乃去，自適天趣。吾故曰：「其無懷、大庭氏[90]之民歟！其葛天氏[91]之民歟！」

白話文(**Vernacular**)：

---

[90]無懷氏是中國在前 5241 年～前 5175 年的古代帝王。大庭氏是中國在前 7361 年～前 7224 年的古代帝王。參見「大庭氏」，維基教科書，https://zh.m.wikibooks.org/zh-hant/%E4%B8%AD%E5%9C%8B%E6%AD%B7%E5%8F%B2/%E4%B8%8A%E5%8F%A4%E5%B8%9D%E7%8E%8B%E5%85%A8%E8%A1%A8　2022 年 10 月 14 日瀏覽。

Wuhuai was an ancient emperor in China from 5241 BC to 5175 BC. Dating was an ancient emperor in China from 7361 BC to 7224 BC. See "Dating", *Wikibooks*, https://zh.m.wikibooks.org/zh-hant/%E4%B8%AD%E5%9C%8B%E6%AD%B7%E5%8F%B2/%E4%B8%8A%E5%8F%A4%E5%B8%9D%E7%8E%8B%E5%85%A8%E8%A1%A8　October 14, 2022 retrieved.

[91] 葛天氏，是中國在前 5649 年～前 5539 年的部落首領。同上註。

Ge Tian was the tribal leader of China from 5649 BC to 5539 BC. *Ibid.*

雖然該地沒有特出的物產，人民沒有居室，山洞中住有男女數十人，怪形而異狀，他們穴居而野處。沒有穿衣服，每天吃山菓和魚蝦，晚上就睡在樹上的巢，很像獵捕野鹿之時代，我不知道他們為何會如此生活。凡是船隻遇到惡風而灣泊在該島，男女羣聚觀看，撫掌而笑，很長一段時間才離去，他們自己覺得很有趣。所以我說：「他們若不是無懷、大庭氏之子民，就是葛天氏之子民。」

Although the land has no different products and people have no living room, there are dozens of men and women huddled in the valley, they look weird, living in caves and wild places. They have no clothes, eat mountain fruits, fish, and shrimps in the daytime, and sleep in tree nests at night. It seems they lead a life of hunting wild deer; I don't know why they live like this. If the boats are parked under the mountain in the strong wind, the men and women gather together and look, clap, and laugh, and after a long time, they go away. They have fun in it. Therefore, I said: "They are either the people of the Wuhuai and Dating or the people of the Ge Tian!"

51. 靈山[92]
51. Língshān

嶺峻而方，石泉下咽。民居星散，以結網為活。田野闢，

---

[92]藤田豐八認為靈山位在 Qui-nhon 城北的 Lang-son 港。Lang-son 即靈山之對音。參見藤田豐八校註，前引書，頁 100。

Fujita Toyohachi believed that Língshān is located in Lang-son Port, north of Qui-Nhon City. Lang-son is the same pronunciation as Língshān. See Fujita Toyohachi notes, *op. cit.*, p.100.

宜耕種，一歲，凡二收穀。舶至其所，則舶人齋沐三日。其
什事，崇佛誦[93]經，燃水燈，放彩船，以禳本舶之災，始度
其下。風俗、氣候、男女與占城同。

白話文(**Vernacular**)：

山嶺高峻而呈方形，山腳下有泉水。人民散居各處，以
結魚網維生。田野有開墾，適宜耕種，一年稻米收穫兩次。
船隻到此，船人要齋戒沐浴三日。主要要做的事，是拜佛誦
經，燃水燈，放彩船，以消除本船之災難，然後該船才繼續
下一個行程。該地的風俗、氣候、男女都與占城相同。

The ridge is steep and square, and there is a spring in the
foothills. The people's dwellings are scattered, and they live by
making nets. The fields are wide and suitable for cultivation.
There are two harvests of grain in one year. When the ship
arrives at this place, the shipmen fast for three days. What's more,
worshiping the Buddha, chanting sutras, burning water lanterns,
and setting off colorful boats, to eliminate the disaster of the ship.
Then the ship proceeds on its next voyage. Customs, climate,
men, and women are the same as Champa.

地產藤枝，輕小黑紋[94]相對者為冠，每條可互易一花斗
錫；粗大而紋疎者，一花斗錫互易三條。舶之往復此地，必
汲水、採薪以濟日用。次得檳榔、荖葉，餘無異物。貿易之
貨，用粗碗、燒珠、鐵條之屬。

白話文(**Vernacular**)：

---

[93] 原文寫為「諷」，故改之。
The original text was written as "sarcasm", so I correct it.
[94] 原文寫為「文」，故改之。
The original text was written as "Wen", so I correct it.

當地生產藤枝，重量輕而且有小黑花紋的是最佳，每條可換一花斗錫；粗大而花紋較疎者，一花斗錫可換三條。船隻來往此地，必定要汲水、採薪以作為日常所用。其次生產有檳榔和荖葉，此外就無其他特異物產。貿易之貨品使用粗碗、燒珠和鐵條等。

The land produces rattan branches, those with light and small black lines are the best ones, and each one can be exchanged for one natural tin nugget; three thick and sparse texture rattan branches can be exchanged for one piece of a natural tin nugget. When ships travel back and forth here, they must draw water and pick wood for daily necessities. The next products are betel nut and piper betel leaves, and there were no other special products. The goods for trade used crude bowls, burning beads, and iron bars.

52. 東西竺[95]
52. Dōngxīzhú

石山嵯峨，形勢對峙。地勢雖有東西之殊，不啻蓬萊方丈之爭奇也。田瘠不宜耕種，歲仰淡洋[96]米穀足食。氣候不

---

[95] 藤田豐八認為東西竺即是 Pulo Aor，意為竹島。（參見藤田豐八校註，前引書，頁 101。）該島現稱為奧爾島（Pulau Aur），位在馬來西亞柔佛州豐盛港（Mersing）以東外海。

　　Fujita Toyohachi believed that Dōngxīzhú is Pulo Aor, which means bamboo island. (See Fujita Toyohachi notes, *op. cit.*, p. 101.) The island, now called Pulau Aur, is located in the South China Sea off the Mersing port in the Johor State of Malaysia.

[96] 淡洋，又作淡水洋、淡水湖。指今柬埔寨的洞里薩湖（Tonle Sap）。參見「淡洋」，古代南海地名匯釋，

http://mall.cnki.net/Reference/ref_search.aspx?bid=R200809105&inputText

齊，四五月淫雨而尚寒。俗朴略。男女斷髮，繫占城布。

　　白話文(Vernacular)：

　　石山高聳，彼此對峙。地勢雖有東西之不同，如同蓬萊山之爭奇一般。田地貧瘠，不適宜耕種，每年要仰賴淡洋進口米穀才夠吃。氣候不穩定，四、五月下雨多而有點冷。風俗樸實。男女剪短髮，繫占城布。

The stone mountains are high and confrontational. Although the terrain is different between the West and the East, it is as peculiar as Fenglai Mountain. The fields are barren and not suitable for cultivation. They depend on importation of the rice grains from Danyang every year. The climate is unstable, and it is still cold and rainy in April and May. The customs are simple. Men and women have their hair cut, and they are tied with Champa cloth.

　　煮海為鹽，釀椰漿為酒。有酋長。地產檳榔、荖葉、椰子簟、木棉花。番人取其椰心之嫩者，或素或染織而為簟，以售唐人。其簟冬暖而夏涼，亦可貴也。貿易之貨，用花錫、胡椒、鐵器、薔薇露水之屬。

　　白話文(Vernacular)：

　　煮海水製鹽，釀椰漿製酒。有酋長。當地生產檳榔、荖葉、椰子草席和木棉花。番人取其椰心之嫩者，或素色或染織做成草席，賣給中國人。其草席冬暖而夏涼，價格昂貴。

=%E6%B7%A1%E6%B4%8B　2022 年 10 月 19 日瀏覽。

　　Danyang, also known as Dànshuǐ Ocean and Dànshuǐ Lake. It refers to the Tonle Sap Lake in Cambodia. See "Danyang", *An Interpretation of Ancient South China Sea Place Names*, http://mall.cnki.net/Reference/ref_search.aspx?bid=R200809105&inputText=%E6%B7%A1%E6%B4%8B　October 19, 2022 retrieved.

貿易之貨品使用花錫、胡椒、鐵器和薔薇露水等。

The people boil the sea for salt and brew coconut milk for wine. There is a chief. The land produces betel nut, piper betel leaves, coconut mats, and kapok. The barbarians used the tender heart of coconut, either plain or dyed and woven, to make mats for sale to the Chinese people. The mats are warm in winter and cool in summer and are expensive. The goods used for trade are tin, pepper, iron, and rose dew perfume.

53. 急水灣[97]
53. Jí Shuǐ Wān (Turbulence Bay)

灣居石綠嶼之下，其流奔鶩。舶之時月遲延，兼以潮汐南北人莫能測，舶洄漩於其中，則一月莫能出。昔有度元之舶，流寓在其中二十餘日，失風，針迷舵折，舶遂擱[98]淺。人船貨物，俱各漂蕩。偶遺三人於礁上者，枵腹五日，又且斷舶往來，輒采礁上螺蚌食之。當此之時，命懸於天。忽一日大木二根，浮海而至礁旁。人抱其木，隨風飄至須門荅剌

---

[97]急水灣，今印尼蘇門答臘島北部鑽石角（Diamond Point）以西的司馬威（Lhokseumawe）。多暗沙和珊瑚礁，水流湍急，因此而得名。參見「急水灣」，澳典辭典，
http://cidian.odict.net/zh-tw/856977773/857117776/857129450/
2022 年 10 月 16 日瀏覽。

Jí Shuǐ Wān, now Lhokseumawe, west of Diamond Point in northern Sumatra, Indonesia. There are many shoals and coral reefs, and the currents are fast, hence the name. See " Jí Shuǐ Wān ", odict. Net, http://cidian.odict.net/zh-tw/856977773/857117776/857129450/ October 16, 2022 retrieved.

[98] 原文寫為「閣」，故改之。
The original text was "Ge", so I correct it.

[99]之國，幸而免溺焉。

白話文(Vernacular)：

該灣位在石綠嶼之下方，其海流奔騰。船隻來此時間不對，再加上潮汐南北人莫能測，船隻會迴漩當中無法脫出，有時一個月還無法脫出。從前有一艘前往元國之船隻，在該地停留二十餘日，沒有風，針路迷失，船舵也折斷，船隻遂擱淺。人船貨物，都漂蕩海上。剛好有三人逃到礁上，五天沒吃東西，又沒有船隻前來，就採集礁上螺蚌吃。當此之時，生命懸於天。忽然有一天有大木二根浮海而至礁旁。每人抱著木頭，隨風飄至須門答剌國，幸而獲救。

The bay is located under Shilu Island, and its water is fast. The ship came at the wrong time and the North and the South people did not know the tides. Consequently, the ship was swirling in it, and it couldn't come out for a month. In the past, there was a ship voyaging to Yuan Dynasty, and it stayed in it for more than 20 days. It lost the wind, lost the needle, and broke the rudder, and the ship was stranded. People, ships, and cargo are drifting into the sea. Even if three people are left on the reef, they have no foods to eat for five days, and no ships come to rescue them. They pick up conch and clams on the reef to eat. At this time, life hangs in the sky. Unexpectedly one day, two large trees floated to the side of the reef. Everyone hugs the tree and floats with the wind to the country of Xū Mén Dā Lá, fortunately, they were saved from a drowning death.

---

[99] 須門答剌，是指位在蘇門答臘島北端的亞齊。
　　Xū Mén Dā Lá refers to Aceh located at the northern tip of Sumatra Island.

54. 花面[100]

54. Huāmiàn (Flower Face)(tattoo on the face)

其山逶迤，其地沮洳，田極肥美，足食有餘。男女以墨汁刺於其面，故謂之花面，國名因之。氣候倍熱。俗淳，有酋長。

白話文(Vernacular)：

此地的山曲折蜿蜒，其地低溼，田極肥美，足食有餘。男女以墨汁在臉上刺青，故謂之花面，國名也取花面。氣候倍熱。風俗純樸，有酋長。

The mountains are winding, and the land has low humidity. The fields are extremely fertile, and there are sufficient foods to eat. Men and women pierce their faces with ink, so they are called Huāmiàn, and the country is named after it. The climate is hotter. The customs are vulgar. There is a chief.

地產牛、羊、雞、鴨、檳榔、甘蔗、茗葉、木棉。貨用鐵條、青布、粗碗、青處器之屬。舶經其地，不過貿易以供日用而已。餘無可與販也。

白話文(Vernacular)：

當地生產牛、羊、雞、鴨、檳榔、甘蔗、茗葉和木棉。

---

[100] 花面，指蘇門答臘島北部的巴塔克（Batak）國。參見「花面」，古代南海地名匯釋，

　http://mall.cnki.net/Reference/ref_search.aspx?bid=R200809105&inputText=%E8%8A%B1%E9%9D%A2　2022 年 10 月 19 日瀏覽。

　Huā Miàn refers to the country of Batak in the north of Sumatra. See " Huā Miàn ", *An Interpretation of Ancient South China Sea Place Names*, http://mall.cnki.net/Reference/ref_search.aspx?bid=R200809105&inputText=%E8%8A%B1%E9%9D%A2　October 19, 2022 retrieved.

貨品使用鐵條、青布、粗碗和處州的青瓷器等。船隻經過此地，不過貿易只供日用而已。沒有多餘的物產可供做生意。

The land produces cattle, sheep, chickens, ducks, betel nut, sugar cane, piper betel leaves, and kapok. The goods used for trade are iron bars, green cloth, crude bowls, and green Chuzhou porcelains. Ships pass through the land, but they only trade for daily use. Otherwise, there are no other goods to trade with them.

55. 淡洋[101]
55. Dàn Yáng

港口通官場百有餘里，洋其外海也。內有大溪之水，源二千餘里，奔流衝合於海。其海面一流之水清淡，舶人往往經過乏水，則必由此汲之，故名曰淡洋。過此以往，未見其海洋之水不鹹也。嶺窩有田，常熟，氣候熱，風俗淳。男女椎髻，繫溜布。有酋長。

白話文(Vernacular)：

港口通往官場有一百多里，其外海有大洋。內有大溪之水，河流長達二千餘里，奔流衝向海洋。其海面一邊流之水是清淡的，船人經過時往往缺水，就從這兒汲水，所以叫淡洋。過了此處，海洋之水都是鹹的。山嶺的谷地有田，頗肥

---

[101]陳佳榮等認為毯陽即淡洋之異譯，指蘇門答臘東北岸的 Tamiang 河流域。參見陳佳榮、謝方和陸峻嶺等編，古代南海地名匯釋，中華書局，北京，1986 年，頁 774。

　　Chen Jiarong and others believed that Tǎn Yang is a different translation of Danyang, referring to the Tamiang River basin on the northeastern coast of Sumatra. See Chen Jiarong, Xie Fang and Lu Junling, etc., *An Interpretation of Ancient South China Sea Place Names*, Zhonghua Book Company, Beijing, 1986, p.774.

沃，氣候熱，風俗純樸。男女椎髻，繫溜布。有酋長。

The port is more than 100 miles away from the official office and the Dàn Yáng is its outer ocean. There is a big stream which is more than 2,000 li long and rushing flows into the sea. The stream flows into the sea, and the water on the sea surface tastes very fresh. When the ships often pass through here, if they lack water, they must draw from this water, hence named it Danyang. When passing elsewhere, the sea water is salty. There are fields in the valleys of the mountains, which are fertile. The climate is hot and the customs are pure. Men and women wear a bun on their heads, tied with slippery cloth. There is a chief.

地產降眞香，味與亞蘆[102]同。米穀雖小，炊飯則香。貿易之貨，用赤金、鐵器、粗碗之屬。

---

[102] 亞蘆，應是阿魯（Aru）之別譯。陳能宗認為阿魯位在今北蘇門答臘省卡若縣（Karo）馬達山（Berastagi）及其北面丹絨籠葛鎮（Tanjung Langkat）地區。（參見陳能宗，「古爪哇文『納卡拉柯爾塔卡麻』史詩贊頌滿者伯夷帝國版圖的三首詩譯注」，東南亞史論文集，第一集，暨南大學歷史系東南亞研究室出版，廣州，1980年，頁226。）陳佳榮等人認為阿魯，約在今蘇門答臘北方靠近馬六甲海峽的日里（Deli）和棉蘭（Medan）一帶。（參見陳佳榮、謝方和陸峻嶺等編，前引書，頁593。）

Yalu should be the other translation of Aru. Chen Nengzong believed that Aru is located in what is now Berastagi, Karo County, North Sumatra Province, and the area of Tanjung Langkat to the north. (See Chen Nengzong, "Annotation of Three Poems of the Ancient Javanese 'Nakara Koltakama' Epic Praising the Territory of the Majapahit Empire", *Collected Papers on the History of Southeast Asia*, Volume 1, published by the Southeast Asia Research Office, Department of History, Jinan University, Guangzhou, 1980, p. 226.)

Chen Jiarong and others believed that Aru is located in the area of Deli and Medan in north Sumatra near the Strait of Malacca. (See Chen Jiarong, Xie Fang and Lu Junling, eds., *op. cit.*, p. 593.)

白話文(**Vernacular**)：

當地生產降眞香，味道與亞蘆相同。米穀雖小粒，炊飯則香。貿易之貨品使用赤金、鐵器和粗碗等。

The land produces Jiangzhen incense, and the taste is the same as that of Yalu (Aru). Although the rice grains are small, their rice is fragrant. The goods used for trade are red gold, ironware, and crude bowls.

56. 須文答剌[103]
56. Xū Wén Dá Lá

峻嶺掩抱，地勢臨海，田磽穀少。男女繫布縵。俗薄。其酋長人物修長，一日之間必三變色，或靑或黑或赤。每歲必殺十餘人，取自然血浴之，則四時不生疾病，故民皆畏服焉。男女椎髻，繫紅布。

白話文(**Vernacular**)：

群山高聳，地勢臨海，田地貧瘠，穀物產量少。男女繫布縵。風俗淺薄。其酋長人物修長，一日之間必定換三種顏色的衣服，或靑色或黑色或紅色。每年必殺十餘人，取人血洗浴，認為這樣可以四時不生疾病，故人民皆害怕而服從他。男女椎髻，繫紅布。

This place is surrounded by high mountains, the terrain is facing the sea, and there are few fields and grains. Men and women wear cloth. The customs are vulgar. Its chief is slender and will change the cloth's color three times a day, either green

---

[103]須文答剌，又寫為蘇門答剌。
　　Xū Wén Dá Lá also written as Sū Mén Dá Lá(Sumatra).

or black, or red. Every year, the chief must kill more than ten people, and bathe in human blood, so that he will have no disease in the four seasons. So the people are all afraid of him and are obliged to obey him. Men and women wear a bun on their heads and tie them with red cloth.

土產腦子、粗降眞香（味短）、鶴頂、斗錫。種茄樹，高丈有餘，經三四年不萎，生茄子，以梯摘之，如西瓜大，重十餘斤。貿易之貨，用西洋絲布、樟腦、薔薇水、黃油傘、靑布、五色緞之屬。

白話文**(Vernacular)**：

土產腦子、粗降眞香（味道短暫）、鶴頂和斗錫。種茄樹，高丈有餘，經三、四年不凋謝，生茄子，要用階梯摘之，如西瓜大，重十餘斤。貿易之貨品使用西洋絲布、樟腦、薔薇水、黃油傘、靑布和五色緞等。

The land produces local Borneol, crude Jiangzhen incense (short taste), Heding, and natural tin nuggets. The eggplant tree is planted, more than 10 meters tall, and will not wilt after three or four years and then grow the eggplant. The eggplant is picked with a ladder, which is as big as a watermelon and weighs more than ten pounds. The goods used for trade are the West Ocean silk cloth, camphor, rose water, butter umbrella, green cloth, and five-color satin.

57. 僧加剌[104]

---

[104]僧加剌，即師子國，今之斯里蘭卡。(參見藤田豐八校註，前引書，頁105。) W. P. Groeneveldt 亦持相同觀點。(參見 W. P. Groeneveldt, *op.cit*, p.29.)

57. Sēng Jiā La

疊山環翠，洋海橫縶。其山之腰，有佛殿巋然，則釋迦肉身所在，民從而像之，迨今以香燭事之若存。海濱有石如蓮臺，上有佛足跡，長二尺有四寸，闊七寸，深五寸許。跡中海水入其內，不鹹而淡，味甘如醴，病者飲之則愈，老者飲之可以延年。

白話文(**Vernacular**)：

群山高聳，像綠色翠環，洋海相聯繫。其山的腰部，有佛殿矗立，是釋迦肉身所在地，人民從而敬拜他，至今以香燭敬拜好像他還活著一樣。海濱有石如蓮臺，上有佛陀足跡，長二尺四寸，闊七寸，深五寸許。跡中有海水進入，不鹹而淡，味甘如甜酒，生病的人喝了就會痊癒，老年人喝了可以延年益壽。

The mountains are surrounded by greenery, and the oceans and seas are connected. On the waist of the mountain, there is a Buddhist temple, where the body of Sakyamuni is located, and the people worship him. Today people worship him with incense and candles as if he were still existing. On the seashore, there is a stone like a lotus pedestal, with Buddha footprints on it, two feet and four inches long, seven inches wide, and five inches deep. Seawater flows into the footprint depression; it is not salty but bland, and the taste is like sweet wine. The sick drink it to be cured, and the old to prolong life.

Sēng Jiā La is the country of Shī Zǐ, present-day Sri Lanka. (See Fujita Toyohachi notes, *op. cit.*, p. 105.) W. P. Groeneveldt also held the same view. (See W. P. Groeneveldt, *op.cit*, p.29.)

土人長七尺餘，面紫身黑，眼巨而長，手足溫潤而壯健，聿然佛家種子，壽多至百有餘歲者。佛初憐彼方之人貧而為盜，故以善化其民，復以甘露水灑其地。產紅石。土人掘之，以左手取者為貨，右手尋者設佛後，得以濟貿易之貨，皆令溫飽而善良。佛案前有一鉢盂，非玉非銅非鐵，色紫而潤，敲之有玻璃聲，故國初凡三遣使以取之。至是則舉浮屠之敎以語人，故未能免於儒者之議。然觀其土人之梵相，風俗之敦厚，詎可弗信也夫！

白話文(Vernacular)：

土人身高七尺餘，面紫身黑，眼巨大而長，手足溫潤而壯健，真是佛家種子，高壽一百多歲。佛陀剛開始憐憫此地人貧窮而做強盜，所以教化其民，又以甘露水灑其地。該地生產紅石。土人掘之，以左手拿紅石，用右手設立佛壇後，就可以用紅石作為貿易之貨，使得他們得以溫飽而善良。佛案前有一鉢盂，非玉非銅非鐵，色紫而潤滑，敲之有玻璃聲，故元國建國初三度遣使欲取得該物。但是當地人以佛陀之教誨告訴我們，所以還未能免於儒者之議論。然觀察其土人之佛相，風俗之敦厚，我們能不相信嗎？

The natives are more than seven feet tall, with purple faces and black bodies, huge and long eyes, warm and strong hands and feet, like the seeds of Buddhism, and their lifespan is more than a hundred years old. The Buddha first took pity on the poor who were thieves, so he transformed the people with good deeds and then sprinkled the ground with nectar water. The land produced red stone. The natives dig it up, take the goods with their left hand, and set up the Buddha altar with the right hand so that they can use red stone for trade, and they all get well-fed and are kind in character. There is a bowl in front of the Buddha altar. It is neither jade, copper, nor iron. The color is purple and moist. When it is knocked, there is a glass sound. At the beginning of the Yuan Dynasty, envoys were dispatched three times to take it. In the end, the teaching of the Buddha was cited by a speaker, so it was not exempt from the discussion of the Confucians. However, looking at the Buddha appearance of the natives, they have very honest customs, can we not believe it?

58. 勾欄山[105]
58. Gōulán Shān (Goulan Mountain)

嶺高而樹林茂密，田瘠穀少，氣候熱。俗射獵為事。國初，軍士征闍婆，遭風於山下，輒損舟，一舟倖免，唯存釘灰。見其山多木，故於其地造舟一十餘隻。若檣柁、若帆、若篙，靡不具備，飄然長往。有病卒百餘人不能去者，遂留山中。今唐人與番人叢雜而居之。男女椎髻，穿短衫，繫巫崙布。

白話文(Vernacular)：
山嶺高聳，樹林茂密，田地貧瘠，穀物產量少，氣候熱。風俗是從事射獵。元國建國初期，派軍征爪哇，遭風停靠於山下，船隻損壞，有一舟倖免，保存釘灰。見其山多木，故於其地造舟十餘艘。製造檣柁、帆和篙等，飄然航向爪哇。

---

[105]勾欄山在婆羅洲西南松巴角（Sambar）附近的格拉姆島（Gelam I.）。參見李則芬，元史新講（二），頁493-494。格羅尼維德特則認為勾欄山在今天的勿里洞島（Billiton）。參見 W. P. Groeneveldt, op.cit., p.22.
　　Goulan Mountain is located on Gelam I. near Sambar, southwest Borneo. See Li Zefen, *New Lectures on Yuan History* (2), pp. 493-494. W. P. Groeneveldt believes that Goulan Mountain is in today's Billiton Island. See W. P. Groeneveldt, *op.cit.*, p. 22.

有病卒百餘人不能去的，遂留該島。今中國人與番人叢雜而居。男女椎髻，穿短衫，繫巫崙布。

The ridge is high and the woods are dense. The fields are barren, and grains are few. The climate is hot. It is common for people to shoot and hunt. At the beginning of the Yuan Dynasty, when the troops conquered Java, they suffered from the wind at the foot of the mountain, and the boats were damaged. Only one boat survived and kept the nails and marl. Seeing that this island has many trees in the mountains, more than ten boats were built, including mast, sail, and barge pole. Then they continued to voyage. There were more than 100 soldiers who were sick and could not go on, so they stayed on the island. Today, the Chinese people and the barbarians live together. Men and women wear a bun on their heads, short shirts, and tied Wu Lun cloth.

地產熊、豹、鹿、麂皮、玳瑁。貿易之貨，用穀米、五色絹、青布、銅器、青器之屬。

白話文(Vernacular)：

當地生產熊、豹、鹿、麂皮和玳瑁。貿易之貨品使用穀米、五色絹、青布、銅器和青器等。

The land produces bears, leopards, deer, suede, and tortoiseshell. The goods which are used for trade are grains and rice, five-color silk, green cloth, copper utensils, and green utensils.

59. 特番里[106]

---

[106] 特番里，可能位在埃及尼羅河東部支流杜姆亞特（Damietta、Damiata

59. Tèfān Lǐ

國居西南角，名為小食。官場深邃，前有石崖當關以守之，後有石洞，周匝以居之。厥土塗泥，厥田沃饒臨溪，溪又通海。海口有閘，春月則放水灌田耕種。時雨降則開閘[107]，或歲旱則閉焉。民無水旱之憂，長有豐稔之慶，故號為樂土。氣候應節。俗淳，男女椎髻，繫青布。

白話文(Vernacular)：

該國位在西南角，名為小食。官場位在較遠的地方，前有石崖當關口來守護，後有石洞，周遭有人民居住。該地的土可用來塗泥牆，田地肥沃，前面臨溪，溪又通海。海口有閘門，春天則放水灌田耕種。下雨時則關閘門，如遇乾旱則關閉。所以人民無需擔憂水旱災，他們有長期的豐收慶典，故號為樂土。氣候變化符合節序。風俗純樸，男女椎髻，繫青布。

The country is located in the southwest corner and is also called Xiaoshi. The officialdom is located in a distant place, with stone cliffs in front to guard it, and there is a cave in the back, and the people live around it. The soil from this area can be used to paint the walls of houses. The fields are fertile, and it has a river connecting to the sea. There is a sluice in the outlet of the

---

或 Domyat）支流的出海口。參見藤田豐八校註，前引書，頁 113。

Tèfān Lǐ is probably located on the estuary of the Damietta tributaries of the eastern Nile in Egypt. See Fujita Toyohachi notes, *op. cit.*, p. 113.

[107] 原文寫為「閉閘」，有誤，蓋下大雨，為防氾濫，應該是「開閘」。乾旱時，水量不足，應是「關閘」。故改之。

The original text was written "close the gate", which is wrong. It was raining heavily. To prevent flooding, it should be "open the gate". During droughts, the water supply is insufficient and should be "shut off". So I correct it.

river into the sea, and in the spring season, they open sluice to irrigate the fields. When the rainy season comes, the sluice is opened, or when there is drought, it is closed. The people do not have to worry about floods and droughts, and they have a long celebration of the harvest, so it is called the Land of Paradise. The climate is correspondent by season change. The customs are vulgar. Men and women wear a bun on their heads and tie it with a green cloth.

煮海為鹽，釀茗葉為酒，燒羊羔為食。地產黃蠟，綿羊高四尺許。波羅大如斗，甜瓜三、四尺圍。貿易之貨，用麻逸布、五色絾緞、錦緞、銅鼎、紅油布之屬。

白話文(Vernacular)：

煮海水製鹽，釀茗葉製酒，燒小羊為食。當地生產黃蠟，綿羊高四尺許。波羅大如斗，甜瓜周徑三、四尺。貿易之貨品使用麻逸布、五色絾緞、錦緞、銅鼎和紅油布等。

The people boil the sea for salt, brew the piper betel leaves for wine, and cook lamb for food. The land produces yellow wax, and the sheep were four feet tall. Polo is as big as a bucket, and the sweet melon is three or four feet in circumference. The goods used for trade are Mayit cloth, five-color satin, brocade, copper tripod, and red oilcloth.

60. 班達里[108]

---

[108]班達里，故地在印度西南岸科澤科德北 16 英里，今已湮沒。參見「Fandaraina」，南溟網，
http://www.world10k.com/blog/index.php?s=%E7%8F%AD%E9%81%94%E9%87%8C　2022 年 10 月 15 日瀏覽。

60. Bān Dá Lǐ

地與鬼屈、波思國[109]為鄰，山峙而石盤，田瘠穀少。氣候微熱，淫雨間作。俗怪，屋旁每有鬼夜啼，如人聲[110]相續，至五更而啼止。次日酋長必遣人乘騎鳴鑼以逐之，卒不見其蹤影也。厥後立廟宇於盤石之上以祭焉，否則人畜有疾，國必有災。

白話文(Vernacular)：

該地與鬼屈、波思國為鄰，高山對峙，石頭盤旋，田地貧瘠，穀物產量少。氣候微熱，偶爾下長雨。風俗怪異，屋旁每有鬼在夜間啼哭，如人聲持續不斷，至五更天亮雞啼才停止。次日酋長必派人騎馬鳴鑼來趕鬼，最後不見其蹤影。後立廟宇於盤石之上以祭拜，否則人畜會生病，國必有災難。

This place is neighboring to Gui Qū and Bō Sī countries, and its territory is mountainous. The fields are barren and grains are few. The climate is mildly hot, sometimes rainy. The customs are fond of ghosts. Every night there is a ghost crying beside the house, like a continuous human voice, and it will stop at the fifth watch of the night (just before dawn) when the cock crows. The next day, the chief must send a man on horseback to sound the gong to chase him away, but finally, there are no traces of him.

Bān Dá Lǐ, whose hometown is 16 miles north of Kozhikode on the southwestern coast of India, has now disappeared. See "Fandaraina", Nanming.Net,
http://www.world10k.com/blog/index.php?s=%E7%8F%AD%E9%81%94%E9%87%8C   October 15, 2022 retrieved.

[109] 波思，可能為波斯之不同音譯。

Bō Sī may be a different transliteration of Persian.

[110] 原文寫為「身」，故改之。

The original text was written as "body", so I correct it.

Later, temples were built on the rock to offer sacrifices, otherwise, people and animals would suffer from diseases, and the country would suffer disasters.

男女椎髻，繫巫崙布，不事針縷紡績。煮海為鹽。地產甸子、鴉忽石、兜羅綿、木棉花、靑蒙石。貿易之貨，用諸色緞、靑白瓷、鐵器、五色燒珠之屬。

白話文**(Vernacular)**：

男女椎髻，繫巫崙布，不從事針線和紡織。煮海水製鹽。當地生產甸子、鴉忽石、兜羅綿、木棉花和靑蒙石。貿易之貨品使用諸色緞、靑白瓷、鐵器和五色燒珠等。

Men and women wear a bun on their heads and tie it with Wu Lun cloth, and they do not engage in needle-weaving. The people boil the sea for salt. The land produces Dianzi, Yahu stone, Douluo cotton, Kapok, and green Meng stone. The goods used for trade are various colors of satin, green and white porcelain, ironware, and five-color burnt beads.

61. 曼陀郎[111]

---

[111] 曼陀郎，今印度西岸古吉拉特邦卡奇（Kutch）南部曼德維（Mandvi）東面 30 英里的蒙德拉（Mundra）。參見「曼陀郎」，古代南海地名匯釋，
http://mall.cnki.net/Reference/ref_search.aspx?bid=R200809105&inputText=%E6%9B%BC%E9%99%80%E9%83%8E　2022 年 10 月 19 日瀏覽。

Màn Tuó Láng is located in present-day Mundra, 30 miles east of Mandvi, south of Kutch, in the state of Gujarat on the west coast of India. See "Màn Tuó Láng," *An Interpretation of Ancient South China Sea Place Names*,
http://mall.cnki.net/Reference/ref_search.aspx?bid=R200809105&inputText=%E6%9B%BC%E9%99%80%E9%83%8E　October 19, 2022 retrieved.

61. Màn Tuó Láng

國界西北隅，與播寧接壤。壤瘠，宜種麥。酋長七尺有餘。二國勢均，不事侵伐，故累世結姻，頗有朱陳[112]村之俗焉。蠻貊之所僅[113]聞，他國之所未見者。

白話文(Vernacular)：

國界西北隅，與播寧接壤。土壤貧瘠，適宜種麥。酋長身高七尺有餘。曼陀郎和播寧二國國力差不多，不事侵伐，故世代結姻親，頗有朱、陳兩姓結親之風俗。未開化國家所僅聞，他國之所未見者。

In the northwest corner of the border, it neighbors Boning. The land is barren and suitable for planting wheat. The chief is more than seven feet tall. The power of the two countries is even, and there is no invasion, so they have married for many generations, which is quite the same as the customs of the Zhu-Chen Villages. This can only be seen among the barbarian countries, and not so in other countries.

氣候少熱。男女挽髻，以白布包頭，皂布為服。以木樨花釀酒。地產犀角、木棉，摘四斗花，可重一斤。西瓜五十斤重有餘。石榴大如斗。貿易之貨，用丁香、荳蔻、良薑、蓽芨、五色布、青器、斗錫、酒之屬。

白話文(Vernacular)：

---

[112] 朱陳村，比喻朱姓和陳姓兩姓締結婚姻的情誼。
Zhu Chen village is a metaphor for the friendship between the surnames Zhu and Chen who concluded their marriage
[113] 原文寫為「近」，故改之。
The original text was written as "near", so I correct it.

氣候稍微熱。男女挽髻，以白布包頭，穿黑布衣服。以木檊花釀酒。當地生產犀角、木棉，摘四斗花，可重一斤。西瓜五十斤重有餘。石榴大如斗。貿易之貨品使用丁香、荳蔻、良薑、蓽茇、五色布、青器、斗錫和酒等。

The climate is a little hot. Men and women wear a bun on their heads, with white cloth wrapping their heads, and wear black cloth. The wine is made from the calamansi flower. The land produces rhino horn, kapok, picking four buckets of flowers, which can weigh a pound. Watermelon weighs more than fifty pounds. Pomegranates are as big as buckets. The goods used for trade are cloves, cardamom, galangal, piper longum, five-color cloth, green utensils, natural tin nuggets, and wine.

62. 喃巫哩[114]
62. Nán Wū Lī

---

[114]喃巫哩，又寫為南無力、南巫里（Lamurai）、藍無里、南無里、喃巫里、南淳里、南勃利。印尼學者薩努西・巴尼說：「南巫里在今大亞齊及其附近地區。」（[印尼]薩努西・巴尼原著，吳世璜譯，前引書，頁214。）克羅姆（H-J,G, Krom）則說三佛齊的屬國藍無里，位在蘇門答臘西北部的亞齊。（引自 K. A. Nilakanta Sastri, *History of Sri Vijaya*, University of Madras, India, 1949, p.90.）陳佳榮的著作說南巫里在今班達亞齊(Banda-Aceh)。（陳佳榮、謝方和陸峻嶺等編，前引書，頁583。）

Nán Wū Lī, also written as Nan Wuli, Lamurai, Lanwuli, Nanwuli, and Nanboli. The Indonesian scholar Sanusi Pane said: "Namburi is in today's Greater Aceh and its surrounding areas." ([Indonesian] Sanusi Pane, *op.cit.*, p. 214.); H-J, G, Krom said that Nán Wū Lī is the vassal of Sanfoqi, and it is located in Aceh in the northwest of Sumatra. (Quoted from K. A. Nilakanta Sastri, *History of Sri Vijaya*, University of Madras, India, 1949, p. 90.) Chen Jiarong's writings said that Nán Wū Lī is in present-day Banda-Aceh. (Chen Jiarong, Xie Fang, and Lu Junling, eds., *op.cit*, p. 583.)

地當喃巫哩洋[115]之要衝，大波如山，動盪日月，望洋之際，疑若無地。居民環山，各得其所。男女椎髻露體，繫布捎。田瘠穀少。氣候暖，俗尚劫掠，亞於單馬錫[116]也。

白話文(Vernacular)：

該地位在喃巫哩洋之要衝，大波浪像山一樣，驚動日月，向海洋望去，好像看不到陸地。居民環山居住，各得其所。男女椎髻，裸體，繫布巾。田地貧瘠，穀物產量少。氣候暖和，俗尚劫掠，次於單馬錫。

This place is the pivotal point of the Nán Wū Lī Ocean, and the waves churning are like mountains, affecting the sun and the moon. When looking at the ocean, it seems like there is no land. Residents live around the mountains, and each has his place. Men and women wear a bun on their heads, tied with cloth towel, and are all naked. There are few fields and few grains. The climate is warm, and the customs are fond of plundering, but it is inferior to Temasek.

地產鶴頂、龜筒、玳瑁，降眞香冠於各番。貿易之貨，用金、銀、鐵器、薔薇水、紅絲布、樟腦、青白花碗之屬。

白話文(Vernacular)：

當地生產鶴頂、龜筒和玳瑁，降眞香冠於各番。貿易之貨品使用金、銀、鐵器、薔薇水、紅絲布、樟腦和青白花碗等。

The land produces Heding, Guī Tǒng, tortoiseshell, and

---

[115] 原文無「洋」字，故加之。
   The original text does not have the word "ocean", so I add it.
[116] 原文寫爲「牛單錫」，故改之。
   The original text was "Niu Tansek", so I correct it.

Jiangzhen incense which is the best one in the various barbarian countries. The goods used for trade are gold, silver, iron, rose water, red silk cloth, camphor, and green and white flower bowls.

夫以舶歷風濤，回經此國，幸而免於魚龍之厄，而又罹虎口，莫能逃之，其亦[117]風汛[118]之乖時使之然歟！

白話文(Vernacular)：

船隻歷經風濤，回來經過此國，幸而免於遭到魚龍吞噬之災厄，但又遭逢虎口，莫能逃脫，此應是風汛來得不是時候所致吧！

When boats traveled through the wind and waves and return to this country, they, fortunately, are freed from the misfortune to be eaten by fishes and dragons, but they fall into the mouth of a tiger and have no way to escape. Is this because the trade winds came at the wrong time?

63. 北溜[119]
63. Běi Liū (North Slip)

地勢居下，千嶼萬島。舶往西洋，過僧伽剌傍，潮流迅急，更值風逆，輒漂此國。候次年夏東南風。舶仍上溜之北，

---

[117] 原文寫為「赤」，故改之。
The original text was written as "red", so I correct it.

[118] 原文寫為「迅迅」，故改之。
The original text was "Xun Xun", so I correct it.

[119]北溜，今印度洋中馬爾地夫（Maldives）群島。參見藤田豐八校註，前引書，頁118。
Běi Liū is located in today's Maldives archipelago in the Indian Ocean. See Fujita Toyohachi notes, *op. cit.*, p. 118.

水中有石槎中牙，利如鋒刃，蓋已不勝舟矣。

白話文(Vernacular)：

地勢低平，有一萬多個島。船隻往西洋，經過僧伽剌傍，潮流迅急，更值逆風，常會漂到此國。等候隔年夏天吹東南風才能離開。船隻經過上溜之北方，水中有礁石，利如鋒刃，船隻到此很難脫困。

The terrain of this place is flat, with thousands of islands spreading wide. Ships to the West Ocean, passing by the Sanghala. The tide is fast and facing the headwind. The ships always drift into this country. They must wait for the southeast wind next summer. If a ship still sails through the north of Běi Liū, it must suffer stone teeth in the water, as a sharp knife, and the boat can't resist it anymore.

地產椰子索、玑子、魚乾、大手巾布。海商每將一舶玑子下烏爹、朋加剌，必互易米一船有餘。蓋彼番以玑子權錢用，亦久遠之食法也。

白話文(Vernacular)：

當地生產椰子索、玑子、魚乾和大手巾布。海商每將一舶玑子運至烏爹、朋加剌，必定可換得米一船有餘。因為該地土番以玑子當錢使用，亦是常久以來的貿易方法。

The land produces coconut rope, Pazi, dried fish, and a large towel cloth. Every time a sea merchant sends a ship to Wū Diē and Bangladesh, he will exchange more than one ship of rice. They used Pazi to replace the money, and it is also a long-standing method of trade.

64. 下里[120]
64. Xià Lǐ

國居小唄喃、古佛里之中，又名小港口。山曠而原平，地方數千餘里。民所奠居，星羅碁布。家給人足，厥田中下。農力耕，氣候暖。風俗淳。民尚氣，出入必懸弓箭及牌以隨身。男女削髮，繫溜布。

白話文(Vernacular)：

該國位在小唄喃、古佛里之中間，又名小港口。山廣大，而土地平坦，地方數千餘里。人民居住的地方，分散各地。家庭人口多，田地屬中下等。農民努力耕種，氣候暖。風俗純樸。人民很有勇氣，出入必隨身攜帶弓箭及盾牌。男女剪短髮，繫溜布。

This country is located in the center of Gǔ Fú Lǐ and Xiǎo Gé Nán also called Small Port. The mountains have no trees and the plain extends more than thousands of miles. The people's residences are built widely. The family is full of people. The

---

[120] 下里，指「鄭和航海圖」中之歇立，今印度西岸卡里庫特（Calicut）北部的 Maunt Delly。或謂今科欽（Cochin）北 20 英里之小港阿爾瓦耶（Alwaye）。參見「下里」，古代南海地名匯釋，http://mall.cnki.net/Reference/ref_search.aspx?bid=R200809105&inputText=%E4%B8%8B%E9%87%8C　2022 年 10 月 19 日瀏覽。

藤田豐八認為下里即是卡里庫特。參見藤田豐八校註，前引書，頁 119。

Xià Lǐ refers to Xiē Lì in the "Zheng He Navigational Chart", which is now Maunt Delly, north of Calicut on the west coast of India. Or in Alwaye, a small port 20 miles north of Cochin. See " Xià Lǐ ", *An Interpretation of Ancient South China Sea Place Names*, http://mall.cnki.net/Reference/ref_search.aspx?bid=R200809105&inputText=%E4%B8%8B%E9%87%8C　October 19, 2022 retrieved.

Fujita Toyohachi believed that Xià Lǐ is Calicut. See Fujita Toyohachi notes, *op. cit.*, p.119.

fields are middle and lower grades. The people work hard to cultivate. The climate is warm. The customs are pure. People have a competitive spirit, and they must hang bows and arrows and shields to carry with them when they go in and out. Men and women have their hair cut and tie with a slippery cloth.

　　地產胡椒，冠於各番，不可勝計。樹木滿山，蔓衍如藤蘿，冬花而夏實。民採而蒸曝，以乾為度。其味辛，採者多不禁。其味之觸人，甚至以川芎煎湯解之。他番之有胡椒者，皆此國流波之餘也。

　　白話文(Vernacular)：

　　當地生產胡椒，是各國最好的，產量不可勝計。胡椒樹種滿山，蔓衍如藤蘿，冬天開花而夏天結實。人民採摘蒸後再曝曬，使之乾燥。其味辛，採者多受不了。其味之嗆人，可用川芎煎湯解之。他國有胡椒者，皆是此國輸出的。

The land produces pepper which is the best one among various countries. Its production is abundant. The mountains are full of pepper trees, spreading like vines, blooming in winter, and fruiting in summer. The people harvested pepper and steamed it and were exposed to dryness. Its pungent smell is unbearable for pickers. Its taste is so choking that even decocted with Chuanxiong decoction can eliminate it. Those foreign countries have peppers that are all coming from this country.

65. 高郎步[121]

[121]高郎步，又作高浪阜，即今斯里蘭卡首都科倫坡（Colombo）。參見藤田豐八校註，前引書，頁 120。

Gāo Láng Bù is also known as Gaolangfu, namely Colombo, the capital

65. Gāo Láng Bù (Colombo)

　　大佛山之下，灣環中，縱橫皆鹵股石。其地濕卑，田瘠，米穀翔貴，氣候暖。俗薄。舶人不幸失風，或駐擱[122]於其地者，徒為酋長之利。舶中所有貨物，多至全璧而歸之，酋以為天賜也，孰知舶人妻子飢寒之所望哉！

　　白話文(Vernacular)：

　　大佛山之下，灣環中，分布著許多鹵股石。其地低濕，田地貧瘠，米穀昂貴，氣候暖。風俗淺薄。船人不幸遭逆風，或擱淺於其地者，對當地酋長有利。船中所有貨物，多數歸酋長所有，以為天賜也，怎知船人妻子飢寒且盼望他歸家呢！

　　Under the Dà Foshān (Big Buddha mountain), in the bay ring; there are many reef stones. The land is wet and low, the fields are barren, and the rice and grains are expensive. The climate is warm. The customs are vulgar. For those boatmen who are unfortunate to lose the wind and be stranded here, the chief becomes the only gainer. All the goods in the ship, as many as the whole, belong to the chief. The chief thinks it is an endowment or gift by God, but who knows if the ship-owners wife is hungry and cold and hopes he comes home!

　　男女撮髻，繫八郎那間布捎。煮海為鹽，釀蔗漿為酒。有酋長，地產紅石頭，與僧加剌同。貿易之貨，用八丹布、斗錫、酒、薔薇水、蘇木、金、銀之屬。

　　白話文(Vernacular)：

---

　　of Sri Lanka. See Fujita Toyohachi notes, *op. cit.*, p. 120.

[122] 原文寫為「閣」，故改之。

　　The original text was "Ge", so I correct it.

男女撮髻，繫八郎那間布巾。煮海水製鹽，釀蔗漿製酒。有酋長，當地生產紅石頭，與僧加剌同。貿易之貨品使用八丹布、斗錫、酒、薔薇水、蘇木、金和銀等。

Men and women wear a bun on their heads and tie it with the Bā Láng Nà Jiān's cloth towel. The people boil the sea for salt and brew sugarcane pulp for wine. There is a chief. The land produces red stones which are the same as Sēng Jiā Lá. The goods used for trade are Bā Dān's cloth, natural tin nuggets, wine, rose water, Biancaea sappan, gold, and silver.

66. 沙里八丹[123]
66. Shālǐ Bā Dān

國居古里佛山之後，其地沃衍，田少俗美。氣候微暖。男女繫布纏頭，循海而居，珠貨之馬頭也。民有犯罪者，以

---

[123]沙里八丹，即印度東南部的納格伯蒂訥姆（Nagapattinam）港口，大唐西域求法高僧傳中譯作那伽鉢亶那，明朝稱之為小瑣里。參見「納加帕蒂南」，維基百科，
https://zh.wikipedia.org/wiki/%E7%BA%B3%E5%8A%A0%E5%B8%9 5%E8%92%82%E5%8D%97 2022 年 9 月 28 日瀏覽。
藤田豐八認為沙里八丹位在納加帕蒂南，而不在馬蘇利派特南。（參見藤田豐八校註，前引書，頁 121-122。）蘇繼卿認為沙里八丹為古代的注輦。（參見蘇繼卿，前引書，頁 216。）
Shālǐ Bā Dān refers to the port of Nagapattinam in south-east India. It was translated as Nagabotan in the *Biography of the Dharma-seeking Monks in the Western Regions of the Tang Dynasty*, and it was called Xiaosuoli in the Ming Dynasty. See "Nagapatinan", *Wikipedia*, https://zh.wikipedia.org/wiki/%E7%BA%B3%E5%8A%A0%E5%B8%95 %E8%92%82%E5%8D%97 September 28, 2022 retrieved.
Fujita Toyohachi believed that Shālǐ Bā Dān is located in Nagapatinan, not in Masuripatnam. (See Fujita Toyohachi notes, *op. cit.*, pp. 121-122.) Su Jiqing believed that Shālǐ Bā Dān is an ancient Chola. (See Su Jiqing, *op. cit.*, p. 216.)

石灰畫圈於地，使之立圈內，不令轉足，此其極刑也。

白話文(Vernacular)：

該國位在古里佛山之後，其地肥沃平坦，田地少，風俗美好。氣候微暖。男女繫布纏頭，沿海而居，珠寶貨品之買賣碼頭也。人民有犯罪者，以石灰畫圈於地，使之站立圈內，命令他不可移動，這是它的嚴酷刑法。

This country is located behind Gullifoshan (Gulli Buddha Mountain), and the land is fertile and wide. The fields are few, but the customs are beautiful. The climate is mildly warm. Men and women tie a cloth around their heads and live along the coast. There are also piers for buying and selling jewelry. If the people commit crimes, they draw a circle on the ground with lime, make them stand inside the circle, and prevent them from turning their feet. This is a cruel punishment.

地產八丹[124]布，珍珠由第三港來，皆物之所自產也，其地採珠，官抽畢，皆以小舟渡此國互易，富者用金銀以低價塌之。舶至，求售於唐人，其利豈淺鮮哉！

白話文(Vernacular)：

該地生產八丹布，珍珠由第三港來，都是當地的土產，其地採珠，官署抽完稅後，皆以小舟運至該國各地交易，富者用金銀以低價買進。船隻來了，求售於中國人，其利潤豐厚。

The land produces Badan's cloth, and pearls coming from the Third Port, and they are all produced by themselves. The

---

[124]原文寫為「舟」，故改之。

The original text was written as "boat", so I correct it.

people produced pearls, and after the officials' tax, they take small boats to trade them with other countries. The rich use gold and silver to buy them at low prices. When Chinese ships come here, they seek to sell to the Chinese, and they get huge profits.

67. 金塔[125]

67. Jīn Tǎ (Gold Pagoda)

古崖之下，聖井傍有塔十丈有餘。塔頂曾鍍以金，其頂頹而石爛，惟苔蘚青青耳。上有鶴巢，寬七尺餘，有朱頂雌雄二鶴長存，每歲巢於其上。酋長子孫相傳以來千有餘年矣。春則育一二雛，及羽翼成，飛去，惟老鶴在焉。其國人書扁曰：老鶴里。土瘠而民貧。氣候不齊，俗朴。男女椎髻，纏白布，繫溜布。

白話文(Vernacular)：

在古崖的下方，聖井傍有塔十多丈高。塔頂曾鍍以金，其頂傾頹而石頭崩落，留下青色苔蘚。上有鶴巢，寬七尺餘，有朱頂雌雄二鶴長期棲息，每年在上頭築巢。酋長子孫相傳該鶴傳世一千多年。春天則育一、二隻雛鳥，羽翼長成後就飛走了，惟老鶴還在。其國人寫說：老鶴里。土地貧瘠，人民窮困。氣候不穩定，風俗純樸。男女椎髻，纏白布，繫溜布。

Under the Gǔ Yá, there is a tower more than ten feet tall nearby the holy well. The top of the tower was once plated with gold, but the top was crumbling and the stone was rotten, except

---

[125]金塔，可能是緬甸仰光的大金塔。

　　Jīn Tǎ Pagoda is probably Shwedagon Pagoda in Yangon, Myanmar.

for the green moss. There is a crane's nest on it, more than seven feet wide, and there are two cranes, male and female, with red tops. The nest is on it every year. According to the descendants of the chieftain, the crane has been handed down for more than a thousand years. In spring, one or two chicks are bred, and when their wings are completed, they fly away, but the old crane is there. The people of this country wrote it "Old Crane." The soil is barren and the people are poor. The climate is unstable and the customs are vulgar. Men and women wear a bun on their heads, wrapped in white cloth and tied with slippery cloth.

　　民煮海為鹽，女耕織為業。壽多至百有餘歲。地產大布手巾、木棉。貿易之貨，用鐵鼎、五色布之屬。

　　白話文(Vernacular)：

　　人民煮海水製鹽，女耕織為業。長壽有一百多歲。當地生產大布手巾、木棉。貿易之貨品使用鐵鼎和五色布等。

　　The people boil the sea for salt, and the women cultivate farms and weave. Longevity is more than one hundred years old. The land produces large cloth towels and kapok. The goods which are used for trade are iron tripods and five-color cloths.

68. 東淡邈[126]

---

[126]東淡邈，一說在今印尼爪哇島或其附近；一說在印度西岸，即果阿（Goa），原名 Chandapur 的譯音。參見「東淡邈」，南溟網，http://www.world10k.com/blog/?p=1142　2022 年 10 月 15 日瀏覽。

　　Dōng Dàn Miǎo, one said that it is located in or near Java Island, Indonᶤsiᶤ; another said that it is located on the west coast of India, that is, Goa (Goa), the transliteration of the original name Chandapur. See "Dōng Dàn Miǎo," *Nanming.Net*, http://www.world10k.com/blog/?p=1142

68. Dōng Dàn Miǎo (East Dàn Miǎo)

　　皋揵相去有間，近希苓數日程。山瘠民閒，田沃稻登，百姓充給。氣候熱。俗重耕牛。每於二月舂米為餅以飼之，名為報耕種之本。男女椎髻，繫八丹[127]布。

　　白話文(Vernacular)：

　　從這裡到皋揵有一段距離，近希苓數日程。山地貧瘠，人民沒有什麼事做，田地肥沃，稻米產量多，百姓夠吃。氣候熱。風俗重視耕牛。每於二月舂米做成餅來餵養，名為報答耕種之本。男女椎髻，繫八丹布。

From here to Gāo Qián there is a distance and it is several days travel to Xī Líng. The mountains are barren, and the people have nothing to do. The fields are fertile and the rice is abundant, and the people get sufficient supplies. The climate is hot. The customs attach importance to farming cattle. Every February, the rice is pounded for feeding the cattle, which is called "In return for their contribution to farming". Men and women wear a bun and tie it with Badan cloth.

　　煮海為鹽，釀椰漿為酒。有酋長。地產胡椒，亞於闍婆，玳瑁、木棉、大檳榔。貿易之貨，用銀、五色布、銅鼎、鐵器、燒珠之屬。

　　白話文(Vernacular)：

　　煮海水製鹽，釀椰漿製酒。有酋長。當地生產胡椒，次於闍婆，另有玳瑁、木棉和大檳榔。貿易之貨品使用銀、五

October 15, 2022 retrieved.

[127] 原文寫為「舟」，故改之。

　　The original text was written as "boat", so I correct it.

色布、銅鼎、鐵器和燒珠等。

The people boil the sea for salt and brew coconut milk for wine. There is a chief. The land produces tortoiseshell, kapok, and betel nut pepper which is inferior to Java. The goods which are used for trade are silver, five-color cloth, copper tripod, ironware, and burnt beads.

69. 大八丹[128]
69. Dà Bā Dān

　　國居西洋之後，名雀婆嶺，相望數百里。田平豐稔，時雨霑渥。近年田中生叢禾，丈有餘長，禾莖四十有八，穀粒一百三十，長半寸許，國人傳玩以為禾王。民掘禾土移至酋長之家，一歲之上，莖不枯槁。後其穗[129]自墜，色如金，養之以檳榔灰，使其不蛀。迨今存，時國人曝之，以為寶焉。

　　白話文(Vernacular)：

　　該國位在西洋之西邊，名雀婆嶺，相望有數百里。田地平坦，生產豐稔，季節雨有利於農作物。近年田中生叢禾，有一丈多高，禾莖四十八，穀粒一百三十，長半寸許，國人

---

[128] 大八丹，在今印度西北沿海地區；或中世紀阿拉伯旅行家所稱 Dehfattan 的對音，在今印度西南沿海的特利切里（Tel-1ieherry）附近。參見「大八丹」，百度百科，
　　https://baike.baidu.com/item/%E5%A4%A7%E5%85%AB%E4%B8%B9/9344661　2022 年 10 月 15 日瀏覽。
　　Dà Bā Dān is located on the northwest coast of India; medieval Arab travelers called it Dehfattan, near Tel-1ieherry on the southwest coast of India. See " Dà Bā Dān ", *Baidu Encyclopedia*,
　　https://baike.baidu.com/item/%E5%A4%A7%E5%85%AB%E4%B8%B9/9344661　October 15, 2022 retrieved.
[129] 原文寫為「國」，故改之。
　　The original text was written as "country", so I correct it.

傳玩以為禾王。人民掘禾土移至酋長家，一年多，莖不枯槁。後其穗自行掉落，色如金，把它放在檳榔灰，使其不蛀。至今還存在，時國人公開展示該稻禾，以為寶貝。

This country is located in the west of the West Ocean; there is a place named Quepo Ling, which is hundreds of miles away from Dà Bā Dān. The fields are flat and have rich harvests, which are benefitted by seasonal rain. In recent years, there have been clumps of grains growing in the fields, with a length of more than 10 feet—the stems are 4.8 feet, the grains are one hundred thirty, and the length is half an inch. People say this is the king of rice. The people dig soil and move it to the chief's house, and the stems will not wither after one year old. After that, the ear of the rice falls, the color is like gold, and it is raised with betel nut ash to prevent it from decay. It exists today, the people of the country exhibit it, and it is regarded as a treasure.

氣候熱。俗淳。男女短髮，穿南溜布。煮海為鹽。地產棉布、婆羅蜜。貿易之貨，用南絲、鐵條、紫粉、木梳、白糖之屬。

白話文(**Vernacular**)：

氣候熱。風俗純樸。男女短髮，穿南溜布。煮海水製鹽。當地生產棉布和婆羅蜜。貿易之貨品使用南絲、鐵條、紫粉、木梳和白糖等。

The climate is hot. The customs are vulgar. Men and women have short hair and wear Southern slippery cloth. The people boil the sea for salt. The land produces cotton, and Jack fruits. The goods used for trade are southern silk, iron bars, purple powder, wooden combs, and white sugar.

70. 加里那[130]
70. Jiālǐ Nà

國近具山，其地磽确，田瘠穀少。王國之亞波下有石穴深邃。有白牛種，每歲逢春產白牛，仍有雌雄，酋長畜之，名官牛，聽其自然孳育於國。酋長因其繁衍，以之互市他國，得金十兩，厥後牛遂不產。

白話文(Vernacular)：

該國近具山，其地多砂石，田地貧瘠，穀物產量少。王國之亞波下有石穴深邃。有白牛種，每年春天產白牛，仍有雌雄，酋長畜養這些牛，名官牛，讓其自然繁衍。由於酋長繁衍牛隻，將它賣到外國，得金十兩，以後牛遂不生產了。

This country is close to Jù Shān (Jù Mountain), the land has many stones, the fields are barren, and the grains are few. There is a deep rock cave below Yapo, which breeds white cattle and gives birth to white cattle every spring. There are males and females of cattle, and the chief keeps them. They are called official cattle, and they are naturally bred in the country. Because

---

[130]加里那，或謂在今波斯灣內伊朗西南部一帶；或謂在今印度沿海，今地不詳。參見「加里那」，古代南海地名匯釋，http://mall.cnki.net/Reference/ref_search.aspx?bid=R200809105&inputText=%E5%8A%A0%E9%87%8C%E9%82%A3 2022 年 10 月 19 日瀏覽。

Jiālǐ Nà is probably in the southwestern part of Iran in what is now the Persian Gulf, or in what is now the coast of India, but unknown where it is. See "Jiālǐ Nà," *An Interpretation of Ancient South China Sea Place Names*, http://mall.cnki.net/Reference/ref_search.aspx?bid=R200809105&inputText=%E5%8A%A0%E9%87%8C%E9%82%A3 October 19, 2022 retrieved.

of their reproduction, the chief uses them to trade with other countries and receives 10 taels of gold, but later the cattle did not produce any new young.

氣候稍熱，風俗淳厚。男女髡髮，穿長衫。煮井為鹽，釀椰漿為酒。地產綿羊，高大者二百餘斤。逢春則割其尾，用番藥搽之，次年其尾復生如故。貿易之貨，用青白花碗、細絹、鐵條、蘇木、水銀之屬。

白話文**(Vernacular)**：

氣候稍熱，風俗淳厚。男女剃髮留辮子，穿長衫。煮井水製鹽，釀椰漿製酒。當地生產綿羊，高大者二百餘斤。逢春則割其尾，用番藥搽之，次年其尾復生如故。貿易之貨品使用青白花碗、細絹、鐵條、蘇木和水銀等。

The climate is slightly hot, and the customs are pure and honest. Men and women have curly hair and wear long gowns. The people boil well water for salt and brew coconut milk for wine. The land produces sheep, the tall ones are more than 200 catties. In the spring, the tail is cut off, it is rubbed with herbal medicine, and the tail is reborn the following year. The goods used for trade are white flower bowls, fine silk, iron bars, Biancaea sappan, and mercury.

71. 土塔[131]

---

[131] 沙里八丹和土塔為同一地點，位在今天印度東南部淡米爾納德邦的 Nagapattinam 港口城市。參見「纳加帕蒂南」，維基百科，https://zh.wikipedia.org/wiki/%E7%BA%B3%E5%8A%A0%E5%B8%95%E8%92%82%E5%8D%97　2022 年 10 月 8 日瀏覽。

　　Shālǐ Bā Dān and Tǔtǎ are the same sites, located in the port city of Nagapattinam in what is today Tamil Nadu in southeastern India. See

71. Tŭtǎ

居八丹[132]之平原，木石圍繞，有土磚甃塔，高數丈。漢字書云：「咸淳三年八月畢工」。傳聞中國之人其年敀彼，為書於石以刻之，至今不磨滅焉。土瘠田少，氣候半熱，秋冬微冷。俗好善。民間多事桑香聖佛，以金銀器皿事之。

白話文**(Vernacular)**：

該國位在八丹之平原，木石圍繞，有土磚造的塔，高數丈。上題漢字書說：「咸淳三年八月畢工」。傳聞中國人在該年到此，刻字在石碑上，至今不磨滅。土地貧瘠，田地少，氣候半熱，秋冬微冷。風俗好善。民間多敬拜桑香聖佛，以金銀器皿奉祀。

This place is located in the plain of Badan, surrounded by wood and stone; there are adobe and brick pagodas, several feet high. The Chinese characters on the stele read: "In August, the third year of Xianchun(in 1267), the work completed." It is said that the Chinese people in that year arrived here and carved it without obliterating it to this day. The fields are barren and few. The climate is semi-hot, and the autumn and winter are slightly cold. The customs are fond of friendliness. The people like to burn incense for the Holy Buddha, and they use gold and silver utensils to serve him.

"Nagapatinan", *Wikipedia*, https://zh.wikipedia.org/wiki/%E7%BA%B3%E5%8A%A0%E5%B8%9 5%E8%92%82%E5%8D%97 October 8, 2022 retrieved.

[132] 原文寫為「舟」，故改之。

The original text was written as "boat", so I correct it.

男女斷髮，其身如漆，繫以白布。有酋長。地產棉布、花布大手巾、檳榔。貿易之貨，用糖霜、五色絹、青緞、蘇木之屬。

白話文(**Vernacular**)：

男女剪短髮，皮膚是黑色，繫以白布。有酋長。當地生產棉布、花布大手巾和檳榔。貿易之貨品使用糖霜、五色絹、青緞和蘇木等。

Men and women have their hair cut, and their bodies are black, tied with a white cloth. There is a chief. The land produces cotton, floral towel, and betel nut. The goods used for trade are icing sugar, five-color silk, green satin, and Biancaea sappan.

72. 第三港[133]
72. Third Port

古號為淵，今名新港，口岸分南北，民結屋而居。田土、氣候、風俗、男女與八丹[134]同。去此港八十餘里，洋名大朗，蚌珠海內為最富。

白話文(**Vernacular**)：

該地古稱為淵，今名新港，口岸分南北，人民築屋而居。田土、氣候、風俗、男女與八丹相同。去此港八十餘里，海

---

[133]第三港，為印度東南海岸的馬八兒（Ma'abar, Mapar）。參見劉迎勝，「宋元時代的馬八兒、西洋、南毗與印度」，歷史（編纂學），http://www.icm.gov.mo/rc/viewer/10033/602　2022 年 10 月 18 日瀏覽。

The Third Port is Ma'abar (Mapar) on the southeastern coast of India. See Liu Yingsheng, "Mabal, Western Ocean, Nanpi and India in the Song and Yuan Dynasties", *History (Compilation)*, http://www.icm.gov.mo/rc/viewer/10033/602 October 18, 2022 retrieved.

[134]原文寫為「舟」，故改之。

The original text was written as "boat", so I correct it.

洋名叫大朗，蚌珠產量是該國最多的。

This place's old name is Wèi Yuan, but today it is called Xingang (New Port). The port is divided into north and south, and people live in houses. The soil, climate, customs, men, and women are the same as in Badan. There is the Dalang Ocean which is distant from this port by more than 80 miles, and the production of clams is the richest in this area.

採取之際，酋長殺人及十數牲祭海神。選日，集舟人採珠，每舟以五人為率，二人盪槳，二人收緪，其一人用圈竹匡其袋口，懸於頸上，仍用收緪，繫石於腰，放墜海底，以手爬珠蚌入袋中，遂執緪牽制，其舟中之人收緪，人隨緪而上，纔以珠蚌傾舟中。既滿載，則官場週回皆官兵守之。越數日，候其肉腐爛，則去其殼，以羅盛腐肉旋轉洗之，則肉去珠存，仍巨細篩閱。於十分中，官抽一半，以五分與舟人均分。若夫海神以取之，入水者多葬於鱷魚之腹。吁，得之良可憫也。舶人幸當其取之歲，往往以金與之互易。歸則樂數倍之利，富可立致，特罕逢其時耳。

白話文(Vernacular)：

在採取蚌珠的時候，酋長殺人及十數牲畜祭海神。選好日子，集舟人採珠，每舟有五人，二人操槳，二人收繩索，一人用竹筐封住其袋口，掛在其脖子上，仍需收緊繩索，將石頭綁在腰上，放墜海底，用手將珠蚌放入袋中，拉動繩索，舟中之人便收繩，人隨繩而上，將珠蚌倒入舟中。船滿載就回去。官署週邊都是官兵守衛。過了數天，候其肉腐爛，則去其殼，以網子盛腐肉旋轉洗滌，則去肉存珠，仍繼續篩檢珍珠的大小顆。於十分中，官抽稅一半，以五分與舟人均分。若有海神來取漁夫之命，入水者多葬於鱷魚之腹。吁，得到珍珠，也是可憐憫。船人幸運在漁夫採珠那一年，可以以黃金和漁夫交易。歸來後快樂得數倍之利，馬上變成富人，但此一機會是很少有的。

When picking the clams, the chief killed people and dozens of animals to sacrifice to the sea god. They select the date and gather the boaters to pick pearls. Each boat is led by five people. Two people swipe the paddles, and two people tighten the rope. One uses a bamboo loop to cover the mouth of the bag and hangs it around the neck. He continues to tighten the rope, ties a stone to his waist, and dives into the sea, to collect the clams into the bag with his hands. Then he pulls the rope, and the people on the boat tighten the rope, and the people follow the rope up, and then they pour the clams into the boat. When it is full, they sail back to the officialdom, which is guarded by the officials and soldiers. After a few days, when the meat is rotten, the shells are removed, and the rotten meat is rotated and washed with a net, and the meat is removed and the pearls are stored, and classified according to size. The official draws half of its profits, and the other half is divided with the boatmen. If the Sea God takes the boatman's life, then those who dive into the water are mostly eaten in the belly of the crocodile. Oh, it's sympathetic that they get the beads. At the right time when the boatman is fortunate enough to take the pearls, they often pay gold to exchange with them. When he returns, he can earn double his interest and be able to get rich immediately. But it is rare to meet at the right time.

73. 華羅[135]

73. Huá Luó

植椰樹為疆理，疊青石為室。田土瘠磽，宜種稻。氣候常熱，秋冬草木越增茂盛。俗怪，民間每創石亭數四，塑以泥牛，或刻石為象[136]，朝夕誦[137]經，敬之若人佛焉。仍以香花燈燭為之供養。凡所坐之壇，所行之地，及屋壁之上，悉以牛糞和泥塗之，反為潔淨。隣人往來，苟非其類，則不敢造其所。

白話文(Vernacular)：

栽種椰樹做為疆界，疊青石建房屋。田土貧瘠，適宜種稻。氣候常熱，秋冬草木越增茂盛。風俗怪異，民間每建造四個石亭，就要塑造泥牛，或刻石象，早晚誦經，敬拜它像人間的佛陀一樣。仍以香花燈燭為之供養。凡所坐之壇，所走之地，及屋壁之上，悉以牛糞和泥塗抹，反而認為這是潔淨的。隣人往來，若非跟其同類，就不敢造訪其住所。

Coconut trees are planted as its boundary, and its room is stacked with stones. The fields are barren and suitable for rice cultivation. The climate is often hot, and the vegetation becomes lusher in autumn and winter. The customs are strange. The people construct four stone pavilions, the cow statues are made

---

[135] 藤田豐八認為華羅位在印度西海岸的胡荼辣（Guzarat）（或譯為古吉拉特）一帶。參見藤田豐八校註，前引書，頁 130-131。

Fujita Toyohachi believed that Huá Luó is located in the area of Guzarat (Gujarat) on the west coast of India. See Fujita Toyohachi notes, *op. cit.*, pp.130-131.

[136] 原文寫為「像」，有誤，故改之。

The original text is written as "image", which is wrong, so I correct it.

[137] 原文寫為「諷」，有誤，故改之。

The original text was written as "sarcasm", so I correct it.

of clay and the elephants are carved of stone. They recite sutras day and night and respect them as if it was Buddha in the world. Still, they offer incense, lanterns, and candles. All the altars on which they sit, the places they walk, and the walls of the houses are all covered with cow dung and mud, and they look clean. When neighbors come and go, if they are not of their kind, they will not dare to enter their house.

男女形黑，無酋長，年尊者主之。語言譸詼。以檀香、牛糞搽其額。以白細布纏頭，穿長衫，與今之南毗人[138]少異而大同。

白話文**(Vernacular)**：

男女皮膚是黑色，無酋長，年尊者統治。語言很難懂。以檀香、牛糞搽其額。以白細布包著頭，穿長衫，與今之南毗人少異而大同。

Men and women are black in the skin, without a chief, and a senior man is a master. Their language is difficult to understand. They smear their forehead with sandalwood and cow dung. Wrapping their head in white fine cloth and wearing a long gown, they are mostly similar to the people of Nanpi but a little different today.

74. 麻那里[139]

---

[138] 南毗人，劉迎勝認為是馬八兒國人。參見劉迎勝，前引文。

A native of Nanpi, Liu Yingsheng believed that he was a native of Maba'er. See Liu Yingsheng, *op. cit.*

[139] 麻那里，位在肯亞的馬林迪（Malindi）。參見 Anshan Li, *A History of Overseas Chinese in Africa to 1911*, Diasporic Africa Press, New York, 2017, p.33.

74. Má Nàlǐ

界迷黎[140]之東南，居垣角[141]之絕島。石有楠樹萬枝，周圍皆水。有蠔如山立，人少至。土薄田瘠，氣候不齊。俗侈。男女辮髮以帶捎，臂用金釧。穿五色絹短衫，以朋加剌布為

---

https://books.google.com.tw/books?id=Xuq7QCmY6jQC&pg=PR5&lpg=PR5&dq=asli,Anshan+Li&source=bl&ots=6OpVBqihdP&sig=ACfU3U1vOjLn2KGD6gAmvzWuwedTzClVdg&hl=zh-TW&sa=X&ved=2ahUKEwi70NPx493nAhXBLqYKHT23AssQ6AEwAXoECAkQAQ#v=onepage&q=asli%2CAnshan%20Li&f=false　2022年10月19日瀏覽。

Má Nàlǐ is located in Malindi, Kenya. See Anshan Li, *A History of Overseas Chinese in Africa to 1911*, Diasporic Africa Press, New York, 2017, p.33.
https://books.google.com.tw/books?id=Xuq7QCmY6jQC&pg=PR5&lpg=PR5&dq=asli,Anshan+Li&source=bl&ots=6OpVBqihdP&sig=ACfU3U1vOjLn2KGD6gAmvzWuwedTzClVdg&hl=zh-TW&sa=X&ved=2ahUKEwi70NPx493nAhXBLqYKHT23AssQ6AEwAXoECAkQAQ#v=onepage&q=asli%2CAnshan%20Li&f=false　October 19, 2022 retrieved.

[140] 迷黎，位在東非沿岸，今肯亞的馬林迪（Malindi）西北面，為東非大陸 Malan 部落名的譯音。參見「迷黎」，南溟網，http://www.world10k.com/blog/?p=1252　2022年10月19日瀏覽。

Má Nàlǐ is located on the coast of East Africa, northwest of present-day Malindi in Kenya, and is the transliteration of the name of the Malan tribe in East Africa. See "Mi Li," *Nanming Net*, http://www.world10k.com/blog/?p=1252　October 19, 2022 retrieved.

[141] 麻那里即馬林迪（Malindi），垣角是其北面之福爾摩沙灣（Formosa Bay），葡萄牙人名之為美麗灣。此灣土名作 Ungama，「垣角」即此土名之對音。參見「Ungama」，南溟網，http://www.world10k.com/blog/index.php?s=%E5%9E%A3%E8%A7%92　2022年10月19日瀏覽。

Má Nàlǐ is Malindi, Yuán Jiǎo is Formosa Bay (Formosa Bay) to the north, and the Portuguese named it Beautiful Bay. The local name of this bay is Ungama, and "Wangjiao" is the opposite sound of the local name. See "Ungama", *Nanming Net*, http://www.world10k.com/blog/index.php?s=%E5%9E%A3%E8%A7%92　October 19, 2022 retrieved.

獨幅裙繫之。

白話文**(Vernacular)**：

該地位在迷黎之東南方，居垣角之孤島。島上有楠樹一萬多顆，周圍皆水。有蠔像山一樣立起來，人跡少至。土地不肥沃，田地貧瘠，氣候不穩定。風俗奢侈。男女辮髮，用手巾綁著，臂上戴著金鈿環。穿五色絹短衫，以朋加剌奢侈布為獨幅裙穿在腰間。

This place is located to the southeast of Mi Li; it is an isolated island which is located in Yuán Jiǎo. There are ten thousand Nan trees on the island, and all around by water. There are oysters that stand like mountains. Few people go to that island. The fields are barren and have few products. The climate is unstable. The customs are extravagant. Men and women braid their hair with belts towel and use golden decorations on their arms. The people wear a five-color silk blouse and tie it with a Bangladesh cloth as a one-piece skirt.

地產駱駝，高九尺，土人以之負重。有仙鶴高六尺許，以石為食。聞人拍掌，則聳翼而舞，其容儀可觀，亦異物也。

白話文**(Vernacular)**：

當地生產駱駝，高九尺，土人以之載重。有仙鶴高六尺許，吃石頭。聽到人拍掌，則聳翼而跳舞，其舞姿可觀，亦是奇異的動物。

The land produces camels that are nine feet tall, and the natives use them to carry the weight. There is a crane that is about six feet tall and feeds on stones. Hearing people clapping their hands, they fluttered and danced, and their appearance is impressive. It is also a strange thing.

75. 加將門里[142]
75. Jiā Jiàngmén Lǐ

去加里二千餘里，喬木成林，修竹高節。其地堰瀦，田肥美，一歲三收穀。通商販於他國。氣候常熱。俗薄。男女挽髻，穿長衫。叢雜回人居之。土商每興販黑囝，往朋加剌互用銀錢之多寡，隨其大小高下而議價。

白話文(Vernacular)：

從這裡到加里有二千餘里，喬木成林，竹林長得很高。其地有堤岸的水塘很多，田肥美，一年可三獲稻穀。有跟外國通商貿易。氣候常熱。風俗淺薄。男女挽髻，穿長衫。跟回教徒混居。當地商人每要到朋加剌賣黑人小孩，值多少銀錢，是根據其年齡大小及身高來議價。

This place is distant from Gary by more than 2,000 miles; the trees have grown into forests, and the bamboo has grown tall. The land has lakes, the fields are fertile, and the grains are harvested three times a year. The people trade with other countries. The climate is very hot. The customs are vulgar. Men and women wear buns on their heads and long gowns. There are many Muslims living together. Every time local businessmen want to sell black children to Bangladesh, they will negotiate the price with silver money according to their age and height.

---

[142] 蘇繼卿認為加將門里位在莫三鼻克的奎里曼尼（Quilimani, Quelimane）。參見蘇繼卿，前引書，頁215。

　　Su Jiqing believed that Jiā Jiàngmén Lǐ is Quilimani (Quelimane) of Mozambique. See Su Jiqing, *op. cit.*, p. 215.

民煮海為鹽，釀蔗漿為酒。有酋長。地產象牙、兜羅棉、花布。貿易之貨，用蘇杭五色緞、南北絲、土紬絹、巫崙布之屬。

白話文**(Vernacular)**：

人民煮海水製鹽，釀蔗漿製酒。有酋長。當地生產象牙、兜羅棉和花布。貿易之貨品使用蘇杭五色緞、南北絲、土紬絹和巫崙布等。

The people boil the sea for salt and brew sugarcane pulp for wine. There is a chief. The land produces ivory, Tūla cotton, and floral cloth. The goods used for trade are Suzhou-Hangzhou five-color satin, north-south silk, local silk, and Wulun cloth.

76. 波斯離[143]
76. Bōsī Lí

境與西夏聯屬，地方五千餘里。關市之間，民比居如魚鱗。田宜麥、禾。氣候常冷。風俗侈麗。男女長身，編髮。穿駝褐毛衫，以軟錦為茵褥。燒羊為食。

白話文**(Vernacular)**：

其邊境與西夏連接，地方五千餘里。設在交通要道的城市，人民像魚鱗一樣排列居住。田地適宜種麥和禾。氣候常冷。風俗侈麗。男女身高，編辮子髮。穿駱駝褐毛衫，以軟錦為褥墊。燒羊肉食用。

---

[143] 波斯離，今伊拉克巴士拉。參見「波斯離」，百度百科，https://baike.baidu.com/item/%E6%B3%A2%E6%96%AF%E7%A6%BB 2022 年 10 月 19 日瀏覽。

　Bōsī Lí is present-day Basra, Iraq. See "Bōsī Lí," *Baidu Encyclopedia*, https://baike.baidu.com/item/%E6%B3%A2%E6%96%AF%E7%A6%BB October 19, 2022 retrieved.

The territory is affiliated with Xixia, and the area is more than 5,000 miles wide. The city is located in the main traffic, and the houses of the people neighboring one by one are like fish scales. The fields are suitable for planting wheat and cereal. The climate is always cold. The customs are extravagant and fond of gorgeous. Men and women have long bodies and braided hair. The people wear a camel brown sweater, use soft brocade as a mattress, and roast mutton for food.

煮海為鹽。有酋長。地產琥珀、軟錦、駝毛、膃肭臍[144]、沒藥[145]、萬年棗。貿易之貨，用氆毹、五色緞、雲南葉金、白銀、倭鐵、大楓子、牙梳、鐵器、達剌斯離香之屬。

白話文**(Vernacular)**：

---

[144]膃肭臍，語源自日語 ottosei，指海狗生殖器做成的一種男性補品，也稱「海狗腎」。參見「膃肭臍」，*Wiktionary*，https://zh.m.wiktionary.org/zh-hant/%E8%86%83%E8%82%AD%E8%87%8D　2022 年 10 月 4 日瀏覽。

「海狗腎」，維基百科，https://zh.m.wikipedia.org/zh-tw/%E6%B5%B7%E7%8B%97%E8%85%8E　2022 年 10 月 4 日瀏覽。

Wànàqí is derived from the Japanese ottosei, which refers to a male tonic made from the genitals of seals, also known as "sea dog kidneys". See "The navel", *Wiktionary*, https://zh.m.wiktionary.org/zh-hant/%E8%86%83%E8%82%AD%E8%87%8D　October 4, 2022 retrieved.

"Sea Dog Kidney", *Wikipedia*, https://zh.m.wikipedia.org/zh-tw/%E6%B5%B7%E7%8B%97%E8%85%8E　October 4, 2022 retrieved.

[145]沒藥（myrrh）是一種活血、化瘀、止痛、健胃的藥材。見「沒藥」，維基百科，https://zh.wikipedia.org/zh-tw/%E6%B2%92%E8%97%A5　2022 年 10 月 4 日瀏覽。

Myrrh is a kind of medicinal material for promoting blood circulation, removing blood stasis, relieving pain, and strengthening the stomach. See "Myrrh", *Wikipedia*, https://zh.wikipedia.org/zh-tw/%E6%B2%92%E8%97%A5　October 4, 2022 retrieved.

煮海水製鹽。有酋長。當地生產琥珀、軟錦、駝毛、膃肭臍、沒藥和萬年棗。貿易之貨品使用氍毯、五色緞、雲南葉金、白銀、倭鐵、大楓子、牙梳、鐵器和達刺斯離香等。

The people boil the sea for salt. There is a chief. The land produces amber, soft brocade, Wànàqí, myrrh, and khurma (date palm). The goods used for trade are rugs, five-color satin, Yunnan leaf gold, white silver, Japanese iron, big maple, an ivory comb, ironware, and Darasili incense.

77. 撻吉那[146]
77. Tà Jí Nà

國居達里之地,卽古之西域。山少田瘠,氣候半熱,天常陰晦。俗與羌同。男女身面如漆,眼圓,白髮鬈鬢。籠軟錦為衣。女資紡織為生,男採鴉鶻石[147]為活。

白話文(Vernacular):

該國位在達里之地,卽古之西域。山少,田地貧瘠,氣

---

[146]撻吉那,位在今印度德干(Deccan)之梵語名 Dakshina 的音譯。參見「Tahiri」,南溟網,
http://www.world10k.com/blog/index.php?s=%E6%92%BB%E5%90%89%E9%82%A3 2022 年 10 月 16 日瀏覽。

Tà Jí Nà is a transliteration of the Sanskrit name Dakshina in today's Deccan, India. See "Tahiri," *Nanming Net*, http://www.world10k.com/blog/index.php?s=%E6%92%BB%E5%90%89%E9%82%A3 October 16, 2022 retrieved.

[147] 鴉鶻石,是一種藍色寶石。見「鴉鶻石」,百度百科, https://baike.baidu.hk/item/%E9%B4%89%E9%B6%BB%E7%9F%B3/89278 2022 年 10 月 4 日瀏覽。

Yā Hú Shí is a blue gemstone. See "Yā Hú Shí," *Baidu Encyclopedia*, https://baike.baidu.hk/item/%E9%B4%89%E9%B6%BB%E7%9F%B3/89278 October 4, 2022 retrieved.

候半熱，天常陰晦。風俗與羌族相同。男女身體和臉孔像黑漆，眼圓，白髮散亂。使用竹籠子裝了軟錦做的衣服。女紡織維生，男採挖鴉鶻石（藍寶石）維生。

This country is located in Dali, namely the Western Regions of ancient times. There are no more mountains and the fields are barren. The climate is semi-hot, and the sky is often gloomy. The customs are the same as the Qiang. Men and women have black color on their bodies and face, round eyes, and white tousled hair. Clothes made of soft brocade were packed in bamboo cages. Women make a living by textiles, and men pluck Yā Hú Shí (Blue gemstone) for a living.

煮海為鹽，釀安石榴為酒。有酋長。地產安息香、琉璃瓶、硼砂，梔子花尤勝於他國。貿易之貨，用沙金、花銀、五色緞、鐵鼎、銅線、琉磺[148]、水銀之屬。

白話文(Vernacular)：

煮海水製鹽，釀安石榴製酒。有酋長。當地生產安息香、琉璃瓶和硼砂，梔子花尤勝於他國。貿易之貨品使用沙金、花銀、五色緞、鐵鼎、銅線、琉磺和水銀等。

The people boil the sea for salt and brew pomegranates for wine. There is a chief. The land produces benzoin, glass bottles, borax, and gardenia, which is better than other countries. The goods used for trade are sand gold, flower silver, five-color satin, iron tripods, copper wire, sulfur, and mercury.

---

[148] 原文寫為「黃」，故改之。
The original text was written as "yellow", so I correct it.

78. 千里馬
78. Qiānlǐmǎ

北與大奮山截界，溪水護市，四時澄徹，形勢寬容。田瘠穀少，氣候乍熱。俗淳。男女斷髮，身繫絲布。

白話文(Vernacular)：

北方與大奮山隔界，溪水環繞城市，四時澄徹，形勢寬大。田地貧瘠，穀物產量少，氣候會突然炎熱。風俗純樸。男女剪短髮，身繫絲布。

The north of this place is bordering with Dafen Mountain; there are streams surrounding the city, the water is clear through the four seasons, and the terrain is wide. The fields are barren and have few grains. The climate is suddenly hot. The customs are vulgar. Men and women have their hair cut and wear silk cloth.

煮海為鹽，釀桂屑為酒。有酋長。地產翠羽、百合、蘿蔔[149]。貿易之貨，用鐵條、粗碗、蘇木、鉛、針之屬。

白話文(Vernacular)：

煮海水製鹽，釀肉桂片製酒。有酋長。當地生產翠羽、百合和山藥。貿易之貨品使用鐵條、粗碗、蘇木、鉛和針等。

The people boil the sea for salt and brew cinnamon chips for wine. There is a chief. The land produces Kingfisher feathers,

---

[149]蘿蔔，俗稱山藥。見「蔔」，百度百科，
https://baike.baidu.hk/item/%E8%95%B7/7000651　2022 年 10 月 4 日瀏覽。

Luó Yù, commonly known as Chinese yam. See "Yù," *Baidu Encyclopedia*, https://baike.baidu.hk/item/%E8%95%B7/7000651 October 4, 2022 retrieved.

lilies, and Luó Yù. The goods used for trade are iron bars, crude bowls, Biancaea sappan, lead, and needles.

79. 大佛山[150]
79. Dà Foshān (Dà Fo Mountain)

大佛山界於迓里[151]、高郎步之間。至順庚午冬十月十有二日,因卸帆於山下,是夜月明如晝,海波不興,水清徹底,起而徘徊,俯窺水國,有樹婆娑。余指舟人而問:「此非青琅玕、珊瑚珠者耶?」曰:「非也。」「此非月中娑羅樹影者耶?」曰:「亦非也。」乃命童子入水採之,則柔滑,拔之出水,則堅如鐵。把而翫之,高僅盈尺,則其樹槎牙盤結奇怪,枝有一花一蘂,紅色天然。既開者彷彿牡丹,半吐者類乎菡萏[152]。舟人秉燭環堵而觀之,眾乃雀躍而笑曰:「此瓊

---

[150] 大佛山,位在斯里蘭卡之 Adam's Peak。參見藤田豐八校註,前引書,頁 137。

　Dà Foshān is located in Adam's Peak in Sri Lanka. See Fujita Toyohachi notes, *op. cit.*, p.137.

[151] 迓里,西洋朝貢典錄溜山國條作牙里大山,錫蘭山國條作牙里,順風相送各處府州山形水勢之圖條作牙里嶼,阿齊往羅里及回針條作牙里坎,皆為僧伽羅語 Gala 之對音,義為岩石。它位在斯里蘭卡西南境之加勒港(Galle)。參見「Galle」,南溟網,http://www.world10k.com/blog/index.php?s=%E8%BF%93%E9%87%8C 2022 年 10 月 16 日瀏覽。

　Yà Lǐ is written as Yali Dashan in the Liushan entry of the *Western Tribute Records*, as Yali in the Ceylonshan, and as Yà Lǐ Yu in the *Bon Voyage*, as Yà Lǐ Kan in the "from Ā Qí to Luó Lǐ" and "Return Needle", all are the opposite sounds of the Sinhala language Gala, which means rock. It is located in the port of Galle in southwest Sri Lanka. See "Galle," *Nanming Net*, http://www.world10k.com/blog/index.php?s=%E8%BF%93%E9%87%8C October 16, 2022 retrieved.

[152] 菡萏,指荷花。見「菡萏」,教育部重編國語辭典修訂本。國家教育

樹開花也，誠海中之稀有，亦中國之異聞。余歷此四十餘年，未嘗覩於此，君今得之，茲非千載而一遇者乎？」余次日作古體詩百首，以記其實。袖之以歸。豫章邵庵虞先生見而賦詩，迨今留於君子堂以傳玩焉。

白話文(Vernacular)：

大佛山介於逛里、高郎步之間。至順庚午冬十月十二日，我在該島卸帆靠港，是夜月明如晝，海波不興，水清徹底，我起床在此地徘徊，俯看水中景色，有樹搖曳舞動的樣子。我問船人說：「這不是綠珍珠、珊瑚珠嗎？」船人回說：「不是。」「這不是月亮照射娑羅樹之影子嗎？」船人回說：「也不是。」我於是命童子入水採之，它有點柔滑，拔之出水，則堅如鐵。我在手上把玩，高僅一尺，它的樹枝長得很奇怪，枝有一花一蕊，天然紅色。它開著很像牡丹，半開則類似荷花。船人拿著蠟燭圍觀，大家雀躍而笑說：「這是瓊樹開花，誠海中之稀有之物，也是中國之異聞。我經歷此四十餘年，未嘗看過此一東西，你今天得到此東西，難道不是千載而難得一見的嗎？」我次日作古體詩百首，以記其實況。將它納入袖中，然後回國。豫章邵庵虞先生見此東西也賦詩，至今留在君子堂以供大家觀賞。

The boundary of Dà Fo Mountain lies between Yà Lǐ and Gaolangbu. On the twelfth day of the tenth month, Zhì Shùn Gēngwǔ year (in 1330), I anchored at the port at the foot of the

---

研究院，

https://dict.revised.moe.edu.tw/dictView.jsp?ID=82057&la=0&powerMode=0　2022 年 10 月 4 日瀏覽。

Hàn Dàn refers to the lotus flower. See "Hàn Dàn," *Ministry of Education Re-edited the Revised Version of the Mandarin Dictionary*. National Academy for Educational Education,

https://dict.revised.moe.edu.tw/dictView.jsp?ID=82057&la=0&powerMode=0　October 4, 2022 retrieved.

mountain. That night moon was as bright as the day, the sea waves were not booming, and the water was completely clean. I got up and wandered on the coast, overlooking the water country, and there were trees swaying. I asked the boatman, "Is this not a green pearl, a coral pearl?" The boatman answered, "No." I continued to ask: "Is this not the shadow of the Saura tree under the moon? The boatman answered, "Also no." So I asked one boy to dive into the water to pick it up. It looks soft and smooth, and when it is pulled out of the water, it turns to be as firm as iron. I play it in my hands. Its height is close to only one foot, the tree has a strange branch which has a flower and a stamen, and the red color is natural. It looks like a peony when it is open, and it is like a lotus when it is half open. The boatmen watched around with a candle, and the crowd cheered and laughed, saying, "This Qiongshu is blooming, it is rare to see in the sea, and it is also strange news in China. I have been here for more than forty years, and I have never seen it here. Is this not a one-time encounter in a thousand years?" I wrote a hundred ancient poems the next day to record the truth. I put this poem into my sleeve and went home (referring to going back to China). Mr. Shao An Yu of Yuzhang wrote a poem when he saw it, and now I put this coral tree on the Junzitang (Gentleman House) for the public to view.

80. 須文（達）那[153]

---

[153] 原文可能少了「達」字，故加之。該國位於蘇門答臘島八昔（Parsei）（巴賽）河口，現在那裏還有一個名叫須文達那（Sumandra）的小村。參見「須文達那」，百度百科，

80. Xū Wén (Da) Nà

　　國居班支尼那接境，山如瓜匏，民樂奠居，田瘠穀少，氣候應節。俗鄙薄。男女蓬頭、繫絲。酋長之家有石鶴，高七尺餘，身白而頂紅，彷彿生像，民間事之為神鶴。四五月間，聽其夜鳴，則是歲豐稔。凡有疾則卜之，如響斯應。

　　白話文(Vernacular)：

　　該國與班支尼那鄰境，山像瓜匏的形狀，人民快樂的住在此地，田地貧瘠，穀物產量少，氣候順應節序。風俗鄙薄。男女蓬頭、繫絲布。酋長的家有一隻石鶴，高七尺餘，身白而頂紅，彷彿活的，老百姓視之為神鶴。四、五月間，會在夜晚聽到它在叫，則該年必是豐收。凡有疾病向它問卜，相當靈驗。

　　This country is bordering with Panchinina. Its mountains are like melons. The people happily built their houses here. The fields are barren and have few grains. The climate is in correspondence with the season change. The customs are vulgar. Men and women have tousled hair tied with silk. There is a stone crane in the chief's house, more than seven feet high, with a white body and red top, as if living. And the people treat it as a "sacred crane". In April and May, if you listen to the singing of the stone crane at night, it must be an abundant year. If you get

---

　　https://baike.baidu.hk/item/%E9%A0%88%E6%96%87%E9%81%94%E9%82%A3/5926616　　2022 年 10 月 16 日瀏覽。

　　The original text may miss the word "Da", so I add it. The country is located at the mouth of the Parsei (Pasai) River in Sumatra, where there is now a small village which is called Sumandra. See "Suvindana", *Wikipedia*, https://baike.baidu.hk/item/%E9%A0%88%E6%96%87%E9%81%94%E9%82%A3/5926616　　October 16, 2022 retrieved.

a disease, then you will be cured by your praying to the stone crane.

民不善煮海為鹽。地產絲布，胡椒亞於希芩、淡邈。孩兒茶一名烏爹土，又名胥實，考[154]之其實檳榔汁[155]也。貿易之貨，用五色細緞、青緞、荳蔲、大小水罐、蘇木之屬。

白話文(Vernacular)：

民不善於煮海水製鹽。當地生產絲布，胡椒產量次於希芩和淡邈。孩兒茶一名烏爹土，又名胥實，研究它其實是檳榔汁。貿易之貨品使用五色細緞、青緞、荳蔲、大小水罐和蘇木等。

The people are not good at boiling the sea for salt. The land produces silk cloth, and the pepper is inferior to Xiling and Danmiao. Hái'ér Chá (Baby tea) is also called Wū Diē Tǔ, also known as Xū Shí. In fact, it is betel nut juice. The goods used for trade are five-color fine satin, green satin, cardamom, large and small water jars, and Biancaea sappan.

81. 萬里石塘[156]

---

[154] 原文寫為「失」，故改之。
The original text was written as "lost", so I correct it.
[155] 原文寫為「汗」，故改之。
The original text was written as "Khan", so I correct it.
[156] 根據宋會要輯稿一書在「真里富國」條說：「嘉定9年(1216年)7月20日，真里富國.....欲至中國者，自其國放洋，五日抵波斯蘭(約在柬埔寨南部沿海)，次崑崙洋，經真臘國，數日至檳達椰（椰）國（即賓同龍，在越南南部的潘朗），數日至占城，十日過洋，傍東南有石塘，名曰萬里，其洋或深或淺，水急礁多，舟覆者十七八，絕無山岸。」（〔清〕徐松，宋會要輯稿，真里富國條。）該文所講的萬里石塘指西沙群島。

81. Wànlǐ Shí Táng

　　石塘之骨，由潮州而生。迤邐如長蛇，橫亙海中，越海諸國。俗云萬里石塘。以余推之，豈止萬里而已哉！舶由岱嶼門，掛四帆，乘風破浪，海上若飛，至西洋或百日之外。以一日一夜行百[157]里計之，萬里曾不足，故原其地脈歷歷可考。一脈至爪[158]哇，一脈至勃泥及古里地悶，一脈至西洋遐崑崙之地。蓋紫陽朱子[159]謂海外之地，與中原地脈相連者，其以是歟！

　　白話文(Vernacular)：

　　石塘之骨幹，是由潮州向南延伸。延展如長蛇，橫亙海中，經過海上好幾個國家。俗云萬里石塘。我推測，它不止萬里啊！船隻由岱嶼門出發，掛四帆，乘風破浪，海上若飛，至西洋百日過幾天可到。以一日一夜行百里計算，不到萬里

According to *The Song Huiyao Compilations* (*A Discourse on Song Dynasty*), in the entry of Zhēnlǐfù Guó, it says: "On July 20, the 9th year of Jiading (1216), Zhēnlǐfù Guó... Those who want to go to China should go abroad from their country and arrive at Bōsī Lán (about the southern coast of Cambodia) in 5 days. Next go to the Kunlun Ocean, through Chenla country, a few days to Bindalan (that is, Bin Tonglong, in Pan Lang in southern Vietnam), a few days to Champa, and ten days across the ocean. In the southeast, there is a stone pond, called Wanli, whose sea may be deep or shallow, with rapid waters and many reefs, seven or eight out of ten boats are overturned, and absolutely no opportunity landing shore." ([Qing] Xu Song, *Song Huiyao Compilations*, the entry of Zhēnlǐfù Guó.) The Wanli Shitang mentioned in this article refers to the Xisha Islands (Paracel Islands).

[157] 原文無「百」字，故加之。
　　The original text does not have the word "hundred", so I add it.
[158] 原文寫為「瓜」，故改之。
　　The original text was written as "melon", so I correct it.
[159] 朱子，即朱熹，號紫陽先生。
　　Zhu Zi, namely Zhu Xi, was named Mr. Ziyang.

之路程，故其原先的地脈歷歷可考。一脈至爪哇，一脈至勃泥及古里地悶，一脈至往西洋的崑崙之地。紫陽朱熹曾說海外之地與中原地脈相連，真是如此啊！

The bone of Shitang (referring to islets and reefs) was born in Chaozhou. It extends like a long snake and stretches across the sea and through many coastal countries. It was called Wànlǐ Shí Táng (referring to islets and reefs extending ten thousand miles). In my opinion, it might be longer than ten thousand miles! The ship sails from the gate of Daiyu, with four sails, riding the wind and breaking the waves, like flying on the sea. It will probably reach the West Ocean in a hundred days or so. If it is calculated by traveling a hundred li in one day and one night, then it is less than ten thousand miles, so the origin of its geology can be traced. One line goes to Java, one line goes to Boni (Borneo) and Guli Dimeng (Timor Island), and the other line goes to the land of Kunlun in the West Ocean. Zhu Xi said that the ley lines of overseas land are connected to the Central Plains. That's true!

觀夫海洋泛無涯涘，中匿石塘，孰得而明之？避之則吉，遇之則凶，故子午針人之命脈所係。苟非舟子之精明，鮮不覆且溺矣！吁！得意之地勿再往，豈可以風濤為徑路也哉！

白話文(Vernacular)：

觀察海洋廣泛無邊界，中間藏匿著石塘，怎能夠看得出來呢？避之則吉，遇之則凶，故船人之性命就靠羅盤了。假若不是船人的精明，無不翻船且溺死矣！吁！已到目的地，就無須繼續前往他地，若要去就需避開風濤的航路了！

Looking at the ocean, there is no end, and there are

submerged reefs hidden in the middle. Who can know it? Avoiding it is auspicious, encountering it is bad, and so the Ziwu needle (compass) is the lifeline of people. If we do have not the shrewdness of the boatman, nobody can escape and will be drowned! Oh! Once you have reached your destination, you don't need to continue to go to another place. If you want to go, you need to avoid the route of wind and waves!

82. 小唄喃[160]
82. Xiǎo Gé Nán (Small Gé Nán)

　　地與都攔礁相近。厥土黑墳，本宜穀、麥。居民懶事耕作，歲藉烏爹運米供給。或風迅到遲，馬船已去，貨載不滿，風迅或逆，不得過喃巫哩洋，且防高浪阜，中鹵股石之厄。所以此地駐冬，候下[161]年八九月馬船復來，移船回古里佛互市。風俗、男女衣著與古里佛同。有村主，無酋長。

　　白話文(Vernacular)：

---

[160] 小唄喃，指印度西南邊的奎隆（Quilon）。參見 Ulrich Theobald, *op.cit.*
　　藤田豐八認為小唄喃位在潘達里納（Pandarina）。(參見藤田豐八校註，前引書，頁141。) 潘達里納位在今印度半島西岸卡里庫特（Calicut）北約 16 英里處。（參見「賓陀蘭納」，南溟網，http://www.world10k.com/blog/?p=1099　2022 年 10 月 21 日瀏覽。

　　Xiǎo Gé Nán refers to the southwest of India's Quilon. See Ulrich Theobald, *op.cit.*

　　Fujita Toyohachi believed that Xiǎo Gé Nán is located in Pandarina. See Fujita Toyohachi notes, *op. cit.*, p. 141.

　　Pandarina is located about 16 miles north of Calicut on the west coast of what is now the Indian peninsula. (See "Bindo Lanna", *Nanming Net*, http://www.world10k.com/blog/?p=1099　October 21, 2022 retrieved.

[161] 原文寫為「夏」，故改之。

　　The original text was written as "Xia", so I correct it.

　　該地與都攔礁相近。它的土地肥沃，本來適宜種穀、麥。居民懶事耕作，每年從烏爹運來米供給。遇到風迅不對，船隻遲到，馬船已去，貨載不滿，風迅有時遇到逆風，不得過喃巫哩洋，且防高浪，中間有鹵股石之災厄，所以會在此地過冬，等候明年八、九月馬船復來，開船回古里佛貿易。風俗、男女衣著與古里佛相同。有村主，無酋長。

　　This land is close to the Dōu Lán Reef. The fields are fertile and suitable for planting grains and wheat. The people are lazy to farm, and they depend upon importing rice from Wū Diē every year. When the seasonal wind comes late, and the horse boat has gone, the loaded cargo is not enough. When it meets the opposite wind, it is not allowed to cross the Nán Wū Lī Ocean. The boat must not only guard against high waves but also avoid the disaster of being hit by the rock and reefs. Therefore, the boatmen must stay here in winter, waiting for the return of the horse boat in August and September of the next year. The boatmen will sail to Gullifo to do business. The customs and clothing of men and women are the same as those of Gullifo. There is a village head, but no chief.

　　地產胡椒、椰子、檳榔、溜魚。貿易之貨，用金、銀[162]、青白花器、八丹[163]布、五色緞、鐵器之屬。

　　白話文(Vernacular)：

　　當地生產胡椒、椰子、檳榔和溜魚。貿易之貨品使用金、

---

[162]原文寫為「錢」，故改之。
　The original text was written as "money", so I correct it.
[163]原文寫為「舟」，故改之。
　The original text was written as "boat", so I correct it.

銀、青白花器、八丹布、五色緞和鐵器等。

　　The land produces pepper, coconut, betel nut, and slippery fish. The goods which are used for trade are gold, silver, green and white flower utensils, Badan cloth, five-color satin, and iron utensils.

83.　古里佛[164]
83. Gullifo

　　當巨海之要衝，去僧加剌[165]密邇，亦西洋諸番之[166]馬頭也。山橫而田瘠，宜種麥。每歲藉烏爹米[167]至。行者讓路，道不拾遺，俗稍近古。其法至謹，盜一牛，酋以牛頭為準，失主仍以犯人家產籍沒而戮之。官場居深山中，海濱為市，以通貿易。

　　白話文(Vernacular)：

　　該地位在大海之要衝，去僧加剌很近，也是西洋諸番之碼頭也。該地多山，田地貧瘠，適宜種麥。每年從烏爹進口米。路上行人要讓路，道不拾遺，風俗稍近古風。其法律嚴謹，盜一牛，酋長以牛頭來辨別是否是被盜的牛，失主可將犯人家產沒收，並將犯人處死。官署設在深山中，海濱為市

---

[164]　藤田豐八認為古里佛位在卡里庫特。參見藤田豐八校註，前引書，頁 141。

　　Fujita Toyohachi believed that Gullifo is located in Calicut. See Fujita Toyohachi notes, *op. cit*., p. 141.

[165]　原文寫為「蜜」，故改之。

　　The original text was written as "honey", so I correct it.

[166]　原文無「番之」，故加之。

　　There is no "fanzhi" in the original text, so I add it.

[167]原文寫為「水」，故改之。

　　The original text was written as "water", so I correct it.

場，以通貿易。

This place is located at the pivot of the great sea, it is quite near to Sēng Jiā Lá. It is also the port of various countries in the West Ocean. There it is mountainous, and the fields are barren, so wheat should be suitable for planting. It depends upon importing rice from Wū Diē every year. Pedestrians give way, the people do not pick up things on the road. The customs are slightly more ancient style. Its law is strict, if a cow is stolen, the chief will use the head of the cow to identify whether it is a stolen cow, and the owner can confiscate the prisoner's property and execute the prisoner. The officialdom lies in the mountains, the seaside is the marketplace, and it is used for trade.

地產胡椒，亞於下里，人間俱有倉廩貯之。每播荷[168]三百七十五斤，稅收十分之二。次加張葉、皮桑布、薇薔水、波蘿蜜、孩兒茶。其珊瑚、珍珠、乳香諸等貨，皆由甘埋里[169]、佛朗來也。去貨與小唄喃國同。蓄好馬，自西極來，故以舶載至此國。每疋互易，動金錢千百，或至四千為率。否則番人議其國空乏也。

白話文(**Vernacular**)：

當地生產胡椒，次於下里，民間都建有倉庫貯藏。每播荷三百七十五斤，稅收十分之二。次產加張葉、皮桑布、薇

---

[168] 播荷是一種商業上秤重量之單位，每個地方其重量均不同。參見 Willem Pieter Groeneveldt, *op.cit.*, p.88.

A bahar is a commercial unit of weight that varies from place to place. See Willem Pieter Groeneveldt, *op.cit.*, p. 88.

[169] 原文寫為「甘理」，應是「甘埋里」之誤，故改之。

The original text was written as "Gan Li", which should be a mistake of "Gān Mái Lǐ", so I correct it.

薔水、波蘿蜜和孩兒茶。其珊瑚、珍珠、乳香諸等貨，皆由甘埋里和佛朗運來。出口的貨品與小唄喃國相同。該地有好馬，自西極來，故以船載至此國。每匹馬交易，需金錢千百，或至四千。否則番人會譏嘲該國是窮國。

The land produces pepper which is inferior to Xiali. The people store it in warehouses. Each bahar is 375 catties, and the tax is two out of ten. The next products include Kajang leaf (one kind of palm leaf), Pisang cloth, rosewater, jackfruit, and Hái'ér Chá (Baby tea). Its corals, pearls, frankincense, and other goods are all from Gān Mái Lǐ and Fú Lǎng. The goods exported are the same as the Xiǎo Gé Nán. They raise good horses which come from Western countries, so they import the horses to this country to sell to local businessmen. They spend one thousand dollars or even four thousand dollars to buy one horse. Otherwise, the barbarians would sneer at them as a poor country.

84. 朋加剌[170]
84. Péng Jiā Lá (Bengal, Bangladesh)

五嶺崔嵬，樹林拔萃，民環而居之，歲以耕植為業，故野無曠土，田疇極美。一歲凡三收谷，百物皆廉，卽古忻都州府[171]也。氣候常熱，風俗最為淳厚。男女以細布纏頭，穿

---

[170]朋加剌，即孟加拉（Bangladesh）。
　　Péng Jiā Lá is namely Bangladesh.

[171] 忻都州府，是 Hindustan 之音譯，指印度之溫德亞山脈（Vidhya Range）以北區域。見「Hindustan」，古代南海地名匯釋 Part II(H)，南溟網，http://www.world10k.com/blog/?p=2243　2022 年 10 月 5 日瀏覽。
　　The ancient Xīn Dōu Zhōu Fǔ is the transliteration of Hindustan, referring to the area north of the Vidhya Range in India. See "Hindustan", *An*

長衫。官稅以十分中取其二焉。國鑄銀錢，名唐加，每箇錢八分重，流通使用。互易趴子一萬一千五百二十有餘，以權小錢便民，良有益也。

白話文(Vernacular)：

該地有五座高山，樹林拔萃，人民環繞居住，每年以耕植為業，故野外沒有空地，田地極美。一年可收穫稻米三次，百物皆便宜，卽是古代忻都州府也。氣候常熱，風俗最為淳厚。男女以細布包著頭，穿長衫。官方稅率是十分之二。由官方鑄造銀錢，名唐加，每箇錢重八分，流通使用。可以交換趴子一萬一千五百二十有餘，可代替小錢使用，非常便民，很有益處。

This country has five high mountains, and the forests are tall. The people live around it, and they engage in farming. There is no vacant land in the suburbs, and the fields are extremely beautiful. It has three harvests in one year; everything is cheap. Here is namely the ancient Xīn Dōu Zhōu Fǔ (Hindustan). The climate is often hot, and the customs are the most simple and honest. Men and women wrap their heads in fine cloth and wear long gowns. The official tax is to take two out of ten. The country casts silver coins, named Tangjia; each coin weighs eight cents and is used in circulation. Each coin can be exchanged for more than 11,520 Pazi, and it is good and beneficial to use it to facilitate business.

產苾布、高你布、兜羅錦、翠羽。貿易之貨，用南北絲、五色絹緞、丁香、荳蔻、靑白花器、白纓之屬。茲番所以民安物泰，皆自乎農力有以致之。是故原防菅茅之地，民墾闢，種植不倦，不辭[172]勞苦之役，因天之時而分地利，國富俗厚，可以淩舊港而邁闍婆也。

白話文(Vernacular)：

產芯布、高你布、兜羅錦和翠羽。貿易之貨品使用南北絲、五色絹緞、丁香、荳蔻、靑白花器和白纓等。此地的土番所以民安物泰，皆由於農民努力的結果。是故原防止茅草過度生長的土地，人民都加以墾闢，種植不倦，不辭勞苦之努力，因天時地利，國家富有，風俗純厚，可以超過舊港而接近闍婆。

The land produces Bi cloth, Gaoni cloth, Douluo brocade, and Kingfisher feathers. The goods used for trade are north-south silk, five-color silk satin, cloves, cardamom, white flower utensils, and white tassels. The reason why this country is safe and peaceful and rich in products is because of the strength of agriculture. Therefore, the people intended originally to prevent the land from being overgrown with weeds, so they reclaimed it and cultivated it, planted it tirelessly, and worked very hard. They get the right time and place, to make the nation rich and customs upright. This country has already exceeded Jiu Gang and is towards Java.

85. 巴南巴西[173]

---

[172] 原文寫為「〇廉」，故改之。
The original text was written as "〇 Lian", so I correct it.

[173] 藤田豐八認為巴南巴西位在印度西岸 Vanawasi。參見藤田豐八校註，前引書，頁 150。

85. Bā Nán Bāxī

國居大響山之南，環居數十里。土瘠，宜種豆。氣候乍涼。俗尚澆薄。男女體小而形黑，眼圓耳長。手垂過膝。身披絲絨單被。凡民間女子，其形窈窕，自七歲，父母以歌舞教之，身摺疊而圓轉，變態百出，粗有可觀。倘適他國呈其藝術，則予以小錢為賞。

白話文(Vernacular)：

該國位在大響山之南方，人民環居數十里。土地貧瘠，適宜種豆。氣候會突然涼。風俗粗俗。男女體形小而顏色黑，眼圓耳長。雙手垂下過了膝蓋。身披絲絨單被。凡民間女子，其體形嬌媚，自七歲，父母以歌舞教之，身柔可摺彎而圓轉，變化百出，舞姿頗有可觀。倘到他國表演其藝術，則可獲得小錢打賞。

This country is located in the south of Daxiang Mountain, a residential area surrounded by dozens of miles. The fields are barren and suitable for planting beans. The climate is suddenly

---

巴南巴西，今印度卡納塔克邦卡爾瓦爾（Karwar）東南的 Banavāsi，其西岸的霍納瓦（Honavar）即為其國主要港口。參見「巴南巴西」，古代南海地名匯釋，
　http://mall.cnki.net/Reference/ref_search.aspx?bid=R200809105&inputText=%E5%B7%B4%E5%8D%97%E5%B7%B4%E8%A5%BF　　2022年 10 月 19 日瀏覽。

Fujita Toyohachi believed that Bā Nán Bāxī is located in Vanawasi on the west coast of India. See Fujita Toyohachi notes, *op. cit.*, p. 150.

Bā Nán Bāxī is located in Banavāsi, southeast of Karwar, Karnataka, India, and Honavar on its west coast is the country's main port. See "Bā Nán Bāxī", *An Interpretation of Ancient South China Sea Place Names*, http://mall.cnki.net/Reference/ref_search.aspx?bid=R200809105&inputText=%E5%B7%B4%E5%8D%97%E5%B7%B4%E8%A5%BF　　October 19, 2022 retrieved.

cool. The customs are vulgar. Men and women are small and black in shape, with round eyes and long ears. Hands are over knees. The people were covered with a velvet duvet. All folk girls have good posture and were taught by their parents to sing and dance at the age of seven. Their body is soft, rotating freely, and it is quite impressive. If they go to other countries to present their dancing art, they will be rewarded with a small sum of money.

地產細棉布，舶人以錫易之。

白話文(**Vernacular**)：

當地生產細棉布，船人可用錫交換。

The land produces fine cotton cloth, and the boatmen exchange it for tin.

86. 放拜[174]
86. Fàng Bài

居巴隘亂石之間，渡橋出入，周圍無田。平曠皆陸地。宜種麥。氣候常暖。風俗質樸。男女面長，目反白，容黑如漆。編髮為繩，穿斜紋木棉長衫。

白話文(**Vernacular**)：

該地位在巴隘亂石之間，有渡橋出入，周圍無田。平坦空曠皆陸地。適宜種麥。氣候常暖。風俗質樸。男女臉長，

---

[174]放拜是位在印度西岸的孟買（Bambay）。參見藤田豐八校註，前引書，頁 151。

Fàng Bài is located in Bambay on the west coast of India. See Fujita Toyohachi notes, *op. cit.*, p. 151.

眼有反白，容貌黑如漆。編織頭髮做繩子，穿斜紋木棉長衫。

This place is located among the rocks at Bā Ai, there is a bridge for entering and going out, and there are no fields around. The land is all plains. It is suitable for planting wheat. The climate is usually warm. The customs are simple. Men and women have long faces, their eyes are white, and their faces are as black as lacquer. They braid their hair as a rope and wear a twill kapok gown.

煮海為鹽，煅鵝卵石為炭以代炊。有酋長。地產絕細布匹，闊七尺長有餘。大檳榔為諸番之冠。貨用金、貼子、紅白燒珠之屬。

白話文(**Vernacular**)：

煮海水製鹽，煅燒鵝卵石為炭，用來炊煮。有酋長。當地生產絕細布匹，闊七尺長有餘。大檳榔為諸番之冠。貨品使用金、貼子和紅白燒珠等。

The people boil the sea for salt and burn pebbles for charcoal to cook. There is a chief. The land produces extremely fine cloth, more than seven feet wide. The big betel nut is the best one among the various countries. The goods used for trade are gold, Pazi, and red and white burnt beads.

87. 大烏爹[175]

---

[175] 大烏爹，在今印度拉賈斯坦邦之烏代普爾（Udeypur, Udeyapur,），或中央邦之烏闍衍那（Ujayana）。參見藤田豐八校註，前引書，頁152-153。

　　Dà Wū Diē is located in Udeypur (Udeyapur) in Rajasthan, India, or Ujayana in Madhya Pradesh. See Fujita Toyohachi notes, *op. cit.*, pp.152-153.

87. Dà Wū Diē

國近巴南之地，界西洋之中峯，山多鹵股，田雜沙土。有黑歲，宜種豆。氣候常熱。俗尚淳。男女身修長。女生髭，穿細布，繫紅絹捎。女善戰，使標鎗，批竹矢毒於蛇，使國人極畏之。仍以金錢、魚兼䏧子使用。

白話文(Vernacular)：

該國接近巴南之地，位在靠近西洋之中峯，山多鹵股石，田雜沙土。有荒年，宜種豆。氣候常熱。風俗樸實。男女身體修長。女生嘴上長鬍鬚，穿細布，繫紅絹巾。女善戰，會使用標鎗，用有毒的竹矢刺殺蛇，使國人極畏之。仍使用金錢、魚以及䏧子。

This country is near Banan, bounded by the middle peak of the West Ocean. The mountains are full of halogen stones, and the fields are mixed with sandy soil. There is a famine. It is suitable for planting beans. The climate is always hot. The customs are pure. Men and women are slender. Girls wear mustaches and wear muslin cloth, tied with red silk towel. Women are good at fighting, use javelins, and poison bamboo arrows at snakes, which makes the people of the country fear them. The people are still using money, fish, and Pazi to do business.

煮海為鹽，以逡巡法釀酒。有酋長。地產布匹、貓兒眼睛、鴉鶻石、翠羽。貿易之貨，用白銅、鼓板、五色緞、金、銀、鐵器之屬。國以䏧子、金錢流通使用，所以便民也。成周[176]之世，用錢幣，漢武造皮[177]幣[178]，鑄白銀，無非子母相權而已。如西洋諸番國，鑄為大小金錢使用，與中國銅錢異。雖無其幣以兼之，得非法古之道者哉！

白話文**(Vernacular)**：

煮海水製鹽，以緩慢的方法釀酒。有酋長。當地生產布匹、貓兒眼睛、鴉鶻石和翠羽。貿易之貨品使用白銅、鼓板、五色緞、金、銀和鐵器等。該國流通使用𧴩子和金錢，所以便民也。成周之世，用錢幣，漢武造皮幣，鑄白銀，無非是讓兩種錢幣交互使用。如西洋諸番國，鑄造大小金錢使用，與中國銅錢有所不同。雖然我們沒有同時兼用其他錢幣，我們並無效法古法之道理！

The people boil the sea for salt and make wine with a slow method. There is a chief. The land produces cloth, cat's eyes (a

---

[176] 成周，為周武王在河南洛陽興建之首都名稱，於周成王 5 年（西元前 1038 年）完成。見「成周」，百度百科，
https://baike.baidu.hk/item/%E6%88%90%E5%91%A8/1860379
2022 年 10 月 6 日瀏覽。

   Chengzhou is the name of the capital built by King Wu of Zhou in Luoyang, Henan. It was completed in the 5th year of King Cheng of Zhou (1038 BC). See "Cheng Zhou", *Baidu Encyclopedia*,
https://baike.baidu.hk/item/%E6%88%90%E5%91%A8/1860379
October 6, 2022 retrieved.

[177] 原文寫為「史」，故改之。
The original text was written as "history", so I correct it.

[178] 白鹿皮幣是西漢武帝元狩四年（前 119 年）發行的貨幣。見「白鹿皮幣」，百科知識，
https://www.easyatm.com.tw/wiki/%E7%99%BD%E9%B9%BF%E7%9A%AE%E5%B9%A3   2022 年 10 月 6 日瀏覽。

   The white deerskin money was issued in the fourth year of Yuanshou (119 B.C.), Emperor Wu of the Western Han Dynasty. See "White Deer Skin Money", *Encyclopedia Knowledge*,
https://www.easyatm.com.tw/wiki/%E7%99%BD%E9%B9%BF%E7%9A%AE%E5%B9%A3   October 6, 2022 retrieved.

gem), crow's stone, and Kingfisher feathers. The goods used for trade are white copper, drum board, five-color satin, gold, silver, and iron utensils. The people use Pazi and money to do business, so it is convenient for the people. In the era of Chengzhou, they used coins, Emperor Hanwu made leather coins and cast silver money. It is nothing more than allowing two kinds of money to be used interactively. For example, in the West Ocean countries, they cast large and small pieces of money for use, which is different from Chinese copper coins. Although we did not use other coins at the same time, we did not follow the principles of ancient methods!

88. 萬年港[179]
88. Wànnián Port

　　凌門正灣為之引從，彷彿相望。中有長闊二十餘丈，其深無底，魚龍之淵藪也。旁有山，如氐環而居。田寬地窄，宜穀、麥，氣候常熱。俗朴。男女椎髻，繫青布捎。

　　白話文(Vernacular)：

　　凌門前面的海灣可作為引導，二者彷彿相望。中間有長闊二十餘丈，其深無底，魚龍居住的深淵。旁有山，有像氐的少數民族環繞居住。田地寬廣，但地呈狹長，適宜種穀和麥，氣候常熱。風俗純樸。男女椎髻，繫青布巾。

　　Along the bay in front of Lingmen, you can reach Wannian

---

[179] 藤田豐八認為萬年港可能為汶萊港，但未可確定。參見藤田豐八校註，前引書，頁153。

　　Fujita Toyohachi thought that Wannian Port may be Brunei Port, but it is uncertain. See Fujita Toyohachi notes, *op. cit*., p. 153.

Port, and from Lingmen go to Wànnián Port, both face each other. This bay is more than twenty feet long and wide, and its depth is bottomless. It is the abyss of fish and dragons. There are mountains next to it. There are ethnic minorities like Di living around it. The fields are wide but less suitable for planting grain and wheat. The climate is often hot. The customs are vulgar. Men and women wear a bun on their heads and tie a green cloth towel on their heads.

煮海為鹽，釀蔗漿為酒。有酋長。地產降眞條、木棉、黃蠟。貿易之貨，用鐵條、銅線、土印花布、瓦瓶之屬。

白話文(Vernacular)：

煮海水製鹽，釀蔗漿製酒。有酋長。當地生產降眞條香、木棉和黃蠟。貿易之貨品使用鐵條、銅線、土印花布和瓦瓶等。

The people boil the sea for salt and brew sugarcane pulp for wine. There is a chief. The land produces Jiangzhen incense, kapok, and yellow wax. The goods which are used for trade are iron bars, copper wires, locally printed cloth, and earthenware vases.

89. 馬八兒嶼[180]

---

[180] 藤田豐八認為馬八兒為 Ma'bar。（參見藤田豐八校註，前引書，頁 155。）按 Ma'bar 一詞有兩個意思，一指印度東南岸淡米爾納德（Tamil Nadu）邦之海岸；二指馬都賴蘇丹國（Madurai Sultanate），該國於 1335-1378 年在淡米爾納德邦成立的獨立國家。參見 "Ma'bar Coast," *Wikipedia*, https://en.wikipedia.org/wiki/Ma%27bar_Coast ; "Madurai Sultanate," *Wikipedia*, https://en.wikipedia.org/wiki/Madurai_Sultanate 2022 年 10 月 19 日瀏覽。

89. Ma'abar Yǔ (Ma'abar Island)

控西北之隅，居加將門里[181]之右，瀕山而民。土鹹，田沃饒，歲倍收。氣候熱，俗淫。男女散髮，以椰葉蔽羞。不事緝織。鑿井煮海為鹽，釀椰漿為酒。無酋長。

白話文(Vernacular)：

該地扼控西北之角落，位在加將門里之右方，老百姓住在鄰近山區的地方。土鹹，田地沃饒，每年收成約兩倍多。氣候熱，風俗淫穢。男女散髮，以椰葉遮蔽私處。不事編織。鑿井、煮海水製鹽，釀椰漿製酒。無酋長。

This country controls the corner of the northwest, and it is located on the right of Jiā Jiàngmén Lǐ. The people live close to the mountains. The soil is salty, the fields are fertile, and the harvests are double. The climate is hot. The customs are licentious. Men and women tousled their hair, and use coconut leaves to cover their bodies. They don't engage in weaving. They

---

蘇繼卿認為馬八兒位在印度東岸的注輦海岸（Coromandel coast）。參見蘇繼卿，前引書，頁 215。

Fujita Toyohachi believed that Mabar is Ma'bar. (See Fujita Toyohachi note, *op. cit.*, p. 155.) According the word Ma'bar, there are two meanings. One refers to the coast of the state of Tamil Nadu on the southeastern coast of India; the other refers to the Sultanate of Madurai (Madurai Sultanate), an independent state established in Tamil Nadu from 1335 to 1378. See "Ma'bar Coast," *Wikipedia*,
 https://en.wikipedia.org/wiki/Ma%27bar_Coast ; "Madurai Sultanate," *Wikipedia*, https://en.wikipedia.org/wiki/Madurai_Sultanate October 19, 2022 retrieved.

Su Jiqing believed that Ma'bar is located on the Coromandel Coast on the east coast of India. See Su Jiqing, *op. cit.*, p. 215.

[181] 加將門，應是加將門里，原文漏了「里」字，故補加上。

Jiā Jiàngmén should be Jiā Jiàngmén Lǐ. The original text omitted the word "li", so I add it.

drill a well and boil the sea for salt, and brew coconut milk for wine. There is no chief.

地產翠羽、細布，大羊百有餘斤。穀米價廉。貿易之貨，用沙金、青緞、白礬、紅綠烧珠之屬。

白話文(Vernacular)：

當地生產翠羽、細布，大羊百有餘斤。穀米價廉。貿易之貨品使用沙金、青緞、白礬和紅綠烧珠等。

The land produces Kingfisher feathers and fine cloth, and the sheep weigh more than 100 kilograms. Rice is cheap. The goods used for trade are sand gold, green satin, alum, and red and green beads.

次曰拔忽，曰里達那，曰骨里傍，曰安其，曰伽忽，皆屬此國之節制焉。

白話文(Vernacular)：

其他地名有拔忽、里達那、骨里傍、安其、伽忽，皆由該國管轄。

It also is called Bahu, called Lidana, called Gǔ Lǐ Bàng, called Anqi, and called Jiahu, all of which belong to the jurisdiction of this country.

90. 阿思里[182]
90. Ā Sī Lǐ

---

[182]阿思里，位在埃及紅海西岸的柯色爾（Quseir, Kosseir）。參見蘇繼卿，前引書，頁197。

Ā Sī Lǐ is located in Quseir (Kosseir) on the west coast of the Red Sea in Egypt. See Su Jiqing, *op. cit.*, p. 197.

極西南達國里[183]之地，無山林之限，風起則飛沙撲面，人不敢行。居人編竹以蔽之。氣候熱，半年之間多不見雨。掘井而飲，深至二、三百丈，[184]味甘而美。其地防原[185]，宜種麥，或潮水至原下，則其地上潤，麥苗自秀。

白話文(Vernacular)：

該國最西南邊到達國里之地方，無山和林，刮風就飛沙撲面，人不敢行走。居民編竹來檔風沙。氣候熱，半年之間多不見雨。掘井而飲，深至二、三百丈，味甘而美。沿岸隆起的土地高於潮水，適宜種麥，或潮水只到岸邊高地以下，地上是濕潤的，麥苗長得很好。

Its extreme southwest reaches the country of Guó Lǐ, and there are no mountains or forests. When the wind blows, the sand blows on the face, and people dare not walk. Residents weave bamboo to protect against wind and sand. The climate is hot, and there is no rain for more than half a year. They have dug a well down to a depth of two or three hundred zhang. The well water tastes sweet. The land is uplifted and suitable for planting wheat. The uplifted land along the coast is higher than the tidewater,

---

[183] 蘇繼卿認為國里是指埃及。(參見蘇繼卿，前引書，頁 197。)不過柯色爾之西南方向應是埃及、蘇丹和利比亞交會之處。

Su Jiqing believed that Guó Lǐ refers to Egypt. (See Su Jiqing, *op. cit.*, p. 197.) However, to the southwest of Quseir should be where Egypt, Sudan, and Libya meet.

[184] 1 丈約等於 3.33 公尺。因此說井深 200-300 丈的說法是不可靠的。

One zhang is equal to 3.33 meters. So it is unreliable to say that the well is 200 -300 zhang deep.

[185] 蘇繼卿認為「防原」，指的是隆起之地。參見蘇繼卿，前引書，頁 197。

Su Jiqing believed that "Fáng Yuán" refers to the uplifted land. See Su Jiqing, *op. cit.*, p. 197.

which is suitable for growing wheat, or the tidewater is only below the highland on the bank, the ground is moist, and the wheat seedlings grow well.

俗惡。男女編髮，以牛毛為繩，接髮捎至齊膝為奇。以鳥羽為衣，搗麥作餅為食。民不善煮海為鹽。地產大棉布、小布匹。貿易之貨，用銀、鐵器、靑燒珠之屬。

白話文(Vernacular)：

風俗粗俗。男女留辮子髮，以牛毛編織成繩子，把它綁在頭髮末稍一直到膝蓋，很是奇怪。以鳥羽為衣，搗麥作餅食用。人民不善煮海水製鹽。當地生產大棉布和小布匹。貿易之貨品使用銀、鐵器和靑燒珠等。

The customs are vulgar. Men and women have braided hair, braided with ox hair into a rope, and tied it from the end of the hair to the knee, which is very strange. They use bird feathers for clothing and pound wheat for cake food. The people are not good at boiling the sea for salt. The land produces large cotton cloth and small cloth. The goods which are used for trade are silver, iron utensils, and green burnt beads.

91. 哩伽塔[186]
91. Licata

---

[186]蘇繼卿不認為哩伽塔位在地中海內，而是指阿丹，即亞丁。（蘇繼卿，前引書，頁 275。）筆者查閱地圖，在義大利西西里島南邊確有 Licata 港地名，而國王海應是指地中海，故以此解之。

Su Jiqing did not think that Licata was located in the Mediterranean Sea, but referred to Aden. (Su Jiqing, *op. cit*, p. 275.) But I checked the map and found that there is indeed the name of the port of Licata to the south of Sicily, Italy and the King Sea should refer to the Mediterranean Sea.

國居遼西[187]之界，乃國王海[188]之濱。田瘠，宜種黍。民疊板石為居。掘地丈有餘深，以藏種子，雖三載亦不朽也。氣候秋熱而夏涼。俗尚朴。男女瘦長，其形古怪，髮長二寸而不見長。穿布桶衣，繫皂布捎。

白話文**(Vernacular)**：

該國位在遼西之邊界，乃國王海之海濱。田地貧瘠，宜種黍。人民疊板石居住。掘地丈有餘深，以藏種子，雖經過三年也不朽壞。氣候秋熱而夏涼。風俗純樸。男女身高瘦長，樣子很古怪，髮長二寸就不再長大。穿布桶衣，繫皂布巾。

This country is located on the border of Liáoxī, and it is on the coast of the King Sea. The fields are barren and suitable for planting millet. The people stack slabs for their homes. Dig the ground to a depth of more than one zhang, to hide the seeds which will not be damaged for three years. The climate is hot in autumn and cool in summer. The customs are simple. Men and women are slender, their shape is strange, and their hair is two inches long, it won't grow any longer. The people wear bucket clothes and tie them with black cloth towel.

煮海為鹽，釀黍為酒，以牛乳為食。地產青琅玕、珊瑚樹，其樹或長一丈有餘，或七、八尺許，圍一尺有餘。秋冬民間皆用船採取，以橫木繫破網及紗線於其上，仍以索縛木

---

[187] 遼西，指遼河以西的地區，泛指西域或極遠之地。

　　Liáoxī refers to the area west of the Liaohe River, generally referring to the Western Regions or extremely far places.

[188] 國王海，應是指地中海。

　　The King Sea should refer to the Mediterranean Sea.

兩頭，人於船上牽以拖之，則其樹槎牙，掛挽而上。貿易之貨，用金、銀、五色緞、巫崙布之屬。

　　白話文(Vernacular)：

　　煮海水製鹽，釀黍製酒，以牛乳為食。當地生產青琅玕、珊瑚樹，其樹或長一丈有餘，或七、八尺許，圍一尺有餘。秋冬民間皆用船採取，在橫木上面綁著破網及紗線，仍以繩索綁木兩頭，人在船上牽引，則其樹枝掛在網上被拖上來。貿易之貨品使用金、銀、五色緞和巫崙布等。

The people boil the sea for salt and brew millet for wine and eat milk. The land produces green jade and the coral tree which may be more than one zhang long, or seven or eight feet long, with a circumference of more than one foot. In autumn and winter, the people use boats to take them. A broken net and yarn are tied to the cross wood, and the two ends of the wood are still tied with ropes. When people on a boat pulled the wood, the coral branches are hung on the net and dragged up. The goods used for trade are gold, silver, five-color satin, and Wu Lun cloth.

92. 天堂[189]
92. Tiāntáng

　　地多曠漠，卽古筠沖[190]之地，又名為西域。風景融和，

---

[189]藤田豐八認為天堂，又作天房，今沙烏地阿拉伯的麥加（Mecca）。參見藤田豐八校註，前引書，頁155。

　　Fujita Toyohachi thought that Tiāntáng, also written as Tiān Fáng, is located in Mecca in Saudi Arabia. See Fujita Toyohachi notes, *op. cit.*, p. 155.

[190] 明史·西域傳四·天方：「天方，古筠沖地，一名天堂，又曰默伽。」默伽，今譯為麥加，是回教的聖城。

四時之春也。田沃稻饒，居民樂業。雲南有路可通，一年之上可至其地。西洋亦有路通。名為天堂。有回回厤(曆)，與中國授時厤(曆)前後只[191]爭三日，其選日永無差異。

白話文(**Vernacular**)：

該地多是空曠的沙漠，即古代筠沖之地方，又名為西域。風景和諧，如同四時之春天。田地肥沃，稻作豐饒，居民樂業。雲南有路可通，一年以上可至其地。西洋亦有路通。名為天堂。有回教厤(曆)，與中國授時厤(曆)相較前後只差三日，其選的吉日永無差異。

This land is vast and deserted, namely the ancient Yún Chōng, also known as the Western Regions. The scenery is harmonious as it is spring for the four seasons. The fields are fertile, the rice is plentiful, and the residents are happy. Yunnan has a road to go there with the trip lasting more than one year. There are also roads to go there from the West Ocean. This city is called heaven. They use the Hijri calendar which is only three days away from China's Time calendar, but choosing auspicious days makes no difference.

氣候暖，風俗好善。男女辮髮，穿細布長[192]衫，繫細布捎。地產西馬，高八尺許。人多以馬乳拌飯為食，則人肥美。貿易之貨，用銀、五色緞、青白花器、鐵鼎之屬。

In the Western Regions Biography Four, Tianfang, *Ming History*, records: "Tianfang was the place of Yún Chōng in the ancient times. It is also called Tiāntáng, also known as "Maka". "Maka", now translated as Mecca, and is the holy city of Islam.

[191] 原文寫為「至」，故改之。

The original text was written as "to", so I correct it.

[192]原文寫為「布」，故改之。

The original text was written as "cloth", so I correct it.

白話文(**Vernacular**)：

氣候暖，風俗好友善。男女辮髮，穿細布長衫，繫細布巾。當地生產西馬，高八尺許。人多以馬乳拌飯食用，則人長得肥美。貿易之貨品使用銀、五色緞、青白花器和鐵鼎等。

The climate is warm, and the customs are fond of friendliness. Men and women braid their hair, wear muslin gowns, and tie them with muslin towel. The land produces west horses, eight feet high. People mostly eat horse milk bibimbap, so they are fat. The goods used for trade are silver, five-color satin, green and white flower utensils, and iron tripods.

93. 天竺[193]

93. Tiānzhú (Hindu, India)

居大食之東，隸秦[194]王之主。去海二百餘里。地平沃。氣候不齊。俗尚古風。男女身長七尺，小目長項。手帕繫額，編髮垂耳，穿百結衣，以藤皮織鞋，以棉紗結襪，仍將穿之，示其執禮也。

白話文(**Vernacular**)：

---

[193] 藤田豐八認為天竺位在西印度的信度（Sind）。（參見藤田豐八校註，前引書，頁 161。）信度是位在巴基斯坦東南部，與印度的古吉拉特邦接壤。

　　Fujita Toyohachi believed that Tianzhu is located in Sind of West India. (See Fujita Toyohachi note, *op. cit.*, p. 161.) Sind is located in southeastern Pakistan, bordering the Indian state of Gujarat.

[194] 秦，指大秦國。「秦」是中國在西元第 1 世紀對東羅馬帝國的稱呼，汪大淵寫作本書時是第 14 世紀，使用該詞有點奇怪。

　　Qin refers to the Great Qin State. "Qin" was the Chinese name for the Eastern Roman Empire in the 1st century AD, and Wang Da-yuan was in the 14th century when he wrote this book, so it's a bit odd to use that word.

位在大食之東方，隸屬大秦國王之領主。距離大海二百餘里。土地平坦肥沃。氣候不穩定。俗尚古風。男女身長七尺，小眼睛，長脖子。手帕繫在額頭，編辮子髮垂到耳朵，穿補綴很多的衣服，以藤皮織鞋，以棉紗結襪，他們穿襪子，示其重禮節也。

This country is located in the east of Dashi and belongs to the lord established by the King of Ta-tsin. It is distant from the sea more than two hundred miles. The land is flat and fertile. The climate is unstable. The customs are fond of the old fashion. Men and women are seven feet tall, with small eyes and long necks. A handkerchief is tied around their forehead, their hair is braided and their ears are drooped. The people wear patched clothes and knit shoes with rattan skin. They knit socks with cotton yarn and wear socks as a courtesy.

不善煮海為鹽，食仰他國。民間以金錢流通使用。有酋長。地產沙金[195]、駿馬。貿易之貨，用銀、青白花器、斗錫、酒、色印布之屬。

白話文(Vernacular)：
不善於煮海水製鹽，糧食仰賴他國進口。民間以金錢流通使用。有酋長。當地生產沙金、駿馬。貿易之貨品使用銀、青白花器、斗錫、酒和色印布等。

The people are not good at boiling the sea for salt and depend on other countries for food. People use the money to circulate. There is a chief. The land produces sand gold and

---

[195]原文寫為「金沙」，故改之。

The original text was written as "Jinsha", so I correct it.

horses. The goods for trade used silver, green and white flower utensils, natural tin nuggets, wine, and colored printed cloth.

94. 層搖羅[196]
94. Céng Yáo Luó

　　國居大食之西南，崖無林，地多淳，田瘠谷少，故多種薯以代糧食。每貨販於其地者，若有穀米與之交易，其利甚溥。氣候不齊，俗古直。男女挽髮，穿無縫短裙。民事網罟，取禽獸為食。

　　白話文(**Vernacular**)：

　　該國位在大食之西南方，有山崖但無林，地景單純，田

---

[196] 藤田豐八認為層搖羅位在馬達加斯加島（Madagascar）。參見藤田豐八校註，前引書，頁 162。

　　Anshan Li 認為層搖羅位在坦尚尼亞的 Kilwa Kisiwani。參見 Anshan Li , *A History of Overseas Chinese in Africa to 1911*, Diasporic Africa Press, New York, 2017, p.33.

　　https://books.google.com.tw/books?id=Xuq7QCmY6jQC&pg=PR5&lpg=PR5&dq=asli,Anshan+Li&source=bl&ots=6OpVBqihdP&sig=ACfU3U1vOjLn2KGD6gAmvzWuwedTzClVdg&hl=zh-TW&sa=X&ved=2ahUKEwi70NPx493nAhXBLqYKHT23AssQ6AEwAXoECAkQAQ#v=onepage&q=asli%2CAnshan%20Li&f=false　2022 年 10 月 19 日瀏覽。

　　Fujita Toyohachi believed that Céng Yáo Luó is located in Madagascar. See Fujita Toyohachi notes, *op. cit.*, p. 162.

　　Anshan Li thought that Céng Yáo Luó is located in Kilwa Kisiwani in Tanzania. See Anshan Li, *A History of Overseas Chinese in Africa to 1911*, Diasporic Africa Press, New York, 2017, p.33.

　　https://books.google.com.tw/books?id=Xuq7QCmY6jQC&pg=PR5&lpg=PR5&dq=asli,Anshan+Li&source=bl&ots=6OpVBqihdP&sig=ACfU3U1vOjLn2KGD6gAmvzWuwedTzClVdg&hl=zh-TW&sa=X&ved=2ahUKEwi70NPx493nAhXBLqYKHT23AssQ6AEwAXoECAkQAQ#v=onepage&q=asli%2CAnshan%20Li&f=false October 19, 2022 retrieved.

地貧瘠，穀物少，故多種蕃薯以代替糧食。每有貨物賣至該地，若有穀米與之交易，其利潤甚大。氣候不穩定，風俗樸實。男女將頭髮盤在頭上，穿無縫短裙。人民從事以魚網捕魚，捕禽獸食用。

This country is located in the southwest of Dashi, there are cliffs but no forests, the land is a monotonous landscape, and the fields are barren and have few grains, so many sweet potatoes are planted to replace grains. If businessmen transport grains and rice to trade with them, it will be very profitable. The climate is unstable. The customs are vulgar and simple. Men and women tie up their hair and wear seamless short skirts. The people are engaged in fishing with nets and taking animals for food.

煮海為鹽，釀蔗漿為酒。有酋長。地產紅檀、紫蔗、象齒、龍涎香[197]、生金、鴨嘴膽礬。貿易之貨，用牙箱、花銀、五色緞之屬。

白話文(Vernacular)：

煮海水製鹽，釀蔗漿製酒。有酋長。當地生產紅檀、紫蔗、象齒、龍涎香、生金和鴨嘴膽礬。貿易之貨品使用牙箱、

---

[197] 原文無「香」字，故加之。龍涎香之主要功效是開竅化痰，活血利氣，主治神昏氣悶，心腹諸痛，消散癥結，咳喘氣逆。參見「龍涎香」，醫學百科，

　http://cht.a-hospital.com/w/%E9%BE%99%E6%B6%8E%E9%A6%99
2022 年 10 月 19 日瀏覽。

　The original text does not have the word "fragrance", so I add it. The main effect of ambergris is to open the orifices and resolve phlegm, promote blood circulation and invigorate qi, treat dizziness and suffocation, pain in the confidants, and dissipate the symptoms, cough, and dyspnea. See "Ambergris", *Medical Encyclopedia*,

　http://cht.a-hospital.com/w/%E9%BE%99%E6%B6%8E%E9%A6%99
October 19, 2022 retrieved.

花銀和五色緞等。

The people boil the sea for salt and brew sugarcane pulp for wine. There is a chief. The land produces red sandalwood, purple sugar cane, ivory, ambergris, raw gold, and duck-billed alum. The goods used for trade are silver ingots, flower silver, and five-color satin.

95. 馬魯澗[198]
95. Mǎ Lǔ Jiàn

國與遐邇沙喃之後山接壤，民樂業而富。週[199]迴廣一萬八千餘里。西洋國悉臣屬焉。有酋長。元臨漳人，陳其姓也。幼能讀書，長練兵事。國初領兵鎮甘州，遂入此國討境不復返。

白話文(Vernacular)：

該國與遠近有名的沙喃之後山接壤，人民樂業而富有。它的周圍廣一萬八千餘里。西洋各國都臣屬於他。有酋長。元臨漳人，陳姓幼能讀書，長練兵事。元國開國初領兵鎮守甘州，遂入此國征討，以後就沒有回國了。

This country is bordered by the back hill behind the well-known Shanan, and the people are happy and prosperous. The

---

[198] 蘇繼卿認為馬魯澗為伊朗的 Maragha 或 Maragak。（參見蘇繼卿，前引書，頁 62。）因為 Maragha 位在伊朗西北部山區，其位置仍有待研究。

Su Jiqing thought that Mǎ Lǔ Jiàn was the Maragha or Maragak of Iran. (See Su Jiqing, *op. cit.*, p. 62.) Because Maragha is located in the mountains of northwestern Iran, its location still needs to do further study.

[199] 原文寫為「遮」，故改之。

The original text was written as "covered", so I correct it.

wide size of the country is more than 18,000 li. The countries of the West Ocean are all vassals. There is a chief. The Linzhang people from the Yuan Dynasty, surnamed Chen, can read, and get long military training. At the beginning of the Yuan Dynasty, they led troops to stay at Ganzhou, and then entered this country to fight but never returned.

茲地產馬，故多馬軍。動侵番國以兵凡若干萬。歲以正月三日則建高壇以受兵賀。所至之地，卽成聚落一所。民間互易，而卒無擾攘之患。蓋以刑法之重如此。觀其威逼諸番，嚴行賞罰，亦豪酋中之表表者乎！

白話文(Vernacular)：

該地產馬，故多馬軍。它常率軍一萬多人侵略各番國。每年在正月三日建高壇閱兵受慶賀。所至之地，卽成聚落一所。民間互相貿易，而沒有紛亂之危險。因為它的刑法處罰很重。觀察它之所以能威逼諸番，嚴行賞罰，亦是豪酋中之最傑出者！

The land produces horses, so there are many horse troops. They invade the neighboring country with tens of thousands of soldiers. On the third day of the first lunar month, a high altar was built to receive congratulations from soldiers. Wherever they went, that place became a settlement. There is mutual exchange among the people, and there is no danger of disturbance. That is because they practice strict criminal law. Watching this coercion and strict enforcement of rewards and punishments, there must also be an outstanding chief!

96. 甘埋里[200]
96. Gān Mái Lǐ

　　國居西南馮之地，與佛朗相近。乘風張帆二月可至小唄喃。其地造舟為馬船，大於商舶，不使釘灰，用椰索板成片。每舶二三層，用板棧，滲漏不勝，梢人日夜輪戽水不竭。下以乳香壓重，上載馬數百匹，頭小尾輕，鹿身吊肚，四蹄削

---

[200] 藤田豐八認為甘埋里位在荷姆茲。參見藤田豐八校註，前引書，頁165。

Rockhill 認為甘埋里位在於非洲東南海岸莫三比克東部與馬達加斯加西南部上的一座火山群島葛摩洛（Comoro）群島。（W. W. Rockhill, "Notes on the Relations and Trade of China with the Archipelago and the Coasts of the Indian Ocean during the Fourteenth Century", *T'oung Pao* 15 (1914), pp. 419-447, and 16 (1915), pp. 61-159, 236-271, 374-392, 435-467, 604-626.）

但蘇繼卿則認為是位在荷姆茲（Hormuz）。（Su Jieqin, "Zhongguo he Yilang lishi shang de youhao guanxi," *Lishi Yanjiu*, No.7, 1978, pp. 72-82.）

Kauz Ralph 和 Ptak Roderich 認為甘埋里就是荷姆茲。（Kauz Ralph, Ptak Roderich, "Hormuz in Yuan and Ming sources," *Bulletin de l'Ecole française d'Extrême-Orient*, Tome 88, 2001, pp. 27-75, p. 39.
https://www.persee.fr/doc/befeo_0336-1519_2001_num_88_1_3509
2022 年 10 月 11 日瀏覽。）

　　Fujita Toyohachi believed that Gān Mái Lǐ is located in Homuz. See Fujita Toyohachi notes, *op. cit.*, p. 165.

　　Rockhill believed that Gān Mái Lǐ is located in the Comoro Archipelago, a volcanic archipelago on the southeastern coast of Africa to eastern Mozambique and southwestern Madagascar. See W. W. Rockhill, "Notes on the Relations and Trade of China with the Archipelago and the Coasts of the Indian Ocean during the Fourteenth Century", *T'oung Pao* 15 (1914), pp. 419-447, and 16(1915), pp. 61-159, 236-271, 374-392, 435-467, 604-626.

　　Kauz Ralph and Ptak Roderich believed that Gambiri is Hormuz. See Kauz Ralph, Ptak Roderich, "Hormuz in Yuan and Ming sources," *Bulletin de l'Ecole française d'Extrême-Orient*, Tome 88, 2001, pp. 27-75, p.39.
https://www.persee.fr/doc/befeo_0336-1519_2001_num_88_1_3509
October 11, 2022 retrieved.

鐵，高七尺許，日夜可行千里。

白話文(**Vernacular**)：

該國位在西南馮之地，與佛朗相近。乘風張帆二月可至小唄喃。該地造的船稱為馬船，大於商船，不使用釘和灰，用椰索板成片。每船有二、三層，用板棧，會有滲漏，因此需請人日夜用勺子將水舀出。船隻下層以乳香壓重，上載馬數百匹，頭小尾輕，鹿身大肚，四蹄釘了鐵蹄，高七尺許，日夜可行千里。

This country is located in the southwest of Feng, which is close to Fú Lǎng. A ship riding the wind with open sail can reach Xiǎo Gé Nán in two months. The boats built here are called horse boats, which are larger than commercial boats; they do not use nails and stucco, but use coconut rope to tie the pieces of boards together. Each ship has two or three decks, because of using wood splicing, leaks are inevitable. They have to have people drain out the water with scoops day and night. The bottom is heavy with frankincense, and there are hundreds of horses on it. The head of the horse is small and the tail is light, looks like a deer's body, and has a big abdomen. The horse, nailing four iron horseshoes on its heels, stands seven feet tall and can travel thousands of miles day and night.

所有木香、琥珀之類，均產自佛朗國來，商販於西洋互易。去貨丁香、荳蔻、青緞、麝香、紅色燒珠、蘇杭色緞、蘇木、青白花器、瓷瓶、鐵條，以胡椒載而返。椒之所以貴者，皆因此船運去尤多，較商舶之取，十不及其一焉。

白話文(**Vernacular**)：

所有木香、琥珀之類，均產自佛朗國運來，商人在西洋各地互易商品。賣去的貨有丁香、荳蔻、青緞、麝香、紅色燒珠、蘇杭色緞、蘇木、青白花器、瓷瓶和鐵條等，而將胡椒運回來。胡椒之所以貴，皆因為船運出去賣很多，但商船買回胡椒之數量卻不及其十分之一。

All wood incense, amber, etc., are produced in Fú Lǎng, and merchants trade it in the West Ocean. They export cloves, cardamom, green satin, musk, red burnt beads, Suzhou and Hangzhou satin, Biancaea sappan, green and white flower utensils, porcelain vases, iron bars, and carry pepper back. The reason why peppers are expensive is that many goods are exported by boat, but ten boats are less than the price of one ship's pepper.

97. 麻呵斯離[201]
97. Má Hē Sī Lí

去大食國八千餘里，與鯨板奴[202]國相近。由海通溪，約

---

[201] 麻呵斯離，又作勿斯離，今伊拉克西北部摩蘇爾（Mosur, Mosul）。參見藤田豐八校註，前引書，頁166。

Má Hē Sī Lí, also written as Wù sī lí, is now Mosur (Mosul) in northwestern Iraq. See Fujita Toyohachi notes, *op. cit.*, p. 166.

[202] 鯨板奴，則為 Kbara 之對音。Kbara 亦作 Okbara，古城名，在今伊拉克巴格達北百餘里，此城在摩蘇爾下游底格里斯河東岸，久已荒廢。參見「Okbara」，南溪網，

http://www.world10k.com/blog/index.php?s=%E9%AF%A8%E6%9D%BF%E5%A5%B4%E5%9C%8B 2022年10月17日瀏覽。

但筆者查相關資料，Kbara 可能是誤寫，應該是 Kuara，它位在巴格達以南百餘里，早期是通往波斯灣的重要港口。參見 "Kuara (Sumer)," *Wikipedia*, https://en.wikipedia.org/wiki/Kuara_(Sumer) 2022年10月21日瀏覽。

Jīng Bǎn Nú is the opposite sound of Kbara which is also known as

二百餘里。石道崎嶇，至官場三百餘里。地平如席。氣候應節。風俗鄙儉。男女編髮，眼如銅鈴。穿長衫。

白話文(**Vernacular**)：

從此地到大食國有八千餘里，與鯨板奴國很近。由海溯河流而上，約二百餘里。石道崎嶇，至官署有三百餘里。土地平坦像草席。氣候符合節序。風俗鄙儉。男女編辮子髮，眼如銅鈴。穿長衫。

This country is distant from Dashi more than 8,000 miles and close to the Jīng Bǎn Nú Guó. From the sea to the river, it is about 200 miles. The stone road is rugged, reaching the officialdom about more than 300 miles. The land is as flat as a straw mat. The climate is in correspondence with seasonal change. The customs are frugal. Men and women braid their hair, and their eyes are like copper bells. They wear long shirts.

煮海為鹽，釀荖葉為酒。有酋長。地產青鹽、馬乳、葡萄、米、麥。其麥粒長半寸許。甘露每歲八九月下，民間築淨池以承之，旭日曝則融結如水，味甚糖霜。仍以瓷器貯之，調湯而飲，以辟瘴癘。古云：「甘露王如來即其地也。」貿易之貨，用剌速斯離布、紫金、白銅、青琅玕、闍婆布之屬。

Okbara and is the name of the ancient city. It is more than a hundred miles north of Baghdad, Iraq. This city is on the east bank of the Tigris River downstream of Mosul and has been abandoned for a long time. See "Okbara," *Nanming Net*,

http://www.world10k.com/blog/index.php?s=%E9%AF%A8%E6%9D%BF%E5%A5%B4%E5%9C%8B　October 17, 2022 retrieved.

But I checked the relevant information, Kbara may be misspelled, it should be Kuara, which is located more than a hundred miles south of Baghdad, and was an important port leading to the Persian Gulf in the early days. See " Kuara (Sumer)," *Wikipedia*,

https://en.wikipedia.org/wiki/Kuara_(Sumer)　October 21, 2022 retrieved.

白話文(**Vernacular**)：

煮海水製鹽，釀荖葉製酒。有酋長。當地生產青鹽、馬乳、葡萄、米和麥。其麥粒長半寸許。甜美的露水每年八、九月下，民間築淨池以承接，太陽上升曝曬則融解如水，味比糖霜，仍以瓷器貯之，調湯而飲，以避免瘴癘。古人說：「甘露王如來郇其地也。」貿易之貨品使用剌速斯離布、紫金、白銅、青琅玕和闍婆布等。

The people boil the sea for salt and brew the piper betel leaves for wine. There is a chief. The land produces green salt, horse milk, grapes, rice, and wheat. The wheat's grain is half an inch long. In the eighth and ninth month of every year, the sky drops down manna, people build a clean pond to hold it. When exposed to the sun, it dissolves into the water. It tastes like icing sugar. The people still store it in a porcelain utensil, mixed with soup, and drink it to prevent miasma. The ancients said: "King of Nectar Tathagata is coming here." The goods used for trade are Lá Sù Sī lí cloth, purple gold, white copper, green jade, and Java cloth.

98. 羅婆斯[203]
98. Luó Pó Sī

國與麻加那之右山聯屬，奇峰磊磊，如天馬奔馳。形勢

---

[203]羅婆斯，可能在今孟加拉灣東南方的尼科巴羣島（Nicobar Islands）。參見藤田豐八校註，前引書，頁 169。

　　Luó Pó Sī is located probably in the Nicobar Islands in the southeastern part of what is now the Bay of Bengal. See Fujita Toyohachi notes, *op. cit.*, p. 169.

臨海，男女異形，不織不衣，以鳥羽掩身。食無煙火，惟有茹毛飲血，巢居穴處而已。雖然飲食宮室節宣之不可闕也，絲麻絺綌寒暑來往之不可或違也。夫以洛南北之地，懸隔千里，尚有寒暑之殊，而況於窮海諸國者哉！

白話文(Vernacular)：

該國與麻加那之右山有隸屬關係，奇峰很多，如天馬奔馳。該地濱海。男女形體特殊，不織不衣，以鳥羽掩身。飲食不用煙火，惟有生食喝血，巢居穴處而已。雖然飲食宮室節日等不可缺乏，穿絲、麻、絺、綌衣服，要按照寒暑來決定，不可違背。以洛水南北兩地，相隔千里，都有寒暑之分別，更不用提該窮海諸國了！

This country is affiliated with the right mountain of Magana, and the mountains have many towering peaks, like a horse gallop. The terrain is facing the sea. Men and women have different shapes, neither weaving nor clothing, they cover their bodies with bird feathers. There is no smoke and fire to cook food, they only eat raw foods, and they live only in a cave. Although there should be food, a house for living in, and a festival, it is not against the law to wear silk and linen clothes according to the change of cold and hot seasons. In the north and south of Luo (river), separated by thousands of miles, there is still a difference between cold and heat seasons, not to mention the poor sea countries!

其地鐘湯之全，故民無衣服之備，陶然自適，以宇宙輪輿。宜乎茹飲不擇，巢穴不易，相與浮乎太古之天矣！

白話文(Vernacular)：

該地到處都是鍾乳石洞和溫泉，故人民無需準備衣服，陶然自得其樂，以宇宙做為輪子和車子。適合他們任意吃喝，不需更換巢穴，一起遨遊於太古之天空！

The land is full of stalactite caves and hot springs, so the people have no clothes to prepare, and they are naturally comfortable, taking the wheel and cart of the universe. It is suitable for them to eat any raw foods and not change their cave for living, and wander in the ancient sky!

99. 烏爹[204]
99. Wū Diē

---

[204]烏爹，又作烏疊、烏丁，或訛作烏爺。一說烏爹即 Uda 譯音，印度古國，在今印度東部奧里薩（Orissa）邦東北；一說為孟語 Ussa 的音轉，指緬甸孟族所建的白古（Pegu）（勃固）國，烏土則指緬族所建之國，都 於 阿 瓦 （ Ava ）。 參 見 「 烏 爹 」， 南 溟 網 ， http://www.world10k.com/blog/?p=1347 2022 年 10 月 18 日瀏覽。

　　第 18 世紀，清國稱緬甸為「烏肚」國。烏肚即烏土，指仰光。「漾貢，古秘古國也，一名烏土，一名冷宮。」[[清]李尚，海客日譚，光緒丙子(1876 年)抄本，卷三，頁 4。見沈雲龍主編，中國近代史料叢刊，第 318 輯，文海出版社印行，台北縣，民國 55 年重印，頁 162。）

Wū Diē is also known as Wū Die, Wu Ding, or falsely known as Wu Ye. It is said that Wū Diē is a transliteration of Uda, an ancient country in India, located in the northeast of present-day Orissa state in eastern India; another is the Mon language Ussa, referring to the Pegu (Bago) built by the Mon people of Myanmar. Utu refers to the country built by the Burmese, its capital is in Ava. See "Wū Diē," *Nanming Net*, http://www.world10k.com/blog/?p=1347 October 18, 2022 retrieved.

In the 18th century, the Qing Dynasty called Myanmar the "Wudu" country. Wudu is Wutu, referring to Yangon. "Yanggong, the ancient secret, and ancient country, one name is Wutu, the other name is Lenggong." ([Qing] Li Shang, *Haike Ritan (Daily Talk of Sea Men)*, Guangxu Bingzi (1876) manuscript, vol. 3, p. 4. See Shen Yunlong, editor-in-chief, Series of Modern Chinese Historical Materials, Vol. 318, published by Wenhai Publishing House, Taipei County, reprinted in 1955, p. 162).

國因伽里之舊名也。山林益少，其地堰潴而半曠。民專農業，田沃稼茂，旣無絕糧之患，又無蝗蟎之災。歲凡三稔，諸物[205]皆廉，道不拾遺，鄉里和睦，士尤尚義，俗厚民泰，各番之所不及也。氣候男女與朋加刺略同，稅收十分之一。

白話文(Vernacular)：

該國因舊名伽里之關係而有此名稱。山林很少，其地有堰塞水塘，有一半的土地沒有開墾。人民專精於農業，田地肥沃，穀物生產很多，旣無絕糧之患，又無蝗蟲之災。一年有三稔，諸物都便宜，路不拾遺，鄉里和睦，士人尤尚義，風俗厚，人民安樂，為各番國所不能及也。氣候、男女與朋加刺略同，稅收為十分之一。

The country has this name because it has the old name of Gary. There are few mountains and forests, and the land has many swamps and pools. Half of the land is not cultivated. People specialize in agriculture, the fields are fertile and the crops are lush, and there is no danger of food shortages and no plague of locusts. The grains have three harvests per year. All things are cheap. No one picks up leftovers on the road. The village is harmonious, and the scholars are especially righteous. The customs are honest, and the people are peaceful—the other barbarian countries can't match them. The climate, men, and women are similar to that of Bangladesh, and the tax is one-tenth.

地產大者[206]黑囝、翠羽、黃蠟、木棉、細匹布。貿易之

---

[205]原文寫為「佛」，故改之。

The original text was written as "Fú", so I correct it.

[206] 原文無「者」字，故加之。

The original text does not have the word "Zhe", so I add it.

貨，用金、銀、五色緞、白絲、丁香、荳蔻、茅香、靑白花器、鼓瑟之屬。每箇銀錢重二錢八分，准中統鈔一十兩，易趴子計一萬一千五百二十餘，折錢使用。以二百五十趴子糴一尖籮熟米，折官斗有一斗六升。每錢收趴子可得四十六籮米，通計七十三斗二升，可供二人一歲之食有餘。故販其地者，十去九不還也。夫以外夷而得知務農重穀，使國無遊民，故家給人足，歲無飢寒之憂。設知興行禮讓，敎以詩書禮樂，則與中國之風無間然矣。孰謂蠻貃之邦而不可行者乎！

白話文(Vernacular)：

當地生產大者如黑小孩、翠羽、黃蠟、木棉和細匹布。貿易之貨品使用金、銀、五色緞、白絲、丁香、荳蔻、茅香、靑白花器和鼓瑟等。每箇銀錢重二錢八分，約合中統鈔一十兩，兌換趴子計一萬一千五百二十餘，可代替錢使用。以二百五十趴子糴一尖籮筐熟米，折官斗有一斗六升。每錢收趴子可得四十六籮筐米，通計七十三斗二升，可供二人一年吃還有剩餘。故到該地販賣東西的人，十個人有九個人不回國。以這些外夷而得知務農重視穀物，使得國家沒有遊民，故每家糧食充足，每年沒有飢寒之擔憂。若讓他們知道奉行禮讓，敎以詩書禮樂，則與中國之風就沒有差別了。誰說蠻貃之邦就不能成為禮義之邦呢！

The land produces big products including black children, Kingfisher feathers, yellow wax, kapok, and fine cloth. The goods used for trade are gold, silver, five-colored satin, white silk, cloves, cardamom, marigold, green and white flower utensils, drums, and zither. Each silver coin weighs twenty-eight cents and is equivalent to Zhōng Tǒng banknotes of ten taels, and it exchanges for eleven thousand five hundred and twenty Pazi which can be used to replace the money. Using two hundred and fifty Pazi to buy a pointed basket of cooked rice, it is equilibrant to an official bucket of rice of sixteen liters. You can get forty-six grains of rice for ten cents of Pazi, which is seventy-three buckets and two liters in total, enough for two people to eat for one year. Therefore, nine out of ten persons who sell their grains to this country will not return home. Although they are foreign barbarians, they have learned that farming is very important, which gives the people a livelihood, so the family gets sufficient food, and there is no worry of hunger and cold. If they have the knowledge and perform courteousness and humility, and are taught poetry, books, rituals, and music, it is quite similar to the Chinese style. Who said that a savage state could not become a courtesy state?

100. 異聞類聚

100. Dissimilar Cluster

古有奇肱國之民，能為飛車，從風遠行。見於博物志矣。

白話文**(Vernacular)**：

古代有奇肱國之人民，能夠像搭乘飛車一樣，隨風遠行。見於博物志之記載。

In ancient times, the people of the Qí Gong country were able to travel far away following the wind as taking a flying car. See *Record on Natural History*.

次日頓遜國。凡人死，送於廓外，鳥食肉盡乃去，以火燒其骨，即沉於海中，謂之鳥葬。見於窮神祕苑矣。

白話文**(Vernacular)**：

其次有頓遜國。凡人死了，放在棺木外，給鳥吃，鳥食肉盡就飛走了，然後用火燒其骨骸，將骨灰沉於海中，謂之鳥葬。見於窮神祕苑之記載。

The next is called Dunsun Country. When a person dies, he is sent to the outside of the coffin. When the birds eat all their body and fly away, they burn their bones with fire, and drop them into the sea; this is called bird burial. See *Exploring Mysterious Garden*.

次曰骨利[207]國。晝長夜短，薄暮，煮一羊脾方熟，東方已曙。見於神異錄矣。

白話文**(Vernacular)**：

其次有骨利國。晝長夜短，在黃昏時，煮一羊脾剛好熟了，東方已現曙光。見於神異錄之記載。

The next is called the Guli country. Days are long and nights are short, and at dusk, when a sheep spleen is cooked, the East has already dawned. See *Mystery Records*.

次曰大食國。山樹花開如人首，不解語。人借問，惟頻笑。笑則彫落。見於酉陽雜俎矣。

白話文**(Vernacular)**：

其次有大食國。山樹花開像人的頭，不能了解人的話。有人跟它說話，只是一直笑。它一笑花就凋落了。見於酉陽雜俎之記載。

The next is called Dashi country. The mountain trees are

---

[207] 原文無「骨利」，故加之。

　　The original text does not have the word "gǔ lì'", so I add it.

blooming like the head of a person, who can't understand people's words. When people ask questions, he laughs frequently. When he laughs, the tree flowers immediately wither away. See *Youyang Zazu (Youyang Miscellaneous)*.

次曰婆登國。種穀每月一熟，見於神異之記。

白話文 **(Vernacular)** ：

其次有婆登國。種稻穀每月一熟，見於神異之記之記載。

The next is called Pó Dēng country. Seed grains ripen once a month. See *The Record of Miracles*.

次曰繳濮國。人有尾，欲坐，則先穴地以安之。誤折其尾則死。見於廣州之記。

白話文 **(Vernacular)** ：

其次有繳濮國。人長有尾巴，想要坐下來，需先挖一洞，才能安穩坐下來。誤折其尾巴，就會死掉。見於廣州之記之記載。

The next is called Jiǎo Pú country. A person has a tail, and if he wants to sit, he must first make a hole in the ground to fit it. If the tail is broken by mistake, he will die. See *The Chronicles of Guangzhou*.

次曰南方之產翁。獠婦娩子，是擁衾抱雛以護衛之。見於南楚之新聞。

白話文 **(Vernacular)** ：

其次有南方之產翁。獠婦生了小孩，他會擁衾抱幼兒以護衛之。見於南楚之新聞之記載。

The next is called the old man who protects a newborn baby

in the South. When a woman of Laos race gives birth, he hugs the quilt and holds her baby to protect them. See *The News of Southern Chu.*

次曰番禺縣民災蔬園，盜之於百里之外，若浮筏乘流於海上，有縣宰為之判杖。見於玉堂之閒話。

白話文(Vernacular)：

其次有番禺縣民災蔬園，有一盜從別人菜園偷盜蔬菜，搭乘浮筏漂流於海上在百里之外，有縣長判決給予杖刑。見於玉堂之閒話之記載。

The next are the people of Pānyú County. If a thief steals vegetables from a vegetable garden and takes a raft to float on the sea for hundreds of miles, the county magistrate judges and punishes the thief with a caning. See *Yutang Gossip.*

他如女人國，視井而生育；茶弼沙國，入其地，聲震雷霆。至於南方縛婦成姻，多非禮聘；嶺南之好女，不事績織；南海之貧妻，名為指腹[208]賣；南中[209]之師郎，擁婦而食肉，此又人物風俗之不同，錄之以備采覽。故曰「異聞類聚」。

---

[208] 原文寫為「腹指」，故改之。

The original text was written as "Fù Zhǐ", so I correct it.

[209] 南中是中國三國時期古地區名。相當今四川省大渡河以南和雲南、貴州兩省。見「南中」，維基百科，https://zh.wikipedia.org/zh-tw/%E5%8D%97%E4%B8%AD_(%E5%9C%B0%E5%90%8D) 2022年10月6日瀏覽。

Nanzhong is the name of the ancient region during the Three Kingdoms period in China. It is located to the south of Dadu River in Sichuan Province and Yunnan and Guizhou Provinces. See "Nanzhong", *Wikipedia*, https://zh.wikipedia.org/zh-tw/%E5%8D%97%E4%B8%AD_(%E5%9C%B0%E5%90%8D) October 6, 2022 retrieved.

白話文**(Vernacular)**：

其他有女人國，看到井就懷孕生子；茶弼沙國，進入該國，他會聽到聲音大如雷聲。至於南方則是綁架婦女成婚，多非禮聘；嶺南之好女，不事紡織；南海之貧妻，名為指腹賣兒女；南中之教師，擁抱婦女而食肉，各地人物風俗均不同，我記錄這些以供大家閱覽，所以說：「異聞類聚」。

In other countries, for example, in a women's country, a woman gives birth by looking at the well; in Chabisha country, when a foreigner enters this country, he'll hear a voice as loud as thunder. As for the marriage of women in the southern countries, they often kidnap women to marriage and do not pay dowry gifts to marry a woman; the good women in Lingnan do not weave; the poor wives in the South Sea are called belly-selling (refers to selling their fetuses); the teacher in Nanzhong embraces women and eats meat. This is the difference between figures and customs. So I recorded it for watching and reading. That's why it's called a "dissimilar cluster ".

101. 島夷誌後序
101. Postscript of Record on Island Barbarians

皇元混一聲敎，無遠弗屆，區宇之廣，曠古所未聞。海外島夷無慮數千國，莫不執玉貢琛，以修民職；梯山航海，以通互市。中國之往復商販於殊庭異城之中者，如東西州焉。

白話文**(Vernacular)**：

我元國一統全國聲名敎化，無遠不到，宇宙之廣，從古到今都未聽聞。海外島夷有數千國，莫不執珠玉進貢珍寶，以盡臣民之職責；他們走過高山航越大海，以通貿易。中國人之前往商販於外國異城之地者，如同到東西兩州一樣。

Royal Yuan integrated reputation and enlightenment, and there is no distance, and the area is so wide that it was unheard of in ancient times. Overseas island barbarians should have thousands of countries, and they all pay tribute treasures to assume the responsibilities of the people; they climb over mountains and sail the sea to do business with each other. Chinese people engaged in business entering and out of different cities and regions are like entering and going out of the Eastern and Western states.

大淵少年嘗附舶以浮於海，所過之域，竊嘗賦詩以記其山川、土俗、風景、物產之詭異，與夫可怪可愕可鄙可笑之事，皆身所遊覽，耳目所親見。傳說之事，則不載焉。

白話文(Vernacular)：

汪大淵少年時曾搭船到海外，所過之地方，曾賦詩以記其山川、土俗、風景、物產之詭異，以及可怪、可愕、可鄙、可笑之事，都是他親身所遊覽，耳目所親見。傳說之事，則不記載。

When Wang Da-yuan was young, he took a ship going abroad. In those countries he traveled through, he wrote poetry to describe the mountains, rivers, folklore, landscape, and the strangeness of productions. It includes strange, shocking, despising, and funny things. All are what he experienced through his ears and eyes. If it's a legend, then it is beyond the record of this book.

至正己丑冬，大淵過泉南，適監郡[210]偰侯命三山吳鑒明之續[211]清源郡誌，願以清源舶司所在，諸番輻輳之所，宜記錄不鄙。謂余知方外事，囑[212]島夷誌附於郡誌之後，非徒以廣士大夫之異聞，間以表國朝威德如是之大且遠也。

白話文(**Vernacular**)：

至正己丑冬，汪大淵到泉州南部，剛好監郡偰侯命三山吳鑒明撰寫續清源郡誌，願將以清源海關所在，諸番輻輳之所，無所偏見的記錄下來。他說我知道外國事情，囑附我將島夷誌附在郡誌之後，不僅可擴大增廣士大夫之奇異見聞，而且可以表現本朝威德如是之大且遠也。

In the winter of Zhì Zhèng Jǐ Chǒu (in 1349), Wang Da-yuan arrived south of Quanzhou. Xiè Hóu, the ombudsman of the county, ordered Sanshan Wu Jianming continuously to edit *the Chronicle of Qianyuan County*, thereby hoping to record the customs of Qianyuan, and the place where all the ships of various countries converge without prejudice. He said that I know foreign affairs, and asked me to attach the *Daoyi Zhi* after *the Chronicle of Qianyuan County*. It not only expands the strange news of the scholars and officials but also occasionally shows that the mighty reputation of the Yuan Dynasty was so great and far away.

皇明嘉靖戊申五月望，汝南郡。考島夷惟日本重文事，

---

[210]原文寫為「群」，故改之。
The original text was written as "Qún", so I correct it.
[211]原文寫為「序」，故改之。
The original text was written as "Xù", so I correct it.
[212]原文寫為「屬」，故改之。
The original text was written as "Shǔ", so I correct it.

其髹漆、金器、刀紙、屏障最精。此誌不載，故及之。予於
正德初年，日本國使臣朝貢，留寓姑蘇。其正使了庵年已八
十八，詩扎賡酬，尚在陶齋。袁表識。

白話文(Vernacular)：

皇明嘉靖戊申五月十五日，我在汝南郡。據研究，島夷
中唯有日本重文事，其髹漆、金器、刀紙和屏障最精。此誌
沒有記載，所以我在此附記一筆。我在正德初年，日本國使
臣朝貢，留宿在姑蘇。其正使了庵年已八十八歲，以寫詩和
書信相互酬答，那時我還住在陶齋。袁表識。

On May 15, Royal Ming Jiajing Wushen (1548), I am in
Runan County. According to research, among the island
barbarians, it is only Japan that attaches importance to civil
affairs, and its lacquer, gold utensils, knife and paper, and
barriers are the most refined. This chronicle is not contained, so
I write it here. In the early years of Zhengde (1506 or so),
Japanese envoys paid tribute and stayed in Suzhou. The
Japanese formal envoy, Le An, is eighty-eight years old and is
still writing poems and letters for gifts and giving each other. At
that time I am still living in Taozhai. Yuan Biao records.

附錄：古今地名對照表

Appendix: Contrast Table of Ancient and Modern Place Names

古代地名 **Ancient Place Names**	現在地名 **Modern Place Names**
彭湖（Penghu, Pescadores Islands）	彭湖（Penghu (Pescadores Islands)）
琉球（Ryukyu）	北臺灣（northern Taiwan）
三島（Sāndǎo, Three islands）	又寫為三嶼，指菲律賓中部民多洛島、班乃島和巴拉望島（also written as San-yu, refers to Mindoro, Panay, and Palawan in the central Philippines）
處州（Chuzhou）	浙江處州府（Chuzhou Prefecture in Zhejiang Province, China）
麻逸（Máyìt）	菲律賓民多洛島（Mindoro Island, Philippines）
無枝拔（Wú Zhī Bá）	馬來西亞馬六甲（Melaka, Malaysia）
龍涎嶼（Lóng Xián Yǔ）	印尼蘇門答臘島東北邊的 Bulas Island（Bulas Island in the northeast of Sumatra, Indonesia）
交趾（Jiāozhǐ, Cochin）	北越紅河三角洲地區（Red River Delta in North Vietnam）
占城（Zhàn Chéng, Champa）	越南中部地區的國家，首都在歸仁（a country in Central Vietnam, its capital is in Quy Nhon）
民多朗（Mindorang）	指越南東南部的潘郎港（Phanrang in southeastern Vietnam）
賓童龍（Bintonglong）	越南慶和省之婆那加（Po-nagar of Khan-Hoa Province, Vietnam）
眞臘（Zhen-la）	柬埔寨（Cambodia）
丹馬令（Thammarak）	丹馬令（Thammarak）
沙里（Shali）	可能為泰國的蘇叻他尼（probably Surat Thani, Thailand）
佛來安（Folai'an）	位在北大年和關丹之間的登嘉樓州的龍運（Terengganu State's Dungun between Pattani and Kuantan）
日麗（Rì Lì）	位在蘇門答臘島北岸的日裏（Delli, on the north coast of Sumatra）
麻里魯（Málǐ Lǔ）	馬尼拉（Manila）
遐來物（Xiá Lái Wù）	指吉利問、吉里門之異譯。吉利問又譯為卡里蒙群島，位在新加坡島和以西的朗桑島之間。（

	refers to the different translations of Karimun and Gilliman. Karimun Island is located between Singapore and Pulau Rangsang.）
古淚（Gǔ Lèi）	印尼勾欄山或交欄山（Gelam Mountain or Gelam Island, Indonesia）.
彭坑（Péng Kēng）	馬來西亞彭亨（Pahang, Malaysia）
吉蘭丹（Kelantan）	馬來西亞吉蘭丹（Kelantan, Malaysia）
丁家盧（Terengganu）	馬來西亞登嘉樓（Terengganu, Malaysia.）
戎（Rong）	泰南春蓬，亦譯尖噴（Chumpon, Thailand）
羅衛（Luo Wei）	1.泰國叻丕; 2.又寫為羅越，指馬來西亞柔佛（1.Rajaburi, Thailand; 2.Johor, Malaysia）
南真駱（Nanzhenluo）	南真臘（South Cambodia）
羅斛（Luó Hú）	泰國羅斛（Lopburi, Thailand）
東沖古剌（Dōng Chōng Gǔ Lá）	泰國宋卡（Songkhla, Thailand）
忽南圭（佛南圭）（Hu Nangui）	1,泰國南部的巴蜀; 2. 緬甸東南岸的墨吉（1. Prachuab, Thailand; 2. Mergui, Myanmar）
淡港（Dàn Gǎng）	泰國宋卡港（Songkhla Port, Thailand）
蘇洛鬲（Srokam）	馬來西亞吉打(Kedah, Malaysia)
針路（Zhēnlù）	緬甸墨吉（Mergui, Myanmar）
麻來墳（Má Lái Fén）	緬甸馬里萬（Maliwan, Myanmar）
八都馬（Baduma）	緬甸馬塔班（Martaban, Myanmar）
淡邈（Dàn Miǎo）	緬甸土瓦（Dawei, or Tavoy, Myanmar）
尖山（Jianshan）	馬來西亞沙巴的神山（Kinabalu, Sabah, Malaysia）
八節那間（Bā Jié Nà Jiān）	印尼泗水（Surabaya, or Surabaja, Indonesia）
三佛齊（Sanfoqi, Sri-Vijaya）	印尼舊港（Palembang, Indonesia）
嘯噴（Xiào Pēn）	印尼蘇門答臘島新邦（Simpang, Sumatra, Indonesia）
監毗（Kampei）	印尼蘇門答臘島甘巴（Kampar, Sumatra, Indonesia）
吉陀（Jí Tuó）	馬來西亞吉打（Kedah, Malaysia）
淳泥（Bó Ní (Borneo)）	包括馬來西亞砂拉越州及沙巴州和汶萊王國（including Sarawak and Sabah and the Kingdom of Brunei.）
朋家羅（Péng Jiā Luó）	1.斯里蘭卡的朋加拉; 2. 印度 Bangaram 島（1. Pingalla (Pangala), Sri Lankar）; 2. Bangaram Island, India）
故臨（Gù Lín）	印度奎隆（Quilon, or Kollam, India）
暹（Xiān）	泰國素可泰（Sukhothai, Thailand）

新門臺（Xinmentai）	泰國北欖（Paknam, Thailand）
單馬錫（Temasek）	新加坡（Singapore）
昔里（Xī Lǐ）	又寫為實叻、石叻，馬來語稱海峽為 selat（Also written as Shila, Malay called the strait as selat）
爪哇（Java）	印尼爪哇（Java, Indonesia）
門遮把逸（Mén Zhē Bǎ Yì）	又寫為滿者伯夷、麻喏巴歇。其地點在惹班（also written as Majapahit or Mazao Paxie. Its place is in Mojokerto.）
三打板（San Daban）	應是打板，指杜並或稱廚閩（Daban, Du Bing, or Tuban）
吉丹（Gidan）	可能是蘇吉丹或斯吉丹，指吉力石（即印尼錦石）（possibly Sujidan or Sjidan, refers to Gressie (Gresik), Indonesia）
孫剌（Sun La）	1. 印尼的梭羅;2. 巽他（1.Solo, Indonesia; 2. Sunda, Indonesia）
重迦羅（Janggala）	印尼錦石，又稱章加拉（Gresik; Karajan Janggala, Indonesia）
杜瓶（Tu Ping）	又寫為杜並或杜並足，現稱為杜板（also written as Tu Bing or Tu Bing Zu, today's Tuban, Indonesia）
都督岸（Dūdū Àn）	馬來西亞砂拉越 Tanjang Datu（Tanjang Datu, Sarawak, Malaysia）
淡港（Tamgang）	馬來西亞砂拉越的古晉（Kuching, Sarawak, Malaysia）
文誕（Wén Dàn）	1. 印尼之班達島; 2. 萬丹（1.Banda Island, Indonesia ; 2. Banten, Indonesia）
蘇祿（Sulu）	菲律賓蘇祿（Sulu, the Philippines）
龍牙犀角（Lóng Yá Xījiǎo）	又寫為狼牙修、朗迦戌、凌牙斯加、凌牙蘇加，地當在北大年到吉打之間（also written as Langkasuka, Langkashu, Lingyaska, and Lingyasuga, which is located between Pattani and Kedah.）
蘇門傍（Sumen Pang）	1.泰國素攀武里;2. 印尼馬都拉島南岸城市三攀（1. Suphan Buri, Thailand; 2. Sampang, Indonesia）
斯吉丹（Sī Jí Dān）	1. 印尼爪哇島中部，位布格角南面; 2. 印尼卡里曼丹島西南岸蘇卡丹那（1. Bugel , Java, Indonesia ; 2.Sukadana, Kalimantan, Indonesia）
舊港（Jiù Gǎng）	印尼巴鄰旁（Palembang, Indonesia）
彭家門（Péngjiāmén）	印尼穆西河口（mouth of the Musi River, Indonesia）

龍牙菩提（Lóng Yá Pútí）	馬來西亞蘭卡威島（Lankawi Island, Malaysia）
毗舍耶（Pi-sir-ya）	菲律賓毗舍耶（Visaya, the Philippines）
班卒（Bān Zú）	1.馬來西亞麻坡; 2. 蘇門答臘島西岸的班卒（1. Muar, Malaysia; 2. Fansur or Fantsur, Sumatra）
蒲奔（Pu Ben）	印尼馬都拉島南邊的大海（the sea on the south side of Madura Island, Indonesia.）
假里馬打（Jiǎ Lǐ Mǎ Dǎ）	卡利馬達島（Karimata Is., Indonesia）
文老古（Wén Lǎo Gǔ）	印尼的摩鹿加群島（Maluku, Indonesia）
古里地悶（Gǔlǐ De Mèn）	帝汶島（Timor Island）
龍牙門（Lóng Yá Mén）	新加坡和林伽（或譯為龍牙）群島之間的新加坡海峽（the Singapore Strait between Singapore and the Lingga Islands.）
吉利門（Jílì Mén）	印尼卡里蒙島（Karimon Island, Indonesia）
軍屯山（Juntun Mountain）	又寫為軍突弄山、軍徒弄山。指越南湄公河出海口外之崑崙島（also written as Juntunong Mountain and Jūn Tú Nòng Mountain. It refers to Poulo Condore outside the mouth of the Mekong River in Vietnam.）
靈山（Língshān）	越南 Qui-nhon 城北的 Lang-son 港（Lang-son Port, north of Qui-nhon City, Vietnam）
東西竺（Dōngxīzhú）	馬來西亞柔佛州豐盛港以東外海的奧爾島（Pulau Aur, off the Mersing port in the Johor State of Malaysia）
淡洋（Dàn Yáng）	蘇門答臘東北岸的 Tamiang 河流域（the Tamiang River basin on the northeastern coast of Sumatra）
急水灣 Jí（Shuǐ Wān (Turbulence Bay)）	印尼蘇門答臘島北部的司馬威（Lhokseumawe, Sumatra, Indonesia）
須門答剌（Xū Mén Dā Lá）	蘇門答臘島北端的八昔（或譯為巴賽）（Pasei, or Pasai, Sumatra, Indonesia）
花面（Huāmiàn (Flower Face)）	蘇門答臘島北部的巴塔克（Batak, Sumatra）
亞蘆（Yalu）	蘇門答臘阿魯（Aru, Sumatra）
須文答剌（Xū Wén Dá Lá）	蘇門答臘亞齊（Aceh, Sumatra）
僧加剌（Sēng Jiā La）	斯里蘭卡（Sri Lanka）
勾欄山（Gōulán Shān (Goulan Mountain)）	1. 印尼的格拉姆島 2. 印尼的勿里洞島（1.Gelam Island, Indonesia; 2. Billiton, Indonesia）
特番里（Tèfān Lǐ）	埃及杜姆亞特（Damietta, Damiata or Domyat, Egypt）
班達里（Bān Dá Lǐ）	印度西南岸科澤科德（Kozhikode, India）

波思（Bō Sī）	可能為波斯（probably Persian）
曼陀郎（Màn Tuó Láng）	印度西岸的蒙德拉（Mundra, India）
喃巫哩（Nán Wū Lī）	印尼班達亞齊（Banda-Aceh, Indonesia）
北溜（Běi Liū (North Slip)）	印度洋中馬爾地夫群島（Maldives）
下里（Xià Lǐ）	1.印度卡里庫特; 2. 蒙特德里;3.阿爾瓦耶（1. Calicut ; 2. Maunt Delly;3.Alwaye, India）
高郎步（Gāo Láng Bù）	斯里蘭卡可倫坡（Colombo, Sri Lanka）
沙里八丹（Shālǐ Bā Dān）	1.印度的納加帕蒂南; 2. 注輦（1.Nagapatinan, India; 2.Chola, India）
金塔（Jīn Tǎ (Gold Pagoda)）	緬甸仰光的大金塔（Shwedagon Pagoda in Yangon, Myanmar）
東淡邈（Dōng Dàn Miǎo (East Dàn Miǎo)）	1. 印尼爪哇島或其附近; 2. 印度果阿（1. Java. Indonesia; 2. Goa, India）
大八丹（Dà Bā Dān）	1.印度西北沿海地區; 2. 印度西南沿海的特利切里（1. the northwest coast of India ; 2.Tel-1ieherry, the southwest coast of India）
加里那（Jiālǐ Nà）	可能在波斯灣內伊朗西南部（the southwestern part of Iran nearby the Persian Gulf）
土塔（Tǔtǎ）	印度東南部淡米爾納德邦的 Nagapattinam 港（Nagapattinam port, Tamil Nadu, India）
第三港（Third Port）	印度東南海岸的馬八兒（Ma'abar, Mapar, India）
華羅（Huá Luó）	印度西海岸的胡茶辣或譯為古吉拉特（Guzarat, or Gujarat, India）
麻那里（Má Nàlǐ）	肯亞的馬林迪（Malindi, Kenya）
迷黎（Mi Li）	肯亞的馬林迪西北面（northwest of Malindi, Kenya）
加將門里（Jiā Jiàngmén Lǐ）	莫三鼻克的奎里曼尼（Quilimani,or Quelimane, Mozambique）
波斯離（Bōsī Lí）	伊拉克巴士拉（Basra, Iraq）
撻吉那（Tà Jí Nà）	印度德干（Deccan）之梵語名 Dakshina（Dakshina, India）
千里馬（Qiānlǐmǎ）	不可考（unknown）
大佛山（Dà Foshān (Dà Fo Mountain)）	斯里蘭卡之 Adam's Peak（Adam's Peak, Sri Lanka）
逛里（Yà Lǐ）	斯里蘭卡西南境之加勒港（Galle, Sri Lanka）
須文那（Xū Wén Nà）	1. 蘇木都剌西北一帶;2. 印度孟買附近的恭建海岸一帶; 3. 印度西北古吉拉特（Gujarat）邦之蘇姆那; 4.蘇門答臘北端之古打拉惹（1.northwest area of Sumudula, Sumatra; 2. Konkan near Bombay, India; 3. Somanth, India; 4. Kuturadja, Sumatra）

萬里石塘（Wànlǐ Shí Táng）	西沙群島（Paracel Islands）
小唄喃（Xiǎo Gé Nán (Small Gé Nán)）	1.印度潘達里納; 2. 印度奎隆（1. Pandarina, India ; 2,Quilon, India）
古里佛（Gullifo）	印度卡里庫特（Calicut, India）
朋加剌（Péng Jiā Lá）	孟加拉（Bangladesh）
忻都州府（Xīn Dōu Zhōu Fǔ）	印度之溫德亞山脈以北區域（north of the Vidhya Range in India）
巴南巴西（Bā Nán Bāxī）	印度西岸 Vanawasi（Vanawasi, west coast of India）
放拜（Fàng Bài）	印度西岸的孟買（Bombay, India）
大烏爹（Dà Wū Diē）	印度拉賈斯坦邦之烏代普爾，或中央邦之烏闍衍那（Udeypur (Udeyapur), or Ujayana, India）
萬年港（Wànnián Port）	可能為汶萊港（probably Brunei Port）
馬八兒嶼（Ma'abar Yǔ (Ma'abar Island)）	印度注輦海岸外的島嶼（Ma'abar Island, off Coromandel Coast. India）
阿思里（Ā Sī Lǐ）	埃及紅海西岸的柯色爾（Quseir, or Kosseir, Egypt）
哩伽塔（Licata）	義大利西西里島南邊 Licata 港（Licata Port, Sicily, Italy）
國王海（King Sea）	地中海（Mediterranean Sea）
天堂（Tiāntáng）	沙烏地阿拉伯的麥加（Mecca, Saudi Arabia）
天竺（Tianzhu）	西印度的信度（Sind, India）
層搖羅（Céng Yáo Luó）	1.馬達加斯加島; 2. 坦尚尼亞的 Kilwa Kisiwani（1. Madagascar; 2. Kilwa Kisiwani, Tanzania）
馬魯澗（Mǎ Lǔ Jiàn）	伊朗的 Maragha 或 Maragak，但未可確定（Maragha or Maragak, Iran. But not sure.）
甘埋里（Gān Mái Lǐ）	1. 伊朗的荷姆茲; 2. 莫三比克東部與馬達加斯加西南部的一座火山群島葛摩洛群島（1. Hormuz, Iran; 2. Comoro Islands, east of Mozambique and southwest of Madagascar）
麻呵斯離（Má Hē Sī Lí）	伊拉克西北部摩蘇爾（Mosur or Mosul, Iraq）
鯨板奴（Jīng Bǎn Nú）	可能是伊拉克 Kuara（probably Kuara, Iraq）
羅婆斯（Luó Pó Sī）	孟加拉灣東南方的印度的尼科巴羣島（Nicobar Islands, India）
烏爹（Wū Diē）	1. 印度東部奧里薩邦東北; 2. 緬甸孟族所建的白古（Pegu）（勃固）國; 3. 仰光（1.the northeast area of Orissa State in eastern India; 2. Pegu (Bago) was built by the Mon people of Myanmar; 3. Yangon）

國家圖書館出版品預行編目資料

島夷志略中英文對照本/(元)汪大淵作；陳鴻瑜校註及翻譯.
-- 初版. -- 臺北市：蘭臺出版社, 2023.07
　　面；　　公分. --（東南亞史研究；6）
ISBN 978-626-97527-1-3(平裝)

1.CST: 歷史地理 2.CST: 亞洲

730.62　　　　　　　　　　　　　　　112009966

東南亞史研究6

島夷志略中英文對照本

著　　　者：汪大淵
校註及譯者：陳鴻瑜
總　　編：張加君
編　　輯：陳鴻瑜
美　　編：陳鴻瑜
封面設計：陳勁宏
出　　版：蘭臺出版社
地　　址：臺北市中正區重慶南路1段121號8樓之14
電　　話：(02) 2331-1675 或 (02) 2331-1691
傳　　真：(02) 2382-6225
E - MAIL：books5w@gmail.com或books5w@yahoo.com.tw
網路書店：http://5w.com.tw/
　　　　　https://www.pcstore.com.tw/yesbooks/
　　　　　https://shopee.tw/books5w
　　　　　博客來網路書店、博客思網路書店
　　　　　三民書局、金石堂書店
經　　銷：聯合發行股份有限公司
電　　話：(02) 2917-8022　　傳真：(02) 2915-7212
劃撥戶名：蘭臺出版社　　　　帳號：18995335
香港代理：香港聯合零售有限公司
電　　話：(852) 2150-2100　傳真：(852) 2356-0735
出版日期：2023年7月 初版
定　　價：新臺幣450元整（平裝）
ISBN：978-626-97527-1-3